Oscar Browning, Francis Godolphin Osborne Leeds

The political Memoranda of Francis Fifth Duke of Leeds

Oscar Browning, Francis Godolphin Osborne Leeds

The political Memoranda of Francis Fifth Duke of Leeds

ISBN/EAN: 9783337133757

Printed in Europe, USA, Canada, Australia, Japan

Cover: Foto ©ninafisch / pixelio.de

More available books at **www.hansebooks.com**

THE
POLITICAL MEMORANDA

OF

FRANCIS FIFTH DUKE OF LEEDS.

NOW FIRST PRINTED

FROM THE ORIGINALS IN THE BRITISH MUSEUM.

EDITED, TOGETHER WITH OTHER PAPERS, AND WITH NOTES,
INTRODUCTION, AND APPENDIX,

BY

OSCAR BROWNING, M.A.,

SENIOR FELLOW OF KING'S COLLEGE CAMBRIDGE, UNIVERSITY LECTURER
IN HISTORY, AND EXAMINER IN THE UNIVERSITY OF LONDON.

PRINTED FOR THE CAMDEN SOCIETY.

M.DCCC.LXXXIV.

COUNCIL OF THE CAMDEN SOCIETY
FOR THE YEAR 1883-4.

President,

THE RIGHT HON. THE EARL OF VERULAM, F.R.G.S.
J. J. CARTWRIGHT, ESQ., M.A., *Treasurer.*
WILLIAM CHAPPELL, ESQ., F S.A.
F. W. COSENS, ESQ., F.S.A.
THE HON. HAROLD DILLON, F.S.A.
JAMES E. DOYLE, ESQ.
REV. J. WOODFALL EBSWORTH, M.A., F.S.A.
JAMES GAIRDNER, ESQ.
SAMUEL RAWSON GARDINER, ESQ., LL.D., *Director.*
J. W. HALES, ESQ., M.A.
ALFRED KINGSTON, ESQ., *Secretary.*
ALEXANDER MACMILLAN, ESQ., F.S.A.
STUART A. MOORE, ESQ., F.S.A.
THE EARL OF POWIS, LL.D.
REV. W. SPARROW SIMPSON, D.D., F.S.A.
WILLIAM JOHN THOMS, ESQ., F.S.A.

The COUNCIL of the CAMDEN SOCIETY desire it to be understood that they are not answerable for any opinions or observations that may appear in the Society's publications; the Editors of the several Works being alone responsible for the same.

INTRODUCTION.

THE Political Memoranda of Francis fifth Duke of Leeds form part of the valuable collection of the Osborne papers preserved in the British Museum. They are contained in five paper books of the size 6¼ inches by 7¾ inches, four note books, with marbled covers, 4 inches by 7½ inches, and one 4 inches by 6½ inches. There are also included some detached memoranda, which are preserved on loose paper of different sizes. Besides the volume containing the memoranda there are eight volumes of official correspondence from which papers have been selected which either form part of the memoranda or should evidently be classed with them. The sale catalogue preserved in the Museum shows that the Political Memoranda were purchased on July 11, 1868, for £11 11s.; a second instalment of the papers was purchased on April 5, 1869.

Francis Godolphin Osborne, fifth Duke of Leeds, Marquis of Carmarthen, Earl of Danby, Viscount Latimer, and Viscount Dumblaine in Scotland, Baron Osborne of Kiveton, a Baronet, Knight of the Garter, Lord Lieutenant and Custos Rotulorum of the East Riding of the County of York, Governor of the Levant Company, High Steward of Hull, and possessor of many other offices and titles, was born January 29, 1751. He married at the age of twenty-two Lady Amelia D'Arcy, daughter of the Earl of Holdernesse and Baroness Conyers in her own right. We are told in the *Gentleman's Magazine*, vol. lxix. i. p. 168, that "in the early years of

a

their conjugal intercourse this lady displayed the utmost degree of domestic virtue, and held forth the fairest prospect of connubial happiness." The old Duke of Leeds was, indeed, so delighted at his son's choice, " that he often declared no honour which fortune could shower upon his house could give him any enjoyment comparable to the pleasure of having so estimable a daughter-in-law. But, alas, these flattering prospects of nuptial felicity were all blighted, for this accomplished and amiable woman listened to the voice of seduction, and was the mark of public obloquy." In other words, the Duchess of Leeds ran off with Captain Jack Byron, who, after her death in 1784, married Miss Gordon of Gight, and became the father of Lord Byron the poet.

In October, 1783, the Duke of Leeds, who had obtained a divorce from his first wife, married as his second wife Miss Catherine Anguish, whose father, Thomas Anguish, was a Master in Chancery. She and her sister were celebrated for their skill in music and singing. The *Gentleman's Magazine* goes on to say that the Duke of Leeds was a most sincere friend, a nobleman of the most tried integrity, and a man of liberal principles, amiable manners, and higher talents than he was generally supposed to possess. The cultivation of his mind in very early life was particularly attended to by an indulgent, but judicious father, and if his knowledge was not profound it was miscellaneous and extensive. He was generally deemed a much better scholar than many of his rank, and he always showed a taste for as well as tendency towards literature, which was indeed one of his favourite topics of conversation, though he was never forgetful of his situation in life. Genius and learning were always strong recommendations to his attention and regard, and, as he was courteous and affable, he mixed with various classes, and was well acquainted with mankind. If he had any peculiar pride, it was in an acknowledgment that his family sprang from a citizen of London. He delighted in conversation, and was much inclined to take the lead in this respect, but was too well-bred to obtrude even upon his inferiors; and his general intercourse with society enabled him to adapt himself with ease to the habits and talents of his occasional companions. Dramatic literature, our authority goes on to say, was a favourite object of his pursuit; and few men were more conversant with this province of English literature. Indeed, it is understood that the Duke had presented a comedy to the proprietors of the Drury Lane Theatre, which was intended to be brought forth in the course of the present season. Some of his Grace's poetical effusions, if they do not indicate the strong inspiration of the muse, show at least fancy, taste, and sensibility. On the whole the Duke of Leeds was a very amiable nobleman, who knew how to be affable without encouraging undue familiarity, and who was dignified without pride. "If aristocracy," Sylvanus Urban remarks, "were always to appear as mild, as conciliating, and as intelligent, even the rude spirit of Republican violence would be softened into respect and esteem." The Duke of Leeds died on January 31, 1799, at his house in St. James's Square, after a short illness, of an erysipelas in his side, which turned to mortification.

The notice above quoted remarks with conscious or unconscious irony that the Duke of Leeds was not supposed to possess great talents, that his knowledge was not profound, that he was a considerable talker, that he never lost the consciousness of his position, that he had not been very strongly inspired by the muses. If we make these deductions from his qualities the Political Memoranda will be found to give full evidence of his honesty, straightforwardness, and high spirit, and of the interest which he took in public affairs. Written down for the most part day by day immediately after the events to which they allude, they throw an important light on some

INTRODUCTION.

of the most critical periods of our recent history. The name of Mr. Pitt, when once mentioned, occurs in nearly every succeeding page.

The Duke of Leeds was a statesman of the Ciceronian type. He represents a time when the business of the country was conducted by the members of a few privileged families, who, conscious of their position and of their duties, trained themselves carefully for their high behest, and considered that each action of their lives should reflect the magnanimity which properly belonged to so lofty a vocation. The Memoranda commence two years before the outbreak of the American war, but as they were not written down till 1780 the entries of the first six years are deficient in fulness and interest. When that year is reached we find the King supporting Lord North and the war policy against the growing discontent of the country. The Duke of Leeds joins the Opposition, and is dismissed from the Lord Lieutenancy of the East Riding. Under June 1780 some graphic pages are devoted to the Gordon riots. In November a new parliament was returned, which was to witness the downfall of Lord North; the ministries of Lord Rockingham, of Lord Shelburne, and the coalition ministry of Fox and North under the Duke of Portland. It was not to be dissolved until William Pitt, made Prime Minister contrary to its will, had subdued its stubbornness by his own unshaken resolution and prepared the country to rise in enthusiastic support of his administration. A minute account is given of the circumstances of Lord North's resignation. During the Rockingham administration the Duke of Leeds appears to have been in constant communication with Lord Shelburne, and his notes of their conversations throw an interesting light on the character of that mysterious politician, so able and powerful, so mistrusted and disliked. The narrative of the Shelburne ministry is even more copious.

When William Pitt was at last induced by the King to form a

government the Duke of Leeds was one of the first to whom he turned for support. The Memoranda give us a vivid impression of the difficulties under which the young prime minister laboured. We learn from them that even his firmness was at one time nearly overcome by the persistent efforts of the House of Commons. History has perhaps never witnessed a similar crisis—a young man of twenty-three was set to govern a great nation in a time of unusual difficulty, the revenue defective, the country bleeding from the disastrous conclusion of an expensive war, the crown shorn of its fairest jewel, the powers of Europe partly hostile and partly contemptuous, the opposition strong beyond precedent in ability, eloquence, and the success of avowed convictions, the King discredited by the results of shortsighted obstinacy. Pitt was no sooner in the saddle than he was master of his steed. He conquered the faction of opposition, stemmed the flood of national bankruptcy, attempted a sound financial agreement with Ireland, concluded a commercial treaty with France, made England respected in Europe, and shewed that he could make her feared. From 1784 to 1793 every important action of the Government bears the impress of the name of Pitt; the chief despatches are written by his hand, whether they are signed by Sydney, Leeds, or Grenville. Sound, indeed, must have been the political education which Pitt received during his seven years retirement at Cambridge, which sent him thus fully armed into a conflict of giants.

Of the foreign administration of the Duke of Leeds we have only fragments. The first business of England after the peace of Versailles was to obtain allies, and in doing this she followed the inherited tradition of enmity to France. We knocked in vain at the door of Austria and Russia. By the astute diplomacy of Harris we made a union with Holland and Prussia. It was hardly to be expected that even Pitt should see that the best policy of England lay in accepting the proffered hands of Louis XVI. and Vergennes. A revolution in Denmark, so peculiar and interesting that it has been thought right to include a full account of it in the Appendix, gave us the friendship of that country; and, while it brought us nearer to Russia, accentuated our distrust of France and Sweden. The negociations for the commercial treaty with France, which, on this side of the Channel, are due to the personal initiative of Pitt, show that he was far from sharing the narrow prejudice of his colleagues, and that he was a worthy pupil of Adam Smith. William Eden, afterwards Lord Auckland, was sent to Paris to conduct the negociations; and his confidence in the substantial honesty of the French was a constant butt for the ridicule of Leeds and Harris. The Memoranda proper tell us little or nothing about these transactions, but some scattered papers are printed which seemed to be of interest.

A gap of four years brings us to the question of the regency. The King was mad, and it was impossible to say whether his illness would be short or long, or whether he would ever recover at all. The Prince of Wales was entirely in the hands of the Opposition. To make him Prince Regent, as was done at a later period when the King's illness became incurable, would have been to change the whole system of government, and to place ministers in office towards whom the King if he recovered would have the strongest repulsion. The account of the deliberations of the ministry under these circumstances leaves nothing to be desired. The letter written by Pitt to the Prince of Wales on Dec. 30th, 1788, is printed on page 143. The Prince's answer, mentioned on page 137, also from a copy in the Leeds MSS., is here subjoined.

The Prince of Wales learns from Mr. Pitt's letter that the proceedings in Parliament are now in a train which enables Mr. Pitt, according to the intimation in his former letter, to communicate to the Prince the outlines of the Plan which His

Majesty's confidential servants conceive to be proper to be proposed in the present circumstances.

Concerning the steps already taken by Mr. Pitt the Prince is silent. Nothing done by the two Houses of Parliament can be a proper subject of his animadversion, but when previously to any discussion in Parliament the outline of a scheme of Government is sent for his consideration, in which it is proposed that he shall be personally and principally concerned, and by which the Royal Authority and the public welfare may be deeply affected, the Prince would be unjustifiable were he to withhold an explicit declaration of his sentiments. His silence might be construed into a previous approbation of a plan the accomplishment of which every motive of Duty to his Father and Sovereign as well as of regard for the public interest obliges him to consider as injurious to both.

In the state of deep distress in which the Prince and the whole Royal Family were involved by the heavy calamity which has fallen upon the King, and at a moment when Government deprived of its chief energy and support seemed peculiarly to need the cordial and united aid of all descriptions of good subjects, it was not expected by the Prince that a Plan should be offer'd to his consideration by which Government was to be render'd difficult if not impracticable in the hands of any person intended to represent the King's authority much less in the hands of his eldest son, the Heir Apparent of his Kingdoms, and the person most bound to the maintenance of his Majesty's just Prerogatives and Authority as well as most interested in the happiness, the prosperity, and the glory of his people.

The Prince forbears to reason on the several parts of the sketch of a Plan laid before him; he apprehends it must have been formed with sufficient deliberation to preclude the probability of any argument from him producing an alteration of sentiment in the projectors of it, but he trusts with confidence to the wisdom and justice of Parliament when the whole of the subject and the circumstances connected with it shall come under their deliberation. He observes therefore only generally on the heads communicated by Mr. Pitt, and it is with deep regret the Prince makes the observation that there seems to be in the contents of that paper a project for producing weakness, disorder, and insecurity in every branch of the administration of affairs, a project for dividing the Royal Family from each other, for separating the Court from the State, and thereby disjoining Government from its natural and accustomed support, a scheme for disconnecting the authority to command service from the power of animating it by reward, and for allotting to the Prince all the invidious duties of Government without the means of softening them to the People by any one act of Grace, Favour, or Benignity.

The Prince's feelings on contemplating this Plan are also render'd still more painful to him by observing that it is not grounded on any general principle, but is calculated to infuse jealousies and distrust wholly groundless he trusts in that quarter whose confidence it will ever be the first pride and object of his life to receive and merit.

With regard to the motive and object of the Limitations and Restrictions pro-

INTRODUCTION.

posed the Prince can have but little to observe; no light or information whatever is afforded to him by his Majesty's Ministers on these points. They have inform'd him what the Powers are which they mean to refuse to him, not why they are to be withheld.

The Prince, however, holding as he does that it is an undoubted and fundamental principle of this Constitution that all the Powers and Prerogatives of the Crown are vested there as a trust for the benefit of the People, and that they are sacred only as they are necessary to the preservation of that Poise and Balance of the Constitution which experience has prov'd to be the true security of the liberty of the subject, must be allow'd to observe that the plea of public utility ought to be strong, manifest, and urgent, which calls for the extinction or suspension of any one of these essential rights in the supreme Power or its Representative, or which can justify the Prince in consenting that in his Person an experiment shall be made to ascertain with how small a Portion of the kingly Power the Executive Government of this country may be carried on.

The Prince has only to add that, if security for his Majesty's repossessing his rightful government, whenever it shall please Providence in bounty to the country to remove the calamity with which he is afflicted, be any part of the object of this plan, the Prince has only to be convinc'd that any measure is necessary or even conducive to that end to be the first to approve and urge it as the preliminary and paramount consideration of any settlement in which he would consent to share.

If attention to what is presumed might be his Majesty's feelings and wishes on the happy day of his recovery be the object, it is with the truest sincerity the Prince expresses his firm conviction that no event could be more repugnant to the feelings of his Royal Father than the knowledge that the Government of his son and representative had exhibited the sovereign Power of the Realm in a state of degradation, of curtail'd authority and diminish'd energy—a state hurtful in practice to the prosperity and good government of his people and injurious in its precedent to the security of the monarchy and the rights of his family.

Upon that part of the Plan which regards the King's real and personal property, the Prince feels himself compell'd to remark, that it was not necessary for Mr. Pitt, nor proper, to suggest to the Prince the restraint he proposes against the Prince's granting away the King's real or personal property. The Prince does not conceive that during the King's life he is by law entitled to make any such grant, and he is sure that he has never shown the smallest inclination to possess any such Power; but it remains with Mr. Pitt to consider the eventual interests of the Royal Family, and to provide a proper and natural security against the mismanagement of them by others.

The Prince has discharged an indispensable duty in thus giving his free opinion on the plan submitted to his consideration. His conviction of the evils which may arise to the King's interests, to the peace and happiness of the Royal Family, and to the safety and welfare of the nation, from the government of the country remaining longer in its present maimed and debilitated state, outweighs in the Prince's mind

INTRODUCTION.

every other consideration, and will determine him to undertake the painful trust imposed upon him by the present melancholy necessity (which of all the King's subjects he deplores the most) in full confidence that the affection and loyalty to the King, the experienc'd attachment to the House of Brunswick, and the generosity which has always distinguish'd this nation, will carry him thro' the many difficulties inseparable from this most critical situation, with comfort to himself, with honour to the King, and advantage to the Public.

(Signed) GEORGE P.

Carlton House,
January 2, 1789.

Endorsed :—
January 2, 1789.
Copy of a Paper delivred by His R.H. the Prince of Wales to the Lord Chancellor, to be communicated to the King's Ministers.

Happily before the crisis became serious the King recovered.

A further gap of two years brings us to 1791 and to the Duke of Leeds' resignation. It was occasioned by a dispute on the question of what would now be called a spirited foreign policy. The triple alliance of England, Holland, and Prussia, formed by Pitt in 1788, had as its principal object the preservation of the peace of Europe and the checking of the ambitious designs of Joseph II. of Austria and Catherine II. of Russia. Austria and Russia were at war with the Porte. Austria had been induced to make peace at Reichenbach and Szistova; Russia refused to desist from hostilities unless she was allowed to retain in her hands the fortress of Oczakow, situated at the mouth of the Dnieper, which she had wrested from the Turks at such a terrible sacrifice of life. Potemkin had won it after six months' siege and the loss of 40,000 men. The allies insisted that Oczakow should be restored to the Turks, and on the refusal of Russia to do this prepared to send an army into Livonia and a fleet into the Baltic. The Opposition stoutly opposed the employment of English ships in a quarrel so remote from English interests, and it was obvious that they had the country at their back. Pitt reluctantly gave way and deserted Prussia, a desertion which paved the way for the defection of Prussia in 1795, when she concluded the peace of Bâle with the French Republic. The Duke of Leeds felt that the honour of England had been engaged, and retired from the cabinet. It would not however be fair to accuse Pitt of pusillanimity. There is evidence in the unpublished despatches of Lord Auckland that Pitt had ascertained that the possession of Oczakow was of no great military importance and that the Dutch were not anxious to proceed to extremities on this ground.

The Memoranda of 1792, pp. 175-200, give an account of a very interesting negotiation which historians have up to the present time misunderstood; the attempt in the face of the alarming condition of Europe to obtain a coalition between Pitt and Fox. The narrative hitherto received is that given in Lord Malmesbury's diaries, and it leaves an impression that such a coalition was seriously entertained by Pitt. The evidence of the Duke of Leeds, which is more trustworthy than that of Lord Malmesbury, as the conversations are reported immediately after they occurred, is at variance with this view; and the discrepancy is explained by observing that the narrative of Lord Malmesbury rests entirely on the evidence of Lord Loughborough, who was a strongly interested, and a very untrustworthy witness. These conversations admit us to the arcana of cabinet intrigue, but, however interesting they may be, we may regret that the Duke did not report Pitt's conversation when it was turned " for some time to the affairs of France " (p. 195). It is amusing to see how easily the Duke of Leeds was persuaded by his " toad-eaters " to believe that he would be acceptable to the King and Pitt as head of a ministry in which Pitt and Fox held subordinate situations. The next instalment of the Memoranda, pp. 201-206, refers to a later phase of the same negotiation. The Memoranda of 1794-5, pp. 207-220, show us the Duke of Leeds coquetting with the Opposition. Pitt engaged in the war with France with the greatest reluctance, after making every sacrifice for peace. He expected the speedy collapse of the French resources. It was hardly credible that a nation with no settled government, deprived of its chivalry and of its natural leaders, should make head against the united force of Europe. To the surprise of everyone, the French were successful beyond their hopes and the English arms were stained with disaster and ignominy. This roused the hopes of the Opposition, who urged that peace should be made and the French Republic recognised. However reasonable these proposals appear to us, they are a little inconsistent in a statesman who three years before resigned office rather than offer a check to the English system of alliances. The vanity of the Duke of Leeds was a serious deduction from his political influence. The concluding Memoranda refer to the marriage of the Prince of Wales and to the unhappy disputes which followed; a few passages from them have already been printed in Mr. Fitzgerald's *Life of George IV.*

It may be hoped that these Political Memoranda as a whole will be welcome to those who take an interest in one of the most stirring and picturesque periods of our history, which, while sufficiently near to us to be fully intelligible, is becoming sufficiently removed to be treated with historical precision. If they reveal to us no very important secrets, nor make it necessary that we should re-write many pages of our history, they at least enable us to live in the very centre of that aristocratical *régime* which placed England after 1815 at the head of Europe, and which the modern democracy will find it difficult to surpass. Above all they enable us to understand a little better the genius, the eloquence, the magnanimity, and the patriotism of William Pitt.

Athenæum Club,
   July 23rd, 1884.

TABLE OF CONTENTS.

	PAGE
Introduction	
Political Memorandums, No. 1, March 1774—January 1780	1
Political Memorandums, No. 2, January 1780—January 1781	21
Political Memorandums, No. 3, February 1781—January 1782	39
Political Memorandums, No. 4, February 1782—March 1782	52
Political Memorandums, No. 5, March 20, 1782—February 28, 1783	63
Fragment in French, written by Carmarthen	80
Fragment on the Fox and North Coalition	82
Memorandum, February 23, 1783	83
Memorandum, February 26, 1783	84
Secret Memorandum, March 14, 1783	84
Memorandum, March 26, 1783	85
Secret Memorandum, April 2, 1783	86
Conversation with Lord Temple, June 15, 1783	87
Cabinet Memorandums, 1784	90
Memorandum, Foreign Alliances, June 11, 1784	106
Memorandum concerning Denmark, June 25, 1784	108
Reasons for a Danish Alliance	108
Memorandum, April 20, 1785	110

CONTENTS.

	PAGE
Sir James Harris, Memorandum for Cabinet, May 9, 1785	111
Conversation with Count Kazeneck, May 26, 1785	113
Conversation with Count Woronzow, June 14, 1785	115
Letter to the King, January 9, 1787	117
Cabinet Memorandum, September 19, 1787	118
Memorandum, Richmond House, November 26, 1788	119
Political Memorandums, 1788-9	121
Letter of William Pitt to the Prince of Wales	143
Conversation with the Duke of Orleans	145
Minute of Cabinet, November 30, 1789	146
Political Memorandums, 1791	148
Political Memorandums, 1792	175
Political Memorandums, 1794, 1795, 1796	207
Appendix, Sir Hugh Eliot's Correspondence from Denmark	235

MARCH 1774—JANUARY 1780.

POLITICAL MEMORANDUMS.

No. 1.

These Memorandums were not begun to be set down till July 1780, consequently many things of some consequence or at least interesting to myself may be omitted.

In March 1774[1] Lord, then Mr., Onslow[2] came to me to inform me that in order to accommodate the K's service some arrangement was to take place in order to gratify Sr Wm Meredith,[3] newly come over from opposition. That it was wished my father[4] would

[1] The Duke of Leeds was born Jan. 29, 1751, and was therefore at this time 23 years of age.
[2] Mr. Onslow was only son of the Right Honourable Arthur Onslow, Speaker of the House of Commons from 1727 to 1761. He was at this time Member for the county of Surrey and a Lord of the Treasury. He was created Baron Cranley, May 14, 1776, and succeeded to the title of Baron Onslow on October 9 in the same year. On June 19, 1801, he was created Viscount Cranley and Earl of Onslow.
[3] Sir William Meredith, Baronet.—He was made Lord of the Admiralty in 1764 and resigned on the dismissal of the Rockingham Ministry: He was elected Member for Liverpool in 1768.
[4] Thomas, fourth Duke of Leeds, born Nov. 6, 1713, was on Nov. 12, 1748, constituted Warden and Chief Justice in Eyre of all His Majesty's Forests, Chases, &c., south of Trent. On January 13, 1756, he resigned these offices and was appointed Cofferer of the Household; on April 14, 1761, he resigned the office of

CAMD. SOC.   B

resign his place of Chief Justice in Eyre north of Trent (retire upon a pension), in which case Lord Pelham,[1] then Comptroller of the Household, would be appointed in his room, and his lordship' white staff be given to Sr William ; that at the same time I was to be brought into Parliament. I immediately went to my father, who did not much approve the plan;[2] but, seeing my wish to come into the H. of Commons, merely to oblige me consented. The arrangement took place, and Capt. Cornwallis, who wished as much to quit as I did to enter the House of Commons, vacated his seat for Eye, in Suffolk, and I was chose in his room. The Boston Port Bill[3] had just passed, matters with America were coming to extremity: convinced of the necessity of strengthening Gov^t as far

---

Cofferer and was constituted Chief Justice in Eyre of all the Royal Forests north of Trent. Manwood, in his *Treatise of the Forest Lawes*, 1615, p. 230, says : " The office of the Lord Chiefe Justice of the Forest is a place both of great honour and of high authoritie, and the same place is to be executed by some greate Peere of the Realme that is alwais one of the King's most honourable Privie Councell. And then when any such noble person is made Lord Chiefe Justice in Eyre of the Forest by the King's especiall commission, hee hath by that as great authority as any other Justice in Eyre hath and more. For then hee may punish all trespassers of the forest according to the lawes of the Forests; and he may heure and determine all the claims of the liberties and franchises which lie within the Forest, as to have parks, warrens, and vivaries : and also of them which do claim to be quitt of assarts and purprestures, and of them which do claim leets, hundreds, felons' goods, waifes, and fugitives, and other liberties within the Forest : and likewise of them which do claim to kill hares and other beasts of the chase within the Forest. For by lawfull and good claimes men may justifie the doing of many things within the Forest which otherwise were unlawfull ; but these claims must be such claims as have been allowed before the Chief Justice in Eyre within the time of prescription." This post was now nothing more than a sinecure, and in 1789 became the subject of parliamentary investigation.

[1] Thomas, afterwards first Earl of Chichester, was appointed Comptroller of His Majesty's Household, July 20, 1765; which post he resigned in 1774. He was appointed Keeper of His Majesty's Great Wardrobe, November 10, 1775.

[2] The Duke of Leeds did not resign the chief justiceship, but Sir William Meredith received the price of his change of party.

[3] This passed on March 25, 1774.

as so great an object demanded, I had no scruple in voting uniformly with them,¹ except on the Petition from the Massachusets, when I divided with the minority, as I could by no means approve of * the rejecting it unheard. Some time, as well as I recollect, after the Prorogation,² I was stepping into my carriage to go to Mims', when I received a message from the Duke of Northumberland,³ who wished to see me immediately. I instantly waited on his Grace at North⁴ House, who proposed to me to be a candidate for Westminster,⁴ with L⁴ Percy, at the ensuing Gen¹ Election. I thank'd his Grace for his polite proposal, but excused myself on account of my design for standing for Helston⁵ (which had constantly been represented by some of the Godolphin Family), and likewise inform'd him in confidence of my design, in case I lost my election,

---

* The Quebec Bill I never attended.⁶

¹ The Marquis of Carmarthen spoke, on May 2, in favour of the Bill for regulating the government of Massachusett's Bay.

² The King closed the Session on June 22; Parliament was prorogued to August 4. On Sept. 30 the Parliament was dissolved by proclamation, and a new one convened, which met on Nov. 29, 1774.

³ This was the first Duke of the new creation, Sir Hugh Smithson, who married the daughter of the Duke of Somerset, became Earl of Northumberland, and, in 1776, was created Duke. Lord Percy was his son, Hugh, born in 1742.

⁴ The Members, in 1774, were Lord Thomas Clinton, Earl Percy, Lord Petersham, and Lord Malden.

⁵ This borough was represented by Sidney Godolphin in 1714, Francis Godolphin in 1741 to 1747, 1754, 1761. In 1774 Carmarthen and Owen received 24 votes each, Cust and Yorke 6 votes each. After this no Godolphin sat for Helston till 1799.

⁶ This was a Bill to give a strongly centralized government to Canada, including districts extending to the Mississippi, the Ohio, and the Hudson's Bay frontier. It was read a second time on May 26, 1774, after a vigorous protest by Townshend, Dunning, Barré, and Fox. It was considered in Committee, May 31, and June 2, June 6, June 8, and reported June 10, the report being carried by the sudden arrival of Members, who, as Burke said, "had not heard anything that had been said against the Bill, no, not even from its being first agitated in the House." It was finally passed June 13.

to ask to be called up to the House of Peers. In autumn the Parliament was dissolved, and in the new one I was returned* with my relation Mr. Owen (who immediately after lost his life by the falling of a bridge as he was riding over it) for Helston, with a petition against us from Mr. Yorke and Mr. Fr. Cust, which was afterwards (in March) determined in their favour. I took no active part the short time I sat for Helston on account of the uncertainty of my situation; however, I voted with Gov' except upon Ld North's conciliatory plan¹ (in Feb.), when Ld Stanley (now Ld Derby), Mr. Welbore Ellis, and myself, voted with the minority.

* Previous to the meeting of the new Parliament, Lord North sent for me and told me he wished I would propose Sr Fletcher Norton² for Speaker. As I was no great admirer of that gentleman's character, I wished to be excused and objected to it, alledging for my reason that I thought it would come with more propriety from some member who had sat longer than I had. His Lord^p prest me for some time, but on my repeated refusal Lord Guernsey³ (now E. of Aylesford) was applied to and moved for him.

¹ This plan was discussed in Committee, Feb. 20, 1775, and was carried by 274 votes to 88. Mr. Wellbore Ellis spoke against it because it did not provide sufficiently for the acknowledgment of British supremacy by America. Burke, Burning, and other Whigs opposed it as "insidious," and contrary to previous declarations.

² A distinguished lawyer: was chosen Speaker on the retirement of Sir John Cust in Jan. 1770, and held his post till the meeting of the new Parliament in October 1780, when he was succeeded by Mr. Cornwall, a nominee of the Court. Sir Fletcher Norton had offended the King by his words on the presentation of the Household Bill, May 7, 1777, when he said that the House had granted His Majesty a very great additional revenue; great beyond example, great beyond your Majesty's highest *expense*. These words were made capital of by the Whigs. Sir Fletcher was also suspected of favouring the American colonies. He was afterwards created Lord Grantley, on the nomination of Lord Rockingham. He died Jan 1, 1789.

³ Member for Maidstone: he was born July 15, 1721, and so was six months younger than Lord Carmarthen.

During the interval of my being out of Parliament, upon a report of the death of Lord Thomas Clinton (now E. of Lincoln), who with Lord Percy had been return'd Member for Westminster, I was again desired to stand for Westminster, and particularly I remember by Mr. W. Ellis, who said it would be extremely agree able to His Majesty and his Ministers. I again excused myself as politely as I could. My friends and myself had already applied for my being called up, and had received for answer that some new Peers were to be created, and at the same time my writ[1] should be made out. In the month of May 1776* I kissed hands for my

---

* This appointment was in compliment to Lord Holdernesse, who at that time resigned his post of Govr to the P. of Wales, &c. When Lord H. was first appointed in 1771,[2] anxious to provide

[1] Lord Carmarthen was called up to the House of Peers, by writ, as Baron Osborne, of Kineton, May 14, 1776.

[2] The Prince of Wales was now nine years old. An account of the arrangement is given by Horace Walpole, in his *Memoirs of the Reign of George III.* p. 310. He calls Lord Holdernesse a "solemn phantom": Dr. Markham (recommended by Lord Mansfield), "the master of Westminster School, a creature of his own, sprung out of the true prerogative seminary at Christchurch, Oxford, a hard arrogant man." Lord North was not consulted. Jackson he calls "an ingenious young man"—he was afterwards Dean of Christchurch. Lord Holdernesse, he says, owed his appointment " to his insignificance and his wife." In his *Last Journals*, i. 129, Walpole calls Lady Charlotte Finch " a woman of remarkable sense and philosophy " An account of the change of tutors is given by Horace Walpole. *Last Journals*, ii. 49, and is so graphic as to be worth quoting. May 28, 1776.—"It was suddenly declared that the King had dismissed Dr. Markham (Bishop of Chester) and Mr. Jackson from being preceptor and sub-preceptor to the Prince of Wales; and that Lord Holderness and Mr. Smelt, his Royal Highnesses governor and sub-governor, had resigned their posts. No reason was assigned for so great a revolution. All that got out at first was that Lord Holderness had been quarrelling with Jackson for three months, and had said that he could not serve with him. So inadequate a cause could not at all account for so general a change, nor satisfy the extreme curiosity of mankind on so large an event, which Lord Hertford said to me that night must have had weighty causes to surmount the King's disposition to conceal everything as much as he possibly could. The next

MARCH 1774—JANUARY 1780.

Peerage, and the same month was appointed one of the Lords of the King's Bedchamber, which office I held till December 1777,

Note to page 5 continued.

a proper preceptor, and having little acquaintance with such of the clergy whose rank could entitle them to so high an office, he con-

day Lord Bruce was named governor, and Dr. Hurd (Bishop of Lichfield and Coventry) preceptor, both being told that they were not to choose their own substitutes; the former was at the same time created Earl of Ailesbury. Bruce Brudenel, youngest brother of Lord Brudenel Montagu, Duke of Montagu, had been adopted by his uncle Thomas Bruce, Earl of Ailesbury, and he inherited his estate. This new lord was a formal, dull man, totally ignorant of and unversed in the world, and a Tory; very unexceptionable in his character, suited to the mystery affected by the King, but totally unfit to educate the Prince of Wales. Bishop Hurd had acquired a good name by several works of slender merit, was a gentle, plausible man, affecting a singular demeanour that endeared him highly to devout old ladies. . . . Lord Holderness, who had a violent humour in his face, which struck in and had fallen on his hearing and his breath, had been to seek relief in the south of France, whence he had returned in the last autumn, a little mended in his health, but still very deaf. On his return he found great prejudices had been instilled into the mind of his friends the Prince of Wales and Prince Frederick, Bishop of Osnaburgh, against him, and it had grown so bad that from last November they had treated his authority with contempt and often ridiculed him to his face. This he imputed to Jackson. I asked if Prince Frederick, who was thought a great favourite, had behaved as ill as the Prince, who it was known had a high spirit, as I guessed two or three years before from Lord Holderness affecting to say how tractable he was. Lord Hertford said, 'Oh! Prince Frederick has gone the furthest, and has been the instrument to influence his brother.' This was artful as more indirect. I said I heard everybody had observed the day before that the King was much fallen away and looked very ill. Both Lord and Lady Hertford cried out. 'Nobody can tell what he has suffered for six weeks.' Lord Hertford added, 'Think what he must feel at finding already that his son is so headstrong that he has not the least authority over him.' I said I heard the Prince was extremely in awe of the Queen. He replied, 'Faith, I believe he is in awe of neither.' He told me the Bishop of Chester was sorely suspected of being at the bottom of this plot, and was a very ambitious man; and that the King had nothing left but to get rid of him and Jackson. The Bishop of Chester had ambitioned the bishopric of Winchester, on the next vacancy, and had been more than once told that he was not to expect it. Jackson had been taken from Oxford with a marvellous character when I had the Honor of being appointed Lord Chamberlain to the Queen, upon the death of Lord Delaware.[1] Lord and Lady

Note to page 5 continued.

sulted the late E. of Chesterfield, who answered him, My dear Holdernesse, whoever is to be Preceptor must be *Preceptor only;* it is of little consequence who is the Prince's *Schoolmaster*, let the King cast his eye over the list of intended preferment among the Bp⁸ and appoint in consequence of it. The successful candidate, however, was Dr Markham, Bishop of Chester (now Archbishop of York); he appointed Mr Cyril Jackson (now Canon of Ch. Ch. and Preacher at Lincoln's Inn) sub preceptor, both respectable charac-

for parts and learning, but I believe his monarchic principles had been a great recommendation. Lord Holderness, though so good a courtier, had recommended Smelt, a thorough Revolution Whig; and had placed two other persons of the same principles about the Prince, one Bude, a pious Protestant, and Salgas, mentioned lower in the text. Jackson's pension was continued to him, and it was said that the Bishop was promised a better bishopric; however, he was very open in his conversation against Lord Holderness, and represented him as most trifling and unfit for his late charge. Both Markham and Jackson had been the choice of Lord Mansfield, and I did not think it very prudent to choose Dr. Hurd, another professed creature of Mansfield; but it was the maxim of the King to cajole all he parted with or disliked, and between hypocrisy and timidity he generally attempted to soothe those he discarded. To mark approbation of the Earl the King immediately made his son-in-law, the Marquis of Carmarthen, Lord of the Bedchamber, in room of Lord Bruce. He offered a pension too to Smelt, who with his usual incorruptible virtue declined it. 'Why,' said the King, 'you have but a small fortune?' 'Enough, Sir,' said he, 'to keep me independent,' and he absolutely refused any premium—following his patron the Earl, who, it is justice to say, acted wisely and handsomely to the King in his retreat. Lord Hertford told me besides that Salgas, son of a French refugee, and one of the Prince's tutors, insisted on retiring too, from the ungovernable temper of the Prince. All his servants, even to *valets de chambre*, were changed." Lord Bruce shortly afterwards retired from his post, and was succeeded by his brother, the Duke of Montagu.

[1] Lord Delaware was appointed Vice-Chamberlain at the first formation of the Queen's Household in 1761; in 1766 he was appointed Master of the Horse to the Queen, which post he held till his death, in Audley Square, Nov. 22, 1777.

Holdernesse[1] suggested to me the idea of asking for that post, which, considering L.ᵈ Dˢ long illness, I took for granted must have

---

Note to page 5 continued.

ters and of great Erudition; bigotted however, to the Pedantic forms of school learning and not sufficiently conversant with men and manners to be of that service their new situations demanded, it was observable that during the first two or three years of this Estabᵗ the Sub preceptor marked the greatest partiality for P. Frederick and seemed to slight the P. of Wˢ. The Gov. and Preceptor seemᵈ to entertain very different ideas of the proper education of their Royal Pupils. The Former wished to enlarge their minds by the study of modern as well as ancient languages and History. The Latter seemed to think the Dead Languages contained all that was essentially necessary for that purpose; he lookd with contempt upon the Foreign Gentlemen who were put about the Princes and seemed surprized to find one of them a good scholar, as he happened not to be an Englishman (M. de Salgas).

In 1774 Lord H. went abroad so ill that his life was despaired of, the Princes wrote frequently to him during his absence, what intrigues might prevail during this interval are uncertain, but upon his return in 1775 he found or thought he found the Royal Pupils much altered in their behaviour towards him and could not but remark the change in the Sub Preceptor's conduct, who now paid great attention to the P. of W. He was soon convinced that somebody had done him ill offices with the Pˢ, who appeared to have withdrawn not only their confidence but to a great degree their affections from him; he now dispaired of attaining the great object of his ambition, the completion of the Education of his Royal Pupils. Early in 1776, he communicated to me in confidence his

---

[1] Lord Carmarthen had married in Nov. 1773, Lady Amelia Darcy, only daughter and heir of Robert, last Earl of Holdernesse, and Baroness Conyers in her own right.

been promised. However, a fortnight or three weeks after my application, Her Majesty in the most gracious and obliging manner

Note to page 5 continued.

fix^d resolution of resigning an employ in which he found he could be no longer serviceable either to the K., the Princes, or the Public. I tried as much as possible to prevent this step, attempting all I could to persuade him to remain in a post for which he was by all parties esteemed so proper. I prevaild on him for a few months to struggle with daily mortifications; at length in May here signed, to the visible concern of both their Majesties, and I may say of the Public. The K. sent for the Bp. of Chester and informed him of L^d H^s resignation. The Bp. said he was ready to act with any person his Majesty would appoint Gov. His M. said he should make an entire new Establishment. The Prelate seemed surprized, and not very respectfully asked, Has your Majesty consulted Ld Mansfield ? The K., surprised at so strange a question, replied he surely was master to appoint whom he pleased to overlook the education of his children, and repeated his determination. The Bp. from the imperious frown with which he had just addressed his Sovereign now changed to the most abject humility, and with tears begg'd the K. to consider his numerous Family. His Majesty dismist him with assuring him it should make no alteration in his future preferment: the Bp. retired confused, and look'd as if he rather doubted what he heard. However, a few months afterwards, on the death of Dr Drummond, he was translated to the See of York. Lord Bruce was appointed Govr (whom I succeeded in the Bedchamber): two days afterwards he resigned and was made E. of Aylesbury. The D. of Montague was then appointed Govr, Col. Hotham, Sub Gov. (tho' Mr. Smelt remained some time), Dr Hurd, Bishop of Litchfield and Coventry, Preceptor, and Mr Arnold sub-preceptor.

Lady Charlotte Finch, Governess of the Royal Nursery, was

gave me the key, Dec. 14, and Lord Lothian¹ had the gold staff. A few days after my receiving the key I was sworn of the Privy Council, Dec. 24, 1777.

During the course of the year 1777 Lord Holdernesse asked if I should have any objection to his applying for my being appointed Ld Lieut^t of the North Riding of Yorkshire, which had been vacant ever since his resignation several years before; he said it had been for many years in his family, and he was sure the gentlemen of the Riding would like it. I answered him I was much oblig^d to him for his kind proposal, and that I should like it extremely. He mentioned Lord Falconberg² having applied for it some time before. He knew not what answer his Lp. had received; but of course thought it right to mention it to him. Ld F. received the information with great politenes, said he had long wished for that office, that he had some time since applied for it, but had received a vague answer. That he would not oppose Ld H. and me about it, &c.; however it was agreed upon that much inconvenience arose from its not being filled, and it was agreed Ld F. should renew his application. Ld H. must have mentioned me to some of the ministers, for being one day at the King's Levée the late Earl of Suffolk,³ then Secretary of

Note to page 5 continued.

supposed to be secretly at the head of the Cabal, who opposed Lord Holdernesse; we gave her the nick-name of Madame de Chevreuse.⁴

¹ He had succeeded to the title in 1775, and was a great personal friend of the King's.
² Henry, the second Earl, born 1743; appointed a Lord of the Bedchamber Feb. 1777; appointed Lord-Lieutenant of the North Riding of Yorkshire Feb. 1778.
³ He was the twelfth Earl of Suffolk and fifth Earl of Berkshire. He was born in May 1738, and, in 1771, became Keeper of the Privy Seal, and Secretary of State for the Northern Department. He died March 1789.
⁴ The avowed enemy of Richelieu and Mazarin at the Court of Louis XIII.

State, ask'd me if I was not come to kiss hands. I appear'd, as I really was, surprised at his Lordship' question, and asked for what; he answered, for the Lieutenancy of the North Riding of Yorkshire. I told him no, that I understood it had been applied for by and promised to Ld Falconberg; he replied that did not signify, I might have it if I chose it. I told him I could not think of taking it so circumstanced, and begg'd Ld F. might be immediately appointed, which he soon after was. In May, 1778, I had the honour of attending her Majesty, who accompanied the King to Portsmouth [1] to see the Grand Fleet then going upon service under the command of Admiral Keppel, and soon perceived a want of harmony between that commander and the E. of Sandwich, first Lord of the Admiralty, tho' I cannot say I profess'd the same degree of foresight with my friend Jackson, who on my return from Portsmouth prophesyd that if Sr H. Palliser went out with that Fleet he was certain, let what would be the event of the campaign, Mr Keppel would be brought to a court-martial.

On the 16 of May poor Lord Holdernesse died. I remember one day sometime after his resignation being with him at Sion Hill; [2] he told me he had had a nosegay brought to him to smell to; he explain'd himself by telling me Mr Robinson had been to him from Ld North trying to induce him to go Ld Lieutenant to Ireland,

[1] Their Majesties went to Portsmouth on May 2, and returned May 9. The great French fleet, under D'Estaing, had just sailed from Toulon. Keppel did not succeed in stopping it, and returned to Portsmouth. On July 10 he sailed out again. In July he had an unsuccessful engagement with the French off Ushant, and returned to Plymouth. His ill success was attributed to the insufficient support given him by Sir Hugh Palliser. In December 1778, owing to charges brought by Sir Hugh Palliser, Admiral Keppel was tried by court-martial. Keppel was very unpopular with the Court, and Palliser's conduct was stimulated by Lord Sandwich. Keppel was triumphantly acquitted, and the news was received with the greatest joy. London and Westminster were illuminated, and Keppel received the freedom of the City of London, and the thanks of the House of Commons.

[2] In the parish of Isleworth, a house built by Lord Holdernesse, and afterwards inhabited by the Duke of Marlborough.

but he had refused it on account of his health. Soon after the E of Buckinghamshire[1] was appointed.

In July I was appointed Lord Lieutenant of the East Riding of Yorkshire in the room of Ld Vicount Irving,[2] deceased, and soon afterwards went to see the Regiment at Warley,[3] from whom I experienced the greatest kindness and civility, as indeed I did from the whole Riding during my continuance in that office.

The first part of the ensuing session I was very little in Town, being in Yorkshire from the latter end of November till near Christmas. After the recess I absented myself from Parliament as my Divorce bill[4] was then coming on. In January, 1779, the Court Martial sat upon Admiral Keppel, for whose acquittal London was illuminated; the mob destroyed Sr Hugh Palliser's house[5] in St. James' square; one Mackay (son to a tradesman in Piccadilly) was taken up for it. I was desired by some of my friends in opposition to make interest for his not being tryed; my friend Crofts came to me from Lord Fitzwilliam[6] on the subject to

---

[1] He was appointed 1776, and entered on his office Jan. 3, 1777. He was second Earl of Buckinghamshire, and died 1793. The offer to Lord Holdernesse is not mentioned in Walpole's *Diary*, Nov. 21, 1776.

[2] Ninth Visconnt, succeeded in 1763, died June 27. 1778. He lived at Temple-Newsham, near Leeds.

[3] Two miles from Halifax.

[4] Amelia D'Arcy, Baroness Conyers in her own right, and Marchioness of Carmarthen, eloped with Captain John Byron, eldest son of Admiral Byron, and father of the poet. She was divorced in May 1779. Lady Conyers died Jan. 26, 1784, and, by Captain Byron, was the mother of the poet's sister, the Honourable Angusta Leigh.

[5] Walpole, writing to Sir Horace Mann, on Feb. 11, 1793, says, "Palliser escaped from Portsmouth this morning at five . . . We passed twice by his house in *Pall Mall* just now" (the letter is dated midnight), "and found a mob before it, but a strong guard of soldiers and constables." He says, later on, that the mob entirely gutted Sir Hugh Palliser's house at three in the morning, but that the furniture had been removed.

[6] This was the second Earl, who succeeded, in 1782, to Lord Rockingham's estates.

oblige Ld F. I said I would write to Ld North to appoint an interview to talk with him upon the subject, tho by the by I disliked my commission extremely. I accordingly wrote to his Lp., but luckily my application was prevented by the Attorney Genl, Mr Wedderburn[1] (now Ld Chief Justice Loughborogh), not chusing to prosecute, tho he had exprest himself with great violence for prosecution in the H. of Commons. Throughout the whole of Admiral Keppels business there appeared a duplicity in administration, which to me was most disgusting. If a proper person to be employed (which I all along was persuaded he was), he should have been countenanced by Gov. If the thanks which were voted to him after his acquittal were disapproved of by Gov^t. why did they not fairly and openly say as much, and act accordingly.

In August 1779, the combined Fleets[2] of France and Spain appeared off Plymouth. Their appearance naturally struck the Kingdom with the utmost consternation, particularly as our own Fleet under Sr Charles Hardy was cruizing to the Westward and the enemies double (or nearly so) his number; they, however, after a parade of a few days retired, the English Fleet got within and made their retreat to Portsmouth, the headmost ships of the combined Fleets being within sight frequently of our sternmost ships—and an engagement for some time appearing inevitable.

Towards the close of the last session a Bill had been pass'd the H. of Commons for augmenting the Militia.[3] This bill I thought in many essential parts very liable to objection; taking for granted, however, that it would likewise pass the House of Lords, and apprehending some difficulty in the carrying it into execution, I

---

[1] He was made Solicitor-General in Jan. 1771, Attorney-General in July 1778, and Lord Chief Justice of the Common Pleas in 1780, when he was created Lord Loughborough.

[2] We learn from Walpole that the combined fleets numbered about sixty, and the ships under Sir Charles Hardy thirty-six.

[3] The Bill for doubling the militia was rejected by the Lords June 30 1779.

had summoned a meeting of the Deputy Lieutenants and Justices, held at Beverley¹ on the ninth of July on account of Militia Business; at the same time I put an advertisement in the York Paper, desiring the attendance of the Gentlemen of the Riding in General, as I wished to take their sense on the present situation of that part in particular and of the County in General; many similar meetings having been held in different parts to consider of the means for putting the country in a state of defence in case of an attempt of the enemy to land.* The bill, however, was very pro-

---

* In the course of the summer Paul Jones with a small French and American squadron had, after an obstinate engagement, taken the K.'s ships, the Serapis, Captain Pearson, and the Countess of Scarbrough, Captain Peircy; the gallant defence however of these two brave officers preserved the trade under their convoy from falling into the Enemy's hands. The action happened off Filey at the distance of about three leagues. The Inhabitants upon that Coast were greatly alarmed, expecting the Enemy would land and destroy Scarbrough, Burlington, &c. In consequence of this alarm I took a survey of the coast from Filey Bridge, the northern extre-

¹ An account of their progress is found in a letter of Mason to Horace Walpole, dated York, Nov. 12, 1779 (Walpole's *Letters*, vol. vii. p. 262): "My Lord Carmarthen called upon me the other day, on his return from the East Riding of this great county, where he had reviewed the whole coast, and found it so totally defenceless that he had given a ball at Beverley on the occasion; he had withal added twenty men to the militia, and by the addition of two captains had metamorphosed a petty battalion into a complete regiment—a very great military manœuvre, and which I doubt not will be attended with the most salutary consequences to this part of the island, especially as the corps with which they are to be embodied is at Coxheath. From York he retired to Kiveton, where, if he pleases, he may make another ball, and invite Lady Conyers to it, who, I don't doubt, will be pleased with such a fête; for you must know, at Lady Holdernesse's request, I have lent her my parsonage to reside in. while W. Byron is raising recruits at Sheffield and Rotherham.

perly rejected by the Lords; however, the second tho' more important object of our meeting still subsisting, I met the Gentlemen at

Note to page 14 *continued.*
mity of the East Riding as far as to Hornsey, and collected all the information I could of the remainder quite to the mouth of the Humber, and up that River as far as Hull. I divided the coast into different districts, and particular Gentlemen were named for the country People to flock to in case of alarm, viz., from Filey to Flambrough Head, Mr. Osbaldeston, of Hunmanby. From Flambro to Hornsey, the Magistrate of Burlington From Hornsey to Waxham, Mr. Constable. From thence to Spurn Point, Sr R. Hilyard. Up the River, the Mayor of Hull. I had applied to Ld Amherst for Arms, &c. Ld Rockingham, Vice-Admiral of the Coast, had likewise applied, and some few arms were sent down to Hull. The military Force in the Riding at this time consisted of two Regiments of Militia, viz. the 2^d Reg^t of West Yorkshire, commanded by Col. Harvey at Hull, and the Northumberland, commanded by Lord Algernon Percy, divided in the following manner, viz. 6 comps. at Beverley, 2 at Burlington, 1 at Hornsey, and 1 at Weighton. The distances between the different districts I had marked out were as follows:

	Miles.	Miles.
From Filey Bridge to Speeton Cliffe	4	
Speeton to Flambro'	7	
To Flamborough Head	.	11
From Flamborough Head to Burlington	4¾	
Burl^n to Hornsey	14	
To Hornsey	.	18¾
From Hornsey to Waxham		16
From Waxham to Spurn Head or Point		15¾
From Spurn to Hull		27
Total		88½

Beverly on the day appointed. I told them I had nothing particular to propose but wished to hear their opinions; nobody seeming disposed to make any proposal, I suggested the Idea of augmenting our own Militia by Volunteer company² ; this they thought unnecessary; I then started an idea of subscription for recruiting the army: upon this we divided and I was in a minority of nine to, I believe, near thirty; then the navy, to this we agreed unanimously, but finding the bountys at Hull and York were so great that our subscription would be of no great use, we agreed to adjourn till circumstances pointed out what means could be taken most conducive to the Public welfare. My Friends, the officers of the East York Mil. wished much for an augmentation of their Corps, which was a Battallion of six companys; on which I told them I would with the greatest pleasure raise a volunteer company of 60 men, and hoped that by a subscription another might be added which would make them a compleat Regiment. This was accordingly done, the Gentlemen of the Riding unanimously agreeing to subscribe for the eighth company at the meeting in November following.

Previous to the meeting of Parliament in Nov. 1779, Lord Gower * ¹ (Lord President) and Lord Weymouth,² Secretary of

* It is supposed that one great motive for the resignation of Lord Gower was his having in a manner engaged in the preceding session that something should be done with regard to the distracted state of Ireland during the recess, in which very proper measure he found himself abandoned by Lord North, &c.

¹ This was Granville, second Earl, and first Marquis of Stafford. He was appointed President of the Privy Council, December 23, 1767, and resigned Nov. 1779; was again appointed, December 19, 1783, and again resigned 1784, and was, in November of that year, appointed Privy Seal, which office he held till 1791. His oldest son was afterwards ambassador at Paris.

² Afterwards first Marquis of Bath, had been Lord-Lieutenant of Ireland, and Secretary of State for the Northern, and afterwards the Southern, Department. He resigned this post in 1770, was appointed to it again in 1775, and resigned it in 1779.

State for the Southern department resigned their places; the former in the debate upon the address[1] said he would no longer remain in office where he found he could be of no service, and was very severe on L North (tho without naming him) for his indolence in business. I had for some time lamented the notorious want of ability in the ministry, the resignation of Lords Gower and Weymouth (two of the best members who composed it) further persuaded me of the necessity of a change; on the first day of the sessions, however, I voted for the address in its original state as Lord Rockingham's amendment,[2] tho containing many unfortunate truths, was couched in too harsh terms. The Duke of Richmond[3] a few days after proposed an address to the King, recommending the appropriating a part of the civil list towards the public exigency, but leaving the quantum and mode to his Majesty. I own I approved of the measure, but would not vote for it, for, as I had in my own mind already determined upon resigning, unless a change in administration took place, I thought it would appear like making a pretended shew of disinterestedness merely to acquire popularity. Previous to the Recess Lord Shelburne gave notice[4] that on the 8th of Feb he should propose a plan for regulating public economy.

During the Recess I received a summons from a committee of Gentlemen at York[5] to attend a meeting there upon the 30th of

[1] Nov. 25, 1779. The debate was largely concerned with the condition of Ireland. Lord Gower's speech is not reported in the *Parliamentary History*.

[2] Lord Rockingham's amendment was to leave out the whole of the address but the title. The House divided at half-past one in the morning: Content, 41; Non-Content, 62, so the amendment was lost. The "many unfortunate truths" must have been in Lord Rockingham's speech, and not in the amendment itself.

[3] The Duke of Richmond's motion for a reform of the Civil Service was made on Dec. 7, 1779. The division was: Content, 36; Non-Content, 77.

[4] Dec. 15, 1779. Burke gave notice of his plan for economical reforms the same day in the House of Commons.

[5] An account of this meeting is given in a letter from Mason to Horace Walpole Dec. 31, 1779, in Cunningham's edition of Horace Walpole's *Letters*, vii. 298.

December, to consider of the necessity of economy in order to support the expense of the war, and for drawing up a petition for the H. of Commons for the abolishing useless and exorbitant or unmerited pensions and salarys, and applying the produce to the public service. I could not but approve of the petition at this time, but apologizd for my not personally attending the meeting.*

On the 24th of Dec., when I returnd home to dress about four o'clock, I found a note from Lord North desiring to see me that day at three. I went immediately to his house in Downing Street: he came directly to me in the dining room, and told me he wished to speak to me in regard to the York meeting, which he represented as a very improper measure and merely the effect of party, and that he was sure I would readily concur with other noblemen and Gentlemen of the county in expressing our disapprobation, and in preventing our friends from attending it The D. of Northumberland[1] was shown into the room where we were, and entirely agreed with his Lordship. I answerd I did by no means see the measure in that light, that I thought nobody could object to the necessity of economy at the present juncture, and that I could by no means disapprove of the plan of the meeting so far as I was informed of it ; that if confusion was to be apprehended from the meeting I was afraid what his Lordship had suggested would rather augment than prevent such confusion. His Ldp. then desired the D. of N. & myself to walk into the next room where we should

---

* As far as the Petition I agreed with the meeting, but could by no means approve of the idea of forming associations and committees of correspondence which they thought proper to do, as no one could know to what dangerous lengths such institutions might proceed, tho perhaps originating from the best & most constitutional principles.

[1] This was the first Duke, who was now Master of the Horse.

find some more Yorkshire Gentlemen.* The company I found all agreed with his Lordship. I however still retained my former opinion, which I repeated, and added that if they were apprehensive of any improper or dangerous proposals being made at the meeting I rather should think it a reason for encouraging our friends to attend in order to oppose such proposals, which otherwise might go forth (considering the notice for the meeting had been so long given) for the real and general sense of the county. We now took our leaves of his Lordship after I had expressed myself as unfortunate in differing so essentially from his Lordship and the company.

Finding myself differ so much from the sentiments of the K's ministers† upon a subject of this sort, was tho unnecessarily an additional motive with me to resign. Accordingly upon Thursday

---

* As well as I recollect the company consisted of the D. of Northumberland, Lords Dartmouth,[1] Carlisle,[2] Fauconberg,[3] Lewisham,[4] Grantham,[5] S[r] J. Goddrick, S[r] Cha[s] Thompson, Lord Mulgrave,[6] Mr. C. Mellish.

† At the Ball on the Queen[s] Birth Day Lord Hillsborough[7] happened to stand behind the Queen[s] chair: he asked me if he might stay there. I replied certainly, and added, I don't want to remove your Ldp. He answered smiling, I am not so sure of that. He then asked if I did not mean to sign the Hertfordshire protest

[1] Lord Dartmouth was Keeper of the Privy Seal from 1775 to 1782.
[2] Lord Carlisle had just been appointed a Lord of Trade, and was in 1780 made Lord-Lieutenant of the East Riding.
[3] Lord Fauconberg was Lord-Lieutenant of the North Riding.
[4] Lord Lewisham, son of the Earl of Dartmouth, was now M.P. for Plymouth.
[5] Lord Grantham had just returned from Spain, where he had been Ambassador. He was afterwards Secretary for Foreign Affairs.
[6] Lord Mulgrave was an Irish Peer who lived in Yorkshire, and in 1790 received an English peerage.
[7] Lord Hillsborough was appointed Secretary of State in place of Lord Weymouth, Nov. 1779.

Jany 27, 1780, after the Drawing room I resigned the Gold Key[1] into her Majesty' hands, giving my reason", viz. that I found supporting the present ministers was not effectually supporting the K's interests: that I had hoped for a change during the Christmas recess, but that not happening I thought it much more consistent with what I owed their Majesties and myself no longer to receive their pay in that situation, when I could not consistently with my own opinion support those ministers his M^y thought proper to employ.

Note to page 19 continued.

against the petition of that County: he said Lord Cranborne[2] had behaved like an angel. I told him I did not doubt it, but I certainly should not sign ye protest. He was very severe against the county meetings for petitioning. Some days after he met my friend Glover in the Park, and asked whether had he given me offence as he heard I meant to resign; he thought Lord North might from his carelessness have been the cause, and rather made excuses on the subject. Glover of his own accord said he did not know the reason, but thought I might perhaps wish for a place of business; his Lordship said if that was all an arrangement might be made.

[1] Walpole, writing to the Countess of Ossory, Jan. 29, 1780, says: "The weathercock Marquis has taken his part, or rather his leave, and resigned his key on Thursday."

[2] Lord Cranborne, who succeeded as Earl of Salisbury in 1780, was now Lord-Lieutenant of Hertfordshire.

JANUARY 1780—JANUARY 1781.
POLITICAL MEMORANDUMS.
No. 2.

Having upon Thursday, Jan. 27, resigned my office of Lord Chamberlain to the Queen, who behaved in the kindest and most gracious manner, and who condescended to express the most flattering concern upon the occasion, I went the next day to the K's Levee, and afterwards had an audience. I told his Majesty it was the first time it ever gave me pain to enter his closet; that the step I had taken far from proceeding from any fractious motive arose merely from my ardent desire for his prosperity; that tho I had a very high opinion of some * still remaining in his administration, yet there were others † whose removal I humbly conceived necessary

---

* Lord Thurlow, Lord Chancellor.
† Lord North, Lord George Germain,[1] and Lord Sandwich.[2]
At Christmas I wrote a small pamphlet intitled " A Letter to Ld Thurlow," which was published in March following, in which I gave my sentiments on the necessity of a change, and particularly of the removal of Lords N., G. G., and S., whose characters I described.

[1] Lord George Germain was Secretary of State for the American Colonies. He was younger son of the Duke of Dorset, and was afterwards created Viscount Sackville.
[2] Lord Sandwich, " Jemmy Twitcher," was First Lord of the Admiralty. Walpole gives an account of these petitions in a letter to Sir Horace Mann, Feb. 6, 1783 : " One or two and twenty counties and two or three towns have voted petitions. But

for his service; that I flattered myself such removals would have taken place during the recess, but that not being the case, as I could not profess supporting those men I so much disapproved, I thought it incumbent on me to resign my place, the former appointment to which I should always look upon as the greatest honour; and that I flattered myself if any unforseen misfortune should arise in the country I could serve his Majesty more effectually in the country than by remaining about Court. The K. seem'd agitated and frequently made use of the expression "I am very sorry": at the conclusion he said he was sure I acted from conviction, and therfore like a man of honour: this I am sure is the substance of what passed upon the occasion. On the 3d of February I went to the Drawing Room (the first after my resignation). The Queen spoke to me, but purposely avoided it for some time, and then more cooly than usual: afterwards the K. spoke to me and behaved just as at another time. Upon Tuesday, Feb. 8[1] (the Day appointed for Lord Shelburne' intended motion), as I was going to dress in order to attend the House of Lords, I received an official letter from the Earl of Hillsborough, secretary of State, containing my dismission[2] from the offices of Lord Lieutenant and Custos Rotulorum of the East Riding of Yorkshire. My surprise would scarcely have been greater had it been a warrant of commitment to the Tower. I went down to the House and spoke for the motion: in the course

in Northamptonshire Lord Spencer was disappointed and a very moderate petition ordered. The same happened at Carlisle. At first the Court was struck dumb, but have begun to rally. Counter-protests have been signed in Hertford and Huntingdon shires, in Surrey and Sussex. Last Wednesday a meeting was summoned in Westminster Hall; Charles Fry harangued the people finely and warmly; and not only a petition was voted but he was proposed for candidate for that city at the next election, and was accepted joyfully."

[1] This was the day appointed for Lord Shelburne's motion for a committee of both Houses to inquire into the public expenditure, of which he had given notice before the recess.

[2] Lord Pembroke was at the same time dismissed from the Lord-Lieutenancy of Wiltshire, and the Duke of Richmond from that of Sussex.

of my speech I took care to give the real motives[1] for my resignation, as well as to comment upon my dismissal. I had a sharp contest with Lord Sandwich upon our being deprived of the service of several of the best officers in the navy merely on account of his remaining at the Head of the Admiralty; this his Lordship denied being the case, but I again affirmed my believing it to be so, and his Lordship said no more on the subject. Admiral Keppel, who happen'd to be in the house, said he could not have conceived his Lordship would have dared to deny so notorious a truth.

Having in my speech said that I thought it improper for those who disapproved the K's ministers to retain places at Court, I the next evening received a note from my Friend[*] Lord Pembroke

---

[*] Lord Pembroke had mentioned to me a motion he proposed to make some time this session for a bill to enable Duke Ferdinand of Brunswick[2] to take the command of the Army in case his Majesty

[1] In the *Parliamentary History* this part of Lord Carmarthen's speech is reported as follows:—"He could no longer give his support to a ministry which had after a series of repeated trials proved themselves pusillanimous, incapable, and corrupt, who had brought the nation to the brink of destruction, and still persisted to plunge it deeper into calamity and danger. They were the curse of this country, and he feared would prove its ruin. One of them from his deserved ignominy, and the other from his criminal ignorance and neglect [supposed to mean Lords Sandwich and North]: the former, when the talents and abilities were most wanting, driving almost every man of a certain description from the service by insult and bad treatment. These were the reasons which induced him to resign his place in the household." He was answered by the Earl of Chesterfield, on which the Marquis of Carmarthen "restated his words and pointed more definitely at Lord Sandwich, Lord Carmarthen refused to retract. Lord Rockingham, in his speech, took occasion to say that in the great meeting held at York there were persons present in one room who possessed landed property to the amount of 800,000*l.* a year, and that no less than 9,000 gentlemen, clergy, and freeholders had signed the petition. The division was: Content, 55; Non-Content, 101.

[2] Duke Ferdinand of Brunswick had just succeeded his father as Duke; had fought as Prince Ferdinand at Hastenbeck and Crefeld. He married Princess Augusta of Wales, sister of George III. and was, therefore, a member of the royal family of England. He was wounded at Jena, and died shortly afterwards, 1806. He was father of Queen Caroline, consort of George IV.

(who had more than once voted with opposition), saying he hoped he should receive no more such severe reprimands from me, as he had that morning resigned his post of Lord of the Bedchamber to the King. The next day after my dismission Lord Carlisle kiss'd Hands for the Lieutenancy, &c. of the East Riding, and that evening at Lady Milbourne' was extremely polite to me on the occasion, and assured me the first he knew of my Dismission was from my speech in the House of Lords. A few days afterwards Lord Pembroke was dismissed from the Lieutenancy, &c. of Wiltshire, and Lord Aylesbury[1] appointed in his room. It was now supposed that the dismission of all the Lord Lieutenants who voted in opposition would take place, and it was reported that the Duke of Richmond" (Sussex) had been offered to the Lord" Pelham[2] and Ashburnham,[3] the former of whom had begged to be excused and the latter desired time to consider of it: however nothing of the sort has as yet taken

Note to page 23 continued.

would be prevailed upon to send for his S. H. I own in case of invasion I thought that Princes abilities might be of the greatest service both in the closet and the Field. Lord P. mentioned this business to Lord Shelburne, who seem'd to approve the measure, but rather wished (for what reason I know not) to have it postpon'd. I remember one day last year at St. James's, after the Levee, talking with the D. of Northumberland, Lord Nugent,[4] and some others; the conversation happened to turn upon D. Ferdinand, and his Grace said he wished he was to be sent for, and that the K. would make a Friend of him.

[1] Lord Aylesbury was Lord of the Bedchamber.
[2] Lord Pelham had been Comptroller of the Household, and was now Keeper of the Great Wardrobe
[3] Lord Ashburnham had been First Lord of the Bedchamber and Groom of the Stole.
[4] Robert, Earl Nugent, was at this time Treasurer of Ireland; he died in 1788, and his honours passed to his son-in-law, the Marquis of Buckingham.

place since the removal of Lord Pembroke. His Lordship and myself being now fairly *Launch'd* into Opposition received much civility from the members who composed it. Lord P. came to me by desire of Lord Shelburne* to ask my consent for his making a

---

* Lord Shelburne possesses great talents for a Statesman, but is not always to be trusted. It is said he sent private instructions[1] to Lord Rochford when Ambassador at Paris, relative to Corsica, which were diametrically opposite to the determination of the Cabinet, so that when Ld R. went to the Duc de Choiseul, and threatened him with the resentment of his court in case the French persisted in their design on Corsica, the D. said his Lp. must be in joke, for by his dispatches from the Compte (now Duc) de Chatelet, the French Ambassador at London, he found the British Ministry were determined not to interfere in that business.

Lord Shelburne was formerly so indifferent a speaker that in 1761 Mr. Fox (afterwards Lord Holland) hearing him in the H.

[1] In Lord E. Fitzmaurice's *Life of Lord Shelburne* there is nothing to justify this suspicion, but two passages give a different explanation of the facts. Vol. ii. p. 135, note, Lord Rochford writes to Shelburne, June 23, 1768: "Choiseul read to me a great part of Count Châtelet's letter, which was very long, in which he gave an account of the conference he had with your Lordship, and, by the tenour of his despatch, it appeared that he thought our alarms with regard to Corsica were quieted. Some parts of the letter the Duc de Choiseul read to himself, and, after he had finished, he said, ' Je vois avec plaisir que vous êtes un peu adoucis sur cette affaire.'" To this Shelburne replied: "In the meantime I am to acquaint your Excellency that nothing could surprise His Majesty more than the idea mentioned by your Excellency, ' que nous étions un peu adoucis sur cette affaire.'" Again, p. 139, Lord E. Fitzmaurice says: "Weymouth never ceased assuring the ambassadors of the Great Powers that nothing would induce England to go to war for Corsica." These indiscreet utterances did not fail to reach the ears of the watchful Châtelet. He left M. Faurés in charge of the French embassy, and himself hurried over to Paris, to assure Choiseul that he could pursue his schemes in security. He received support from an unexpected quarter. "A great law lord," it was Mansfield, "being then in Paris, declared, at one of the minister's tables, that the English Ministry was too weak, and the nation too wise, to enter into a war for the sake of Corsica." In a moment everything was changed.

CAMD. SOC.   E

motion relative to our dismission, and at the same time expressing a wish to see me (he had called at my house when I was out). I waited upon him and found him at home; he said the measure from its being as unusual as violent had alarmed people in general; that the *City of London* saw it a light which threatened the freedom of Parliament, &c., &c., &c.: he wished therefore to propose an address similar to that presented upon the taking the Regiments from the D. of Bolton and Ld Cobham[1] in 1734. I found his Lordship complaind of having been ill used by the K.: he seemed

---

Note to page 25 continued.

of Lords, told a friend of mine (L.) who stood by him "he will never do; he now, tho not an agreeable is yet a most able speaker, possest of vast information and remarkably fluent." He was very principally concerned with Lord Bute and Count Vivi[2] (the Sardinian Envoy) in bringing about the Peace. L.

His Lordship was certainly at one time a very great favourite of the K's, but, thinking to supplant Lord Bute who had governed the K. from a child, he drove at too furious a rate, and fell a sacrifice to his want of prudence. Great and disappointed ambition joined to great and cultivated abilities, as there is no saying where they will stop, render this nobleman as dangerous as he is powerful.

[1] Feb. 13, 1734, a Bill was introduced "to prevent any Commissioned Officer, not above the rank of a Colonel of a Regiment, from being removed, unless by a Court-Martial, or by Address of either House of Parliament." Smollett says of it: "The Duke of Bolton and Lord Cobham had been deprived of the regiments they commanded, because they refused to concur in every project of the administration. It was in consequence of their dismission that Lord Morpeth moved for a Bill to prevent any commission officer, not above the rank of colonel, from being removed, unless by a court-martial or by Address of either House of Parliament. Such an attack on the prerogative might have succeeded in the latter part of the reign of the first Charles, but at this juncture could not fail to miscarry, yet it was sustained with great vigour and address."

[2] Lord E. Fitzmaurice says (vol. i. p. 137) that this secret negotiation began Nov. 17, 1761, and was continued, with intervals, till May 22, 1763. There is a complete copy of the correspondence in the Lansdowne MSS.; partly in cypher.

to wish to know what had passed at my audience, but I only told him that from the manner of his M^y I had no reason to apprehend the ensuing mark of his displeasure. Ld Shelburne some days afterwards made the motion,[1] but not in its original shape (which was merely to know who advised the measure); grounding it upon a direct attack on the Freedom of debate and Parliamentary proceedings, as supposing we were dismissed for our conduct in that house. I desired the ministry to give any reason for my removal, but they would not. The motion was rejected[2] by a considerable majority; Ld P. and I thinking ourselves too personally interested to judge on the occasion, did not vote. It was in introducing this motion that Lord Shelburne made use of the offensive language[3] which afterwards occasioned a duel between him and Colonel Fullerton.

The night of this debate I supp'd at Ld Rockingham's: there was only his Lordship, Lord Fitzwilliam, and myself. Ld F. went away soon after supper, and I had a long and agreeable tete-a-tete with Ld R. for I believe near two hours, during which I found his Lordship agreed with me in most of the essential matters we conversd upon.

About this time several very important questions relating to future reformation in the finances and general economy of the State were agitated in Parliament. Mr. Burke,[4] in one of the most able speeches ever heard, had delivered his plan, which consisted of a variety of

[1] On March 6, 1780.
[2] The division was—Content, 39; Non-Content, 92.
[3] Lord Shelburne, complaining of "occasional rank," said "he would ask what pretensions a Mr. Fullerton had to be appointed a lieutenant-colonel? This gentleman had never held any rank, or even was in the army before . . . . . . yet this clerk-in-office, this *commis*, contrary to all military establishment, contrary to all the spirit of the army, was now a lieutenant-colonel." Col. Fullerton, who was a Member of the House of Commons, resented being called a *commis*. They met in Hyde Park at 5 a.m. Lord Shelburne was slightly wounded. Walpole says that Shelburne did not call Fullerton a *commis*.
[4] His plan for economical reform was introduced Feb. 11, 1780.

JANUARY 1780—JANUARY 1781.

proposed regulations in order to reduce the enormous expence attending the present establishment of different departments of the State and of the K's Household, in consequence of which several bills were brought in for abolishing some and new modelling other institutions. Upon the question for abolishing the Board of Trade[1] as an useless tho enormously expensive establishment the ministry were beat, it being carried in the affirmative. People in general now expected a change, and they were in a manner confirmed in such expectation when Mr. Dunning's proposed resolution[2] that the "Influence of the Crown had increased, was increasing, and ought to be diminish^d," was carried (tho by the accidental absence of Mr. North and a few other ministerial members), likewise against administration. Opposition, however, as if intoxicated by success, seemed to have lost every idea of prudence, and from eagerly seeking to grasp at too much lost the ground they had so recently gain'd. The shortening the duration of Parliaments, a new mode of election, disfranchising what are vulgarly called rotten boroughs, and an additional number of county members, were now the favourite topics in the committees of the different counties, and seem'd to meet with more advocates (both as to respect and numbers) than could have been, I think, imagined. The most respectable part of the opposition (viz. the Cavendishes, Lord Rockingham, and his Friends, the D. of Richmond excepted) seem'd to disapprove this essential innovation in the constitution, which was however said to be approved of by Lords Shelburne, Camden, &c. but, be this as it may, the opposition (within doors and the committees without) seem'd to neglect or to have forgot the sole ground of the Petitions of the People and to have let go the substance through eagerness to grasp the shadow. The H. of Commons had passed a bill to incapacitate a certain de-

---

[1] This debate took place on March 13. The Ministry were beaten by a majority of eight. For the motion, 207; Against it, 199.

[2] This was carried, on April 6, by a majority of 18; 233 for, and 215 against, the motion.

scription of contractors from sitting in their House. This Bill,* after being artfully misrepresented in the H. of Lords, was there rejected.¹

There certainly was at this time some material difference of opinion among the Principal leaders of Opposition, for I remember (I believe it was in April) calling one day upon Lord Shelburne to return a visit, and, finding him dressing, he shewed me a motion he intended to make relative to the transactions between this country and Holland, as likewise to the measures then taking by the Northern Courts² in conjunction with the Dutch for securing the free navigation of the neutral powers. The motion was to address the K.

---

* Lord Mansfield, in speaking against the Bill, said it was cruel and unjust to those who were serving the public by contract, a species of service unavoidable from the nature of things. He instanced the hardship it would inflict both upon the member and his constituents: for instance, says his Lordship, Mr. Harley now serves for the County of Hereford, why incapacitate so respectable a man from serving or his constituents from sending him to Parlᵗ. With all due deference to his Lordship Mr. Harley³ was by no means a case in point, as the bill expressly defin'd the description of contractors who were to be affected by it, viz. those only who contracts of a clandestine nature either in their own names or any persons (in order to destroy that very notorious instrument of ministerial influence). In this predicament Mr. Harley certainly does not stand nor anybody else who avowedly contracts for Government, and whose contract (to use a vulgar expression) is made fairly and above board.

¹ This was rejected in the House of Lords, April 14, by a majority of 20; 61 against 41.

² The so-called *armed neutrality* was initiated by Russia. It was a declaration made by maritime powers to protest against the right of searching neutral ships in time of war, which had been always claimed and exercised by England. Lord Shelburne went into the whole question in the House of Lords, June 1, 1780. In his speech he denounced the bullying and overbearing behaviour of the English against the Dutch, which had driven them into the arms of Russia.

for papers and was rejected. During our conversation he said, "you must be surprized at coming into opposition to find so little Harmony amongst us (I remember making the same remark to the D. of Grafton), but what can we do? Nothing upon earth, there is no dealing with Mr. Burke,[1] he is so violently attach'd to his own opinion that there is no arguing with him, and has got so much ascendency over Lord Rockingham that I protest I see no method of doing anything." I made no answer to this remark but shall not, I trust, forget it. I carried his Ldp. down to the house, and talking in our way thither about Holland was surprized to hear him speak very contemptuously of Sir Joseph Yorke.[2]

I do not recollect any thing material occurrence till the 2nd of June. The D. of Richmond[3] was to propose his Bill relative to the altering the constitution of Parliaments. I went that morning down to Mims where I staid till next day. The 2^d was the day appointed for presenting the Petition of the Protestant Association to the House of Commons, in consequence of which Ld G. Gordon,[4]

---

[1] Compare Fitzmaurice's *Life of Shelburne*, vol. iii. p. 101, where Col. Barré is reported as saying to the Duke of Richmond, "My Lord, I love Burke, I admire him, even in his wanderings; but when these wanderings come to be adopted seriously and obstinately by men of far higher description than himself, they then become alarming indeed."

[2] Sir Joseph Yorke was English ambassador at the Hague.

[3] The Bill was entitled "An Act for declaring and restoring the natural inalienable and equal rights of all the Commons of Great Britain (in fact, persons of insane mind and criminals incapacitated by law only excepted) to vote in the election of their representatives to Parliament; for regulating the mode and manner of such elections; for restoring Annual Parliaments; for giving an hereditary seat to the sixteen peers which shall be elected in Scotland; and for establishing more equitable regulations concerning the peerage of Scotland." The Bill was thrown out without a division.

[4] He was son of the third Duke of Gordon, and was now about thirty years old. It is said that whilst he was haranguing the mob, his cousin, General Gordon, said to him, "My Lord George, do you intend to bring your rascally adherents into the House of Commons? If you do, the first man of them that enters I will plunge my sword—not into his, but into your, body." Another of his relations, General Grant, said, "For God's sake, Lord George! do not lead these poor people into any danger."

President of the association, had several days before inserted an advertisement setting forth that, whereas no hall in London could contain forty thousand persons, he desired the Friends of the Petition would asemble in St. George's Fields, and thence proceed in four different divisions to the H. of Commons in order to its being presented. No steps seem to have been taken by Gov^t to prevent the mishap likely to ensue from this irregular and illegal assembly. They came in immense numbers, filled the avenues to both H^s of Parl^t, and ill treated and endangered the lives of several Members, both Lords and Commons: they even tried to force their way into the H. of Commons, but I believe were prevented by the timely arrival of the Guards. Ld George was continually running from the House to inform the mob in the lobby what was passing within doors and naming what members spoke for or against the Petition; his Lordship likewise thought proper to tell the House that they were all at his mercy, as with a motion of his finger he could have them torn to pieces. That night the mob destroyed the chapels[1] of the Marquis de Cordon and Count Haslang, the Sardinian and Bavarian Ministers. The next day I returned to Town and went to the H. of Lords, which sat (tho' Saturday) on account of the tumults having interrupted the preceding day's business. Lord Shelburne tried to insinuate that the mob was raised by the ministers, he advised an immediate repeal of the Quebec bill.[2] Ld Rock-

[1] An amusing account of this is given by Horace Walpole to the Countess of Ossory, *Letters*, vol. vii. p. 375, following: "The mob forced the Sardinian Minister's chapel, in Lincoln's-Inn-Fields, and gutted it. He saved nothing but the chalice, lost the silver lamps, &c. and the benches, being turned into the street, were fuel for a bonfire, with the blazing brands of which they set fire to the inside of the chapel, nor, till the Guards arrived, would suffer the engines to play. My cousin, J. Walpole, fetched poor Madam Cardon, who was ill, and guarded her in his house till three in the morning, when all was quiet.

"Old Haslang's chapel [in Golden Square] has undergone the same fate, all except the ordeal. They found stores of massbooks, and run tea." Count Haslang had been Minister of Bavaria since 1740. He died in 1783, at the age of 83.

[2] The *Parliamentary History* says (vol. xxi. p. 677) of the Duke of Richmoud's speech, "His Grace again asserted that the Quebec Act was the cause of the dis-

ingham spoke sensibly and cooly upon the occasion and differed from L^d Sh. The D. of Richmond introduced his Bill[1] with great ability; it was, however, negatived without a division. The mob, I believe, that night destroyed some popish schools and houses near Hockley in the hole. The next night[2] I was present while they were burning the furniture of some popish school, chapel, and houses near Moor Fields, which they were suffer'd to do by the shameful pusillanimity of the Ld Mayor, &c., who were present with a party of the Guards, but would give no order. The K^s Birth day being kept on Monday, the 5th of June, I went to the Levée—the first time I had been there since my dismission, but made a point of going there that day. The mob attackd Sir Geo. Saviles[3] House at night: I stood with him there till half af' four the next morning. On the Tuesday the Rioters got into St James' Park, but by a proper disposition of the Guards were prevented going to the Queen^s House, and quitted the Park. They filled all the avenues to the two Houses. However, Troops being posted thereabouts, things remained tolerably quiet there. Lord Sandwich was very ill-treated and cut with a stone, coming from the Admir-[alty]. Ld Rockingham^s House[4] being threatened I remained there

content, and not the repeal of the Acts relative to Popery .... The Quebec Act absolutely established the Popish religion in Canada, by sending a Popish Bishop there, and allowing every part of the exercise of that dangerous and intolerant religion." Lord Shelburne concluded his speech by saying, "there were three subjects under discussion, the punishment of the rioters, the repeal of the Quebec Act, and the regulation of the police of Westminster. Take them up together, and there could be no doubt of producing all that some considerate politicians could wish for under the present circumstances." The Bill for the government of Quebec received the Royal Assent in 1774. The Marquis of Rockingham opposed the immediate repeal of it.

[1] For Annual Parliaments, &c.
[2] Sunday, June 4.
[3] In Leicester Fields.
[4] Walpole says to Lady Ossory, *Letters*, vol. vii. p. 387: "Lord Rockingham has two hundred soldiers in his house, and is determined to defend it." Lord Rockingham lived in Grosvenor Square.

most parts of the nights of Tuesday and Wednesday the 6 and 7. We had a hundred soldiers there, and near as many more Gentlemen, servants, &c. armed. On the Wednesday I saw the D. of Bolton and Lord Galloway, who wished much to have the repeal of the Bill complaind of moved for. They tried to convince me of the propriety of the measure, but I could not think of being bullied and bludgeon'd by the mob into anything. On Thursday, 8th, Mrs. Granville told me, one Lloyd, a wine merchant whom she employed, said he had heard of a house somewhere beyond Moorfields where money was distributed to the Rioters and the orders given them for their mode of proceeding. I immediately went to Mr. Lloyd in St James' Street. He told me he had heard there was such a place, and that he had of late seen some foreigners, whom nobody knew, come frequently to the York coffee house in St James' Street, and that he suspected they came as spies: he promised me he would get all the information he could upon these matters and let me know. I immediately went to the offices of both the Secretarys of State, but neither of them were there. Thursday night everything was quiet, I walk'd with Mr. Rogers (Secretary to Admiral Keppel) between ten and eleven, from Lord Rockingham's over Westminster Bridge, thro' St George's Fields, Blackfriars Bridge, by Bridewell, the Fleet, thro' Holborn, Bloomsbury Square, &c. but scarce anybody but the Patrols. On Fryday I went down to Mims,[1] and returned the next day, when I found a summons to Council at the Cockpit.[2] I immediately went there and likewise several days afterwards, as I thought it my duty at such a period. I saw Mr. Lloyd; he told me the person who kept the House where it was suspected money was given was gone off; that one of the strangers who came to the York coffee house had been followed from thence, that he walked very composedly to Knights-

[1] North Mims, an estate bought from the Coningshys by Sir Nicholas Hyde, through whose granddaughter it passed to Peregrine Osborne, Duke of Leeds. It was sold by them in 1799.
[2] The cockpit of Whitehall Palace, after the great fire of 1697, was converted into the Privy Council Office.

CAMD. SOC.   F

bridge, but supposing probably he was followed ran off of a sudden thro' the coaches and disappeared. I mentioned these particulars to Lord Stormont, but do not find that the man has been since seen or heard of. On Fryday afternoon, the 9th, Lord George Gordon was committed to the Tower for High Treason.

In Sept' the Parliament was dissolved: the new one met the 31st of October.* The opposition appeared without any settled Plan. they proposed Sir Fletcher Norton† in opposition to Mr. Cornwall for Speaker; the latter, however, was chosen by a considerable majority. In the H. of Lords the next day Lord Westmorland[1] moved the address and was seconded by Lord Brownlow.[2] I was desired to say something, tho nothing I found agreed upon. I proposed[3] the omitting the major part of the proposed address, but leaving the assurances of the House to assist his M. to the utmost of their [power] in the defence of their country and preservation of their dearest interests. I could have willingly taken the Paragraph immediately following,‡ but the D. of Richmond dis-

---

* Lord Rochford told me in the House of Lords he thought the great object of the House of Bourbon was Gibraltar; he lamented the indecision and apparent want of ability of the greater part of the ministers, and added he thought the Bedfords were endeavouring to gain over Charles Fox.

† About ten days before the Parliament met Fl. N.[4] told me he knew Ministers meant to alter their plan with respect to America; but the news of Lord Cornwallis having defeated Gates[5] prevented the intended alteration taking place.

‡ The paragraph I allude to was as follows: " It is with just and heartfelt indignation that we see the Monarchies of France and

[1] John, tenth Earl of Westmoreland, now 21 years old, succeeded in 1771.
[2] Sir Brownlow Cust, created first Lord Brownlow in 1776. Aged now 36.
[3] Lord Carmarthen is reported to have opposed the continuance of the war with America.
[4] Sir Fletcher Norton.
[5] This was in the battle of Camden, fought August 15.

approved of the word Rebellion, and, as the great object with me was if possible to procure unanimity by preserving the spirit of the Address, and at the same time omitting any passage or expression which were likely to be objected to, the address in its original state was carried by 68 to 23, Lord Brownlow and myself Tellers.

On Sat. Nov. 4, I called upon Lord Rockingham, and lamented to him the appearance of a want of union[1] among the opposition : he sincerely agreed with me. He told me Lord Shelburne seemed to insist upon the addition of county members, and that the D. of Richmond was equally strenuous for his plan of new modelling the constitution of Parliament. I told him I had ever been apprehensive of the comittees producing mischief by their proposed innovations, that I wished most sincerely to see things settled, and

---

Note to page 34 *continued.*

Spain leagued in confederacy to support the Rebellion in your Majesty' Colonies in North America, and employing the whole force of those kingdoms in the prosecution of a war waged in violation of all public faith, and for the sole purpose of gratifying boundless ambition by destroying the commerce and giving a fatal blow to the Power of Great Britain."

[1] This difference of opinion is clearly brought ont in a letter of Lord Rockingham's, Feb. 28, 1780 (Lord Albemarle's *Memoirs of Rockingham*, vol. i. p. 397); " Some persons, I know, by the expression of a *more equal representation,* mean *little more* than the abolishing *what are called the rotten boroughs!* Some of these persons think that these boroughs should be taken away from their possessors, without any compensation (as being nnconstitutional); some would allow that the possessors should be compensated. Some persons think that the seats for these boroughs should be filled up by additional members from their respective counties: others think that, like Shoreham, these seats should be filled up by the voice of the persons resident within certain neighbouring districts. Others think that many of the great important towns of trade and manufacture, who have not, at present, their respective local representatives, should fill up the parliamentary vacant seats. It is endless, indeed, to state the variety of ideas which are now, as it were, afloat on these points."

recommended if possible a coalition,[1] particularly recommending the Chancellor and Lord Gower as men of whom I had a great opinion, in which his Lordship seemed to concur with me. Talking of the war, which I owned I saw no prospect of terminating, he said he for one would prefer making peace thro' America rather than thro' France.

In consequence of some strange threatening letters wrote and sent by the Earl of Pomfret[2] to the Duke of Grafton, those two noblemen were ordered to attend in their places in the H. of Lords on Monday, Nov. 6. The letters being read and the D's answers and the accounts given by them both, it plainly appeard that the Duke had given no provocation. I moved to commit Lord Pomfret

[1] An account of an overture made of coalition in the summer of 1780 is to be found in Jeremy Bentham's works (Bowring), x. 102. It was given by Lord Shelburne to Mr. W. Pitt on Sunday, Sept. 16, 1781. The terms were, Lord North to be continued; Lord Sandwich to be continued or compensated; Keppel certainly not to come into his place; "that Charles Fox could not be received, at least immediately, into any of the high and confidential offices, such as that of Secretary of State, but that as to any lucrative office out of the great line of business, such as that of Treasurer of the Navy, there would perhaps be no objection." Lord Rockingham stood out for Keppel, and insisted that the Duke of Richmond and Charles Fox should be Secretaries of State. There was nothing said about Lord Shelburne. "Burke was not to have been neglected." The demands on Lord Rockingham's side being such, no reply was given. Lord Rockingham was perhaps to have Ireland.

[2] He died 1785. The letter to the Duke of Grafton had reference to a discharged servant of the Earl of Pomfret, named Langstaff, whom the Duke was supposed to have befriended. Horace Walpole says (vii. 458): "Our old acquaintance, Lord Pomfret, whose madness has laid dormant for some time, is broken out again— I mean his madness is. . . . The Earl some years ago had some of these flippances, and used to call gentlemen out at the play-houses who he pretended had made faces at him." And again (vii. 462): "Lord Pomfret, after a week's imprisonment in the Tower, made his submission, has been reprimanded, and released on giving his honour—a madman's honour—not to repeat his offence." In the course of the debate in the House of Lords only two precedents for a similar course were mentioned: one in 1663, in the case of a challenge sent by the Earl of Middlesex to the Earl of Bridgewater; and one in 1690, between Lord Granville and Lord Kereton. The Duke of Grafton had been Secretary of State, First Lord of the Treasury, and Lord Privy Seal. He was now Chancellor of the University of Cambridge.

to the Tower for the high contempt of the House he had been guilty of in his behaviour to a Peer in the person of the D. of Grafton, and likewise moved a resolution implying the approbation* of the H. of the D^s conduct. Ld P. was sent to the Tower that night: he sent a very proper Petition on the Monday following, and, having agreed to make a proper acknowledgment of his offence, and engagement to proceed no farther in his resentments, was discharged out of custody on Fryday 17, and made his acknowledgments, &c. in his place. The next Day the Duchess of Cumberland[1] sent a Gentleman to my House to inform me he had been heard to threaten my life the night after his discharge, at the Hotel in Jermyn Street; however upon enquiry I could not make anything of the report. He went out of town immediately after, is certainly much disorderd in his mind at times, and if his Friends do not take great care will most probably do more serious mischief.

In Jan^{ry} 1781, Lord Robert Spencer[2] resigned his place of one of the Lords of Trade. I understand he wished not to come into Parliament, but the D. his brother chose he should. He has long been dissatisfied with the present ministers, and, finding his supporting them incompatible with his own opinion, resigned his office.†

---

* On Thursday, Nov. 24, I received a most polite letter from the Duke of Grafton at Euston in acknowledg^t for the active part I had taken in the business, and expressing himself as under great obligations to me for my conduct on the occasion.

† I had a great deal of conversation during my being at Bath in the Christmas Holydays with the Primate of Ireland (Dr. Robinson, Lord Rokeby)[3] upon our political state in general. His Grace

[1] Duchess of Cumberland, wife of George III.'s brother. She had been Lady Anne Luttrell.
[2] Brother of the third Duke of Marlborough, Member for Woodstock, and afterwards for the city of Oxford. He had been appointed a Commissioner for Trade in 1770. In 1782 he became a Vice-Treasurer for Ireland.
[3] Archbishop of Armagh, created Lord Rokeby in 1777.

JANUARY 1780—JANUARY 1781.

On the delivery of the K's message,[1] in Jan^ry, relative to the rupture with Holland during the recess. The D. of Richmond proposed an amendment to the address equally respectful to the Crown, but expressive of our disapprobation of engaging in this new war without fuller information on the subject than what was contained in the papers laid before us by Lord Stormont. Upon the Division we were only 19 against 70, I believe. I took no part in the Debate, which I thought ill conducted on both sides, particularly so by the opposition, who rested their arguments too much upon the supposed injustice of the measure, instead of considering it only in its true light as at best a rash, impolitic and inexpedient one. There were two Protests[2] enter'd, but I signd neither of them.

Note to page 37 continued.

lamented much the situation to which we were reduced, and regretted the want of consistency so evident in the conduct of those who for a long time past had had the management of Public affaires.

I was much entertained while at Bath by accounts given me of Ireland and the political connections of that country, by Mr. Macartney,[3] who may be said to have govern'd it during the late Earl Harcourt's[4] Administration.

[1] Delivered Jan. 25, 1781. The rupture with Holland arose out of the *armed neutrality*. Holland was always the battle-ground of rivalry between French and English infinence. The division was 19 against 84.

[2] The first protest was signed by Richmond, Portland, Fitzwilliam, Harcourt, Ferrers, Rockingham, Devonshire, Pembroke, Coventry. The second by Wycombe (Shelburne), Camden, Richmond, Ferrers, Portland, Rockingham, Fitzwilliam, Pembroke.

[3] John Macartney was knighted, and afterwards made a baronet in 1799.

[4] Earl Harcourt was Lord-Lieutenant of Ireland from 1769 to 1777.

FEBRUARY 1781—JANUARY 1782.

POLITICAL MEMORANDUMS.

No. 3.

In Feb. 1781, Mr. Burke[1] brought the same economical bill into the H. of Commons as in the last session of the late Parl.; it was however negatived on the question of committment by 233 to 190; neither Col. Barré nor Mr. Dunning were present.* Mr. W. Pitt, son of the late Lord Chatham, began his Parliamentary career on this occasion with one of the finest speeches ever remembered.

---

* Conversing with Lord Rockingham on the subject of the absence of those two members he told me he imagined it arose from Ld Shelburne's unwillingness to support any plan of reform unless his own ideas on that subject were to meet with mutual assistance.

[1] Leave was given to bring in the Bill Feb. 15; it was introduced Feb. 19. Mr. Pitt's speech was made on the Second Reading, Feb. 26. The *Parliamentary History* says with regard to it (xxi. 1262): " The Honble. William Pitt, son to the late Earl of Chatham, now rose for the first time, and in a speech directly in answer to matter that had fallen out in the course of the debate displayed great and astonishing power of eloquence. His voice is rich and striking, full of melody and force, his manner easy and elegant, his language beautiful and luxuriant. He gave in this first essay a specimen of eloquence not unworthy the son of his immortal parent." Pitt was returned for Appleby; he had stood for the University of Cambridge in 1780, but was at the bottom of the poll. His speech was warmly in support of the Bill.

The election for Helston[1] was by the committee again decided against us; and on March 8 Lord Godolphin[2] told me that Lord North was against us, declaring that he lookd upon me as his personal enemy, that he considerd L.ᵈ G. as not likely to live long, and that he would not permit *me* to recover the family interest in that borough. I immediately wrote him a letter inclosing my commission of Captain and Keeper of Deal Castle, which I had received from him in 1778, and which I thought myself obliged to resign, considering the *unjust* light in which his Lordship chose to look upon me.

A week afterwards I received a very polite letter from Lord North apologising for not having sooner answered my letter on account of the extraordinary business he had been engaged in for several days past (it was about the time of the Budget, new loan, &c.), assuring me he did not remember having used any similar expression, which he was the more certain of as he had never entertained an opinion that I was his personal enemy; he very civilly expressed his wish to return me the commission as my re-acceptance would be an additional pledge that I was not his enemy. I immediately wrote him my thanks for the explanation, and for the obliging and polite offer of sending me back my commission, which I could only return by repeating my desire of resigning Deal Castle, which might be a desirable object to some more intimate Friend, who would doubtless accept it with pleasure, but could not receive it with more thankfulness or good humour than I resigned it with.

March 22. Lord Rockingham spoke strongly in the H. of Lords

---

[1] In Oct. 1780, Thomas, Lord Hyde, eldest son of Lord Clarendon, was found not duly elected. Jocelyn Dean, brother to Lord Muskerry, died before the committee could try the merits of his election. A new writ was ordered, Feb. 21, 1781. Philip Yorke was elected; he accepted the Chiltern Hundreds, and a new writ was issued June 15, 1781. William Evelyn was returned, but found not duly elected.

[2] Lord Godolphin was son of Provost Godolphin of Eton. He died without issue in 1785, when the title of Lord Godolphin of Helston became extinct.

against the Loan Bill[1] on account of the extravagance of the terms in favour of the lenders; there was, however, no Debate or division: his Lp. and seven other Lords, myself included, signed a protest on the occasion.

On Sunday the 25 I din'd at Lord Shelburne's. When the rest of the company were gone Lord Coventry[2] and I enter'd into the mischiefs arising from a want of union among the leading persons in opposition. Ld Shelburne most heartily agreed with us and said he had done every thing in his power to forward unanimity, that he wished some great system could be agreed upon; that he had done a great deal to accommodate matters; that the D. of Richmond had done the same, but that there was no such thing as knowing how to proceed with Lord Rockingham;* that they had had several meetings last year, but to no purpose; that Burke had been outrageous with him for his economical plan in the H. of Lords, which he said was a matter wholly belonging to the H. of Commons; he seemed to think very contemptuously of Burke's

---

* Lord Sh. expressed himself with some apparent rancour as well as contempt on the conduct of those who, after having so often called upon the people to exert their own strength, went to St. James', and were officiously forward (as he said) in bringing the insurgents to justice who were concerned in the riots last summer. I could by no means agree with his Lp. as to the fact itself, or to the conclusion he seemed to draw from it. However, I did not say a word on the subject.

[1] The loan was for twelve millions. The terms were, 158*l*., 6 per cent.; 25*l*., 4 per cent.; and four lottery tickets to each subscriber of 1,000*l*. The protest declared the loan to be "improvident in its terms, corrupt in its operation, and partial in its distribution. Twenty-one millions are added to the public debt for the loan of twelve." The protest was signed by Rockingham, Portland, Carmarthen, Bishop of St. Asaph, Ferrars, Fitzwilliam, Bolton, and Bessborough.

[2] Lord Coventry was Lord-Lieutenant of Worcestershire. His first wife was one of the Gunnings.

commendation of the Taxes¹ in the H. of Commons; that he had the highest opinion of Admiral Keppel, but wished well to the other professions, and seemed to think Ld R. did not care about the Law or any other, provided his favourite Admiral was gratified. A few days afterwards I met the D. of Richmond at a committee. I mentioned to him part of the conversation I had had with Lord Shelburne, and told him how much I wished he would exert the influence he had both with L^d R——m and L^d Sh——ne in order to prevail upon them to act with unanimity, and added that, at least as far as to reconcile the leaders of the opposition, I wished they would allow him to act as a temporary dictator. He thanked me for my opinion of him, but seem'd to despair of any good arising at present, and smiling begg'd to decline the dictatorship; he went so far as to say he thought Burke intractable, and seem'd convinced that a great deal of mischief arose from thence. On the 4th of April I dined again at Lord Shelburne's with many of the foreign ministers. After dinner his L^dp and I talked over the present state of the opposition; he said he was sorry Ld Rockingham had suffered himself to be the dupe of the Court last summer;² that he expected Lord R. would have been active this present session, or wholly have absented himself from Parl^t. Talking of the want of conduct of the opposition he said that the plan of economy certainly had great weight with the nation at large, and that the petitions committees, &c. might have been of service if they had been properly conducted, for, said he, when *we* had once raised the Devil we ought to have kept the management of him in our own hands, instead of which it got into other peoples, and they by their folly and misconduct had forfeited every degree of consequence and weight with the public; his Lp. said he was very well disposed to L^d Rm. and could not be such an idiot as not to wish to have his support in case any arrangement could be made, particularly as L^d R^m's principles and his con-

---

¹ This was probably in his speech on the Loan Bill.
² In the proposed coalition (see above).

nections would be of great use to combat any artful and underhand dealings of the closet.

In a debate in the H. of L^{ds}, March 30, relative to an inclosure bill, the propriety of allotting land in lieu of tythes[1] became a matter of discussion. Ld Sandwich spoke much in favour of it, and in replying to the Chancellor made use of some expressions which gave offence to that nobleman, who replied[2] in the severest manner and forced an apology from Ld S. The Bp. of St. David's (Dr. Warren) had moved for the recommitment of the bill, the Ch. supported him, a division[3] took place of a very extraordinary nature, the Ch. the Ld President, the two secretarys of state,[4] and ten or twelve Bp^s being in the minority. A few days after[5] the Ld Pres^t (Ld Bathurst) moved for taking into consideration the present constitution of tythe laws on some other day, and mentioned some resolutions he meant to propose. The Ch. fell upon him in a severe tho ironically conceived speech; the H. adjourned, and nothing farther was done in the business; the Ch. attacking the ministers in so violent a manner occasioned much speculation and gave rise to a report of his being soon to resign; the House of Lords adjourned April 11 (for the Easter recess) to May 1.

On Sat. May 5, I breakfasted by appointment with Lord Towns-

[1] It had become the practice to insert a clause to this effect in bills of enclosure. The Hemington Enclosure Bill was now under discussion.
[2] The Chancellor said, among other things:—"The noble Earl had boasted of the advantage he had derived from enclosures: if he had presumed to suggest that the noble Earl had exerted all his influence to get these bills passed without having attended to the interest of the tenants, with that generosity and nobleness of mind which were the distinguishing features of the noble Earl's character, he should have been guilty of something much nearer calumny than anything which had fallen from the reverend prelate who began the debate." The Chancellor was Lord Thurlow since 1778.
[3] The numbers were: for recommitment, 23; against, 31.
[4] These were, since 1779, Lord Stormont and Lord Hillsborough.
[5] On June 6.

hend¹ at Blackheath, went with him to Woolwich, and returned with him to dinner. He complained much of the conduct of Gov¹ in many respects, said they sacrificed every thing to jobs, that the ministers in general were govern'd by inferior people, who in fact turned every object of Gov¹ to their own private emolument. He said that his own opinion officially given as Master-Gen¹ of the Ordnance, that of Ld Amherst as commander-in-chief, and of the several engineers consulted as to different works, and other military questions, had frequently (when all agreeing on the same plan) been defeated by Gov¹ in order to please some insignificant person or other in a corporation, and for the mere object of some dirty jobb. His Lp. told me he had no connection with Lord Sandwich, that they scarcely spoke when they met, and that all the business between them was transacted thro their respective boards. He told me his fortune had suffered so much from his government of Ireland² that he had now scarce any thing to live upon but the emoluments of his office of Master-Gen¹ of the Ordnance. Captain MacBride told us that day a singular circumstance relative to the conduct of the combined Fleets³ while off our coast in the summer 1779. A French officer, afterwards taken by the Apollo, declared that while the Fleets lay off Plymouth he was detachd in a small vessel to reconnoitre the state of the Harbour; that having sprung his boom in a gale he dared not venture so near as otherwise he would have done, but seeing 17 or 18 sail in the sound he returned and reported them to be line of battle ships (when in reality they were only transports under convoy of the Stag Frigate); upon which the French Admiral, conceiving nothing could then be done against Plymouth with such a force to defend it, ordered his armament to sail for Torbay, there to wait for the Transports with troops from

---

[1] Now Viscount and Marquis in 1787, was Master-General of Ordnance from 1772 to 1782, and again for a short time in 1783. He was father of Lord de Ferrars.
[2] He became Lord-Lieutenant in 1767.
[3] See above.

France in order to make a formidable descent agreeable to his orders in case he found Plymouth inaccessible. Luckily, however, for us, a strong easterly wind sprung up, which forced them down Channel, and so prevented their plan being carried into execution.

On Thursday, May 17, being the anniversary Feast of the Sons of the Clergy, of which I was a steward, Lord Hillsborough who was likewise a steward, sitting next to me at dinner at Merchant Taylors' Hall, begun a conversation relative to my resignation, &c. He said how sorry he was for it, that he thought it a wrong step, and was sure I must have repented of it. I assured his Lp. upon my honour I had not repented of it, and that were the same circumstances to exist again I would act in the same manner. He said, except upon very particular occasions indeed the nobility should always co-operate with the Crown, from whom alone they derived their consequence. I told him that no one was more sincerely attach'd to the Crown than I was, and, notwithstanding the hard treatment I had met (and which I must attribute to my having been totally misunderstood if not misrepresented), the K. had not a subject in his dominions more sincerely anxious for his prosperity. I repeated in pretty plain terms to his Lp. that, as the same causes which had occasioned my resignation still subsisted, my sentiments must of course continue precisely the same; that I could not pretend nor did I wish ever to be above the feeling an obligation or an injury, and that I confessed I had been much more hostile to Government than I should have been had I not been ill treated after the fair and, as I conceive, honorable part I had acted towards the King.

On Thursday, May 24, I came up from Mims to dine with the Archbishop of Canterbury,[1] at a dinner his Grace gave to the Lord Mayor and Stewards of the Sons of the Clergy. After dinner, Lord Hillsborough got again upon the topic of my resignation, and among other things said the K. was determined never more to

[1] The Hon. Frederick Cornwallis since 1768.

FEBRUARY 1781—JANUARY 1782.

be governed or govern by a Faction, and that when any appeared even among the ministers he instantly put an end to it, and that this was a sistem H.M. was determined to preserve.

While at Weymouth I received a letter from my friend Col. Hope, in which he mentioned the Fleet under Admiral Darby[1] being put into Torbay, and that they had received information from a foreign vessel of the combin'd Fleets being seen steering for the Channel. This report was represented in London as groundless. On Sept. 5 I went to the Fleet in Torbay, and, being aboard the Foudroyant, Captain Jervis shewed me a letter from Mr. Jackson of the Admiralty, in which that gentleman thought proper to treat the report of the enemy's approach as merely fabricated for factious purposes. The Agememnon, Capt. Caldwell, and the Protée, Capt. Bulkner, had actually, 32 leagues W. Lizard, been in sight of the combin'd Fleets, and were put back on that account, and had joined Admiral Darby. This is a strong proof either of the plenty of assurance or scarcity of information of our Admiralty.

The Parliament met on Tuesday the 27 of November, on the Sunday evening before I went to Ld Rockinghams, where I first

---

[1] Horace Walpole to H. Mann, Sept. 7, 1781 (vii. 75): "The combined fleets, to the amount of forty-seven or forty-nine sail, brought news of their own arrival at the mouth of the Channel a day or two before your letter of August 18th brought an account of that probability, and of the detachment for Minorca. Admiral Darby had a false alarm, or perhaps a true one, had returned to Torbay a week ago, where he is waiting for reinforcements. It is the fourth or fifth day since the appearance of the enemy off Scilly. It is thought, I find here [Berkeley Square] (whither I came to-day), that the great object is our Jamaica fleet; but that a detachment is gone to Ireland to do what mischief they can to the work before our ally, the Equinox, will beseech them to retire. Much less force than this Armada would have done more harm two years ago, when they left a card at Plymouth, than this can do: as Plymouth is now very strong, and that there are great disciplined armies now in both islands. Of Gibraltar we have no apprehensions. I know less of Minorca." Again on Sept. 9, to Mann: "Gibraltar is besieged, Minorca besieged, New York, I believe, besieged, and I also hear Great Britain is besieged—forty-seven or nine French or Spanish ships at the gates of the Channel, and Admiral Darby, with only twenty-two in Torbay, is a blockade to some purpose."

heard the melancholy news of the surrender of Ld Cornwallis[1] and his army. No plan seem'd to be agreed upon relative to the conduct of opposition in Parliament on the opening of the session. Lord Shelburne moved a short amendment[2] purporting the support of the Crown by such counsels as should point the arms and unite the hearts of the country; it pass'd in the negative.[3] The next day I drew up a protest while taking my coffee, a copy of which I sent to his Lordship, and likewise shewed it to the D of Richmond at the opera, who had already enterd a short protest[4] of his own;* he approved much of mine, and wished I would enter it; however I knew it was then too late. On Thursday 29 I receiv'd a very polite letter from Ld Shelburne thanking me for my communicating my ideas to him, and wishing opposition was sufficiently connected for him to ask my leave to make use of them; he told me in confidence that there was still some public principle wanting to unite upon. Upon Sunday, Dec. 2, I met the D. of Grafton at Brookes; in talking over our present situation he told me he hop'd there would soon be unanimity between the Leaders of opposition. Ld Rockingham confirmd this, and the next morning to Ld Pembroke, who called upon me a second time in order to communicate this news to me.

---

* This Protest of the D. of Richmond^s I declined signing on account of the epithet *unjust* being applied to the American war.

[1] The surrender took place on October 17-19th. It had been known in London for some time that his situation was desperate.

[2] The words were: "And we will without delay apply ourselves with united hearts to prepare and digest such councils to be laid at his royal feet as may excite the efforts, point the arms, and command the confidence of all his subjects."

The numbers were, 31 to 75.

The Duke's protest ran thus: "For reasons too often urged in vain for these last seven years against the ruinous prosecution of the unjust war, carrying on by His Majesty's Ministers against the people of North America, too fatally confirmed by subsequent experience and the late disgraceful loss of a second army, to stand in need of repetition." It was signed by Richmond, Abergavenny, Fitzwilliam, King, Rockingham, Pembroke, Abingdon, and de Ferrars.

On Tuesday, Dec. 11, I dined at Lord Shelburnes;* after dinner we got upon the old subject of Burke's influence with Lord Rockingham; he said he could tell me a great deal of what had passed in order to bring about an union in opposition, and would if I would permit him to call some morning in his boots as it would take up too much time at present. He lamented no medium could be struck out between L^d R^{ms} system of independence and the K^s of unconditional submission. For his own part he lamented L^d R^{ms} attachment to the idea of independence, which must ever be a stumbling block between them, for he himself would never consent to it; weak or treacherous officers might surrender the garrison, but he would not sign the capitulation.

On Saturday, Dec. 15,† I dined at Lord Rockingham's; he asked me after dinner my opinion with regard to applying to the sheriff of Yorkshire for calling a meeting of the county, a measure he rather seem'd to approve. I told him I thought a petition, however well drawn and signd by every respectable name in the county, would be of little use, and would most probably be as little regarded as those lately presented had been; that I thought we should wait quietly a little, the Cabinet certainly was in disorder as appeared

---

* L^d Sh. said publickly at table that the Duty upon the Tea not not being repealed at the same time as the others was owing to Ld Rochford^s Vote in the Cabinet contrary to the wish of the D. of Grafton, who had just made him Secretary of State [1] in the room of Ld Shelburne.

† During the conversation both at and after dinner from the different inquiries about what Barré and Dunning had said in the House of Commons, I thought I could perceive some jealousy with regard to Ld Shelburnes conduct, it had indeed been reported that L^d Sh. was to come into the administration.

[1] Lord Rochford was appointed Secretary of State for the North on Oct. 21, 1768, which he exchanged for the South Dec. 19, 1770. This office he held till Nov. 1775.

by the language Rigby and the Lord Advocate had made use of to L.ᵈ Geo. Germaine in the H. of Commons on Fryday last,[1] which would probably produce some change, that I likewise wish'd for the arrival of Lord Cornwallis, who could probably throw light upon some points of consequence which it would be necessary to be fully informed of. The D. of Manchester had justly observed that the people seemed cold and indifferent to any change, as none could afford any present alleviation of the burdens they laboured under. Both Lord Rockingham and Mr. Burke agreed with me that the committees and associations had done harm, and allowed my position that our present calamities could not be with justice attributed to any fault inherent in the constitution, but arose merely from a mal-administration of Government.

I asked Lord R. if he had seen any thing lately of Lord Shelburne; he said no, that they could not agree upon several weighty points relating to America and other concerns; that Lord Sh. pretended he could do more for the people than any body, and that he objected to the independence of America.[2] I told his Lordship I should think the declaring America independent would be a very bold measure in any minister or anybody else, and only mentioned one single circumstance arising from it, viz. that France

[1] Dec. 14. on the Army Estimates. On Wednesday, Dec. 12, a debate had taken place on a motion of Sir James Lowther for putting an end to the American war. The second debate was, in a certain sense, a continuation of the first. On the 14th Pitt pressed the Ministry most closely with their want of union. Seeing Lord North, Lord George Germaine, and Mr. Wellbore Ellis whisper together, he said " he would pause until the unanimity was a little better settled, till the sage Nestor had brought the Agamemnon and the Achilles of the American war to one mind." He then went through the speeches of the two lords, saying "that they were divided and disunited in sentiment, and that one or both of them had the meanness to continue in office and to stand responsible for measures of which they disapproved." Rigby paid great compliments to Pitt on his speech, and implied that the war in America would be reduced to a war of posts.

[2] Lord George Germaine said, on Dec. 12, " his opinion ever had been what his opinion then was, that the moment the House acknowledged the independence of America the British Empire was ruined."

would of course (and not without reason) claim the merit with America of having so effectually contributed to their independence, and consequently render their connection permanent. His Lp. differed with me in the conclusion I drew from thence, and we parted tho in the most perfect good humour.

The next day Ld Shelburne, Ld Chatham, Mr. Pitt, the D. of Rutland, Dudley Long, and Ld Lothian dined with me: the conversation was general, Ld L. was more entertaining than ever, tho somewhat at the expence of the [king]. On Sunday, Dec. 23, I went to Wilton [1] (where I stayed till Tuesday) on my way to Bath. P.[2] told me he heard from the K's domestic servants that his M. was much soured of late in his temper, that the P. of W. was very uncomfortable in his situation,[3] and had once or twice been on the point of desiring to remove, but had been dissuaded from it.* At Bath had a great deal of conversation with Ld Loughborough,[4] but mostly upon the general state of affairs. On the 28 December I called upon the D. of Northumberland, and sat near an hour with him mentioning to him the circumstance of Govn^t chusing every thing of consequence should originate in Parliamt;[5] he observed that the ministers were, like children, afraid to go alone, and therefore chose Parl^t should hold their leading strings.

* By Lieut.-Gen. Johnston of the 11. Dragoons, who is high in his R. H.'s favour, and had been rather cooly treated by H. M. on a supposition of his having encouraged the P. in some irregularity", which was by no means the case.

[1] Lord Pembroke's house, near Salisbury.
[2] Lord Pembroke.
[3] He had just received a small independent establishment, but was obliged to live in Buckingham House, the "Queen's House," as it was called. His conduct was very loose and riotous, and may well have caused the king anxiety. The prince was now nineteen years old.
[4] Lord Loughborough had just been appointed in 1780 Chief Justice of the Common Pleas.
[5] The Ministry, divided among themselves, unwilling to make peace, unable to continue the war, were content to suffer Parliament to give them a lead.

I came up to town the day before the Queens Birth Day, and on Sunday, Jan. 20, the D. of Richmond told me at Brooks'[1] he meant to take notice in the H. of Lords of the execution of Col. Haynes[2] in America under the authority of Lord Rawdon and Col. Balfour. I told him I owned I thought we had matters of more consequence to attend to, and that I wished not to waste our strength upon secondary considerations; however he seemed fixed upon it, and said Lord Shelburne would certainly attend, he meant it for Monday, Feb. 4.

I told Lord Rockingham, and wrote to my friend Lord Pembroke, that I was sorry for this business, as I was convinced it would appear as a mere opposition squib, and that I thought it particularly ill-timed at this juncture when so much business of real national importance called for the exertion of every man who wished the public welfare.

About this time I publish'd a small Pamphlet entitled "An Address to the independent Members of both Houses of Parliament," in which I called upon them in the strongest tho' most respectful manner to take an active part in the business of the nation, and not sacrifice every thing to the violence of the contending parties.

I shewed it in confidence to General Burgoyne, at Bath, who seemed much pleased with it, and heartily wish'd it might be perused with the same spirit and disposition with which it was written.

[1] The present club-house was opened in October, 1778.
[2] The case of Colonel Isaac Hayne occupied the House of Lords on Jan. 31 and Feb. 4, 1782. After the capitulation of Charlestown he had apparently been taken with arms in his hands and summarily executed, not after a court-martial but only after a court of inquiry. Lord Rawdon held a subordinate command in the army, and Colonel Balfour was commandant of the town of Charlestown. The Duke of Richmond's motion was defeated by 73 to 25. The case of cruelty did not seem to be made out.

FEBRUARY 1782—MARCH 1782.

POLITICAL MEMORANDUMS.

No. 4.

On Monday, Feb. 4, the D. of Richmond, agreeable to what he had said on the Thursday before, moved an address to the Crown for several papers to be laid before the House relative to civil as well as military Government at this time observed in America; the debate, however, almost entirely turned upon the execution of Isaac Haynes, a Rebel Colonel. I had no doubts, myself, with regard to the justice of the sentence, but voted for the address from a desire of information on many other subjects included in it.

Previous to the debate, Lord Shelburne apologized to me for my not seeing him a few days before when I call'd, and told me he had given orders for me to be let in at all times when he was at home; he mentioned he had much to say to me in private. He knew we agreed upon one very important point (objecting to the independence of America), and told me he had seen Lord Rockingham but could not bring him to the point he wish'd. Lord Coventry desired to speak with me in the P's Chamber.¹ When we came there he repeated his wishes of union amongst the Opposition, and shewed me a motion he proposed soon to make. It went to the impracticability of continuing the war in America and to the withdrawing the troops from thence, but wisely avoided any direct determination

¹ Prince's Chamber.

with regard to the independence of that country. I told him I highly approved of it and flattered myself as far as it went we should act cordially and unanimously.

The next day, Feb. 5th, I wrote a confidential letter to the Chancellor on the subject of the report which was strongly circulated of Lord George Germaine[1] being shortly to be created a Peer, a measure which I conceived must prove highly injurious to the Honour of the Crown and the Dignity of the Peerage, as the very heavy sentence pronounced on his Lp. by a court martial in April, 1760, confirmed by the late King and given out in Public orders, had never been reversed, and consequently rendered him unfit to be created a member of that assembly, who ought to be so jealous of their Honour. I wrote to the Ch. in the highest confidence as meaning to communicate my sentiments on this subject to no other person unless I should think myself obliged to take notice of it to the House of Lords.

On Thursday 7, after the ordinary business was gone through, and previous to the order of the day, the House being adjourned during pleasure, the Chancellor took me aside to the Bishops'

[1] Lord George Germaine was commander-in-chief of the British forces in Germany under Prince Ferdinand of Brunswick. After the battle of Minden, August 1, 1759, he was not mentioned in despatches. He returned home, was tried by court-martial at his own request, but in consequence was removed from all his military commands. He was also Secretary of State for the American Colonies since 1775. He resigned this in Feb. 1782, and on Feb. 11 was created Baron Bolebrooke and Viscount Sackville. He died 1785.

Horace Walpole says, Feb. 7, 1782 (vol. viii. p. 149): "Don't imagine that *otium cum dignitate* was his own choice, still less his master's, and still less is that a sacrifice to a ruined nation. No, it is a mere cabal, an effort of a faction, whose fear first dictated it. During the recess the Lord Advocate wrote to Lord North that he could not serve any longer with Lord George, and the letter was delivered most unwillingly. The letter was exceedingly ill received, and Lord George was much pressed to remain; nay, this day sevennight the Lord Advocate was not spoken to. However as mighty emperors must submit now and then to their Janissaries, Hawkins himself is rewarded for this closet insurrection with the place of Treasurer of the Navy (6000*l.* a-year), in the room of old Ellis (*ready for all posts*), who is made Secretary of State for late America."

Bench and told me he had received my letter but had sent no answer as he expected to see me in the House next day. He said he thought a good deal as I did on the subject, but knew not in what shape it could be introduc'd to the House except as part of my speech; he said he thought it not very flattering to the House the making people peers when they did not know what else to do with them. The D. of Chandos' motion,[1] after a good deal of conversation rather than debate, was agreed to. I said a few words to it, in order to introduce the subject of L.ᵈ G.'s Peerage. I told the House I was about to trouble them on a subject extremely disagreeable but in which I conceived the Honour of the Crown and their own dignity to be so materially concerned that I could not but mention it. I then stated the matter to them and wished for the assistance of their Lps. to direct what was fitting to be done, having framed as yet no motion on the subject. Different Lords desiring to frame a question on the matter in question, I moved, by way of resolution, "That it is highly derogatory to the Honour of this House to recommend to the Crown a person labouring under the heavy censures comprehended in the following sentence of a Court-Martial and public orders, viz. (here follow sentence and orders), as a proper person to be raised to the dignity of the Peerage."

This occasioned a debate, and the motion was got rid of[2] not by a direct negative, but the question of adjournment being carried.

The next day I wrote to the Dukes of Richmond and Grafton, Lords Rockingham, Derby, Abingdon, Temple, and Shelburne, to say that I meant to postpone protesting to a future opportunity. I had very obliging answers from them all: the two Dukes did not seem to think a protest necessary, and Lord Temple rather thought there could not be a better occasion than upon the subject of the adjournment. L.ᵈ Effingham protested singly for the reasons contained in the motion.

L.ᵈ Rockingham and Lord Shelburne both called upon me that

---

[1] His motion had reference to the surrender of Cornwallis.
[2] On the question of adjournment the division was 75 against 28.

morning, and the latter was full of compliments upon my behaviour, said it had done great credit both with the army and the public at large, and particularly mentioned the City of London, which he understood meant to give me some public testimony of their approbation. That night at Brookes', Charles Fox, after passing great encomiums on my conduct, recommended to be careful of being advised, saying I was upon good ground and that the leaders of the administration of 1765 who had taken up Ld G. Sackville would probably not be hearty in supporting me. The D. of Grafton had asked me to dine with him that day with Ld Chatham, Ld Camden, and Mr. Pitt, but I was engaged. The next night, Saturday, at the opera my friend Ld Bulkeley told me that the Duke of Dorset[1] was much hurt at my not having mentioned a word to him of the business, considering the footing of friendship we were upon, and the near relationship he was in to Ld G. G. I took an opportunity that night of apologizing to him for my silence, and he seemed pleased with my talking to him about it. I dined with him the two following days[2] at Lord Ligonier's,[3] and Sr Chas Thompson^s: Sir John Irwin dined at the latter's and was remarkably cold in his behaviour to me. I had been that day to the House of Peers and had summoned their Lordships' for the next, but at the desire of Lord Shelburne I moved to have the order discharged, as he wished to have the business postponed; this was much against my own wishes as likewise against the opinion of Chas Fox, who was for having it come on as soon as possible. The next day[4] the House met early, Ld Sackville took his seat and the House adjourned till Fryday. Not having been down, I was ignorant of their having adjourned over two days and wrote to the Lords Abingdon, Shelburne, and Camden to say I proposed bringing the business on the Fryday following. Next day, Ash Wednes-

[1] The Duke of Dorset, ambassador in France in 1763, was Lord George's nephew.
[2] Sunday 10 and Monday 11.
[3] An Irish peer, nephew of the great soldier. He died in this year.
[4] Tuesday 12. The House adjourned over Ash Wednesday till Friday 15.

day, I dined at my Father's, and received there a note from Ld Shelburne who had called at my House after four and wished to see me if not inconvenient before eight o'clock that evening. I took a Hackney Coach and went to his Lordship's about seven; he came to me in his library with the Lords Ossory and Camden, Alderman Townshend and a Mr. Steward. We had a loose kind of conversation on the subject, and then L^d Sh. took me to the other end of the room and talked to me on the whole matter. He advised me to make the question more political in order to engage the Rockingham party heartily in the support of it. I did not like changing my ground but said little at that time as there was company in the room, but wrote him my sentiments at large the next day and my reasons for thinking myself obliged to continue my motion pretty near in the same terms, except that it must be now considered as tending to censure, as the measure was past being prevented. I went to the House on Fryday, the 15, and summoned the Lords for the following Monday. I had some conversation with Ld Rockingham at the House on Fryday; he seemed cool in the business, so I troubled him but little about it. Ld Coventry was very friendly in his advice; the D. of Richmond seemed convinc'd I was right (all things considered) in adhering to my original plan; his Grace was very candid and obliging throughout this whole business, and called upon me one morning to talk upon it. Ld Percy was with me one morning and reprobated the measure tho' he did not attend on Monday, the 18, when I made it. I wrote to him and above thirty other Lords to say I should esteem myself much honoured with their presence on the occasion. Ld Pembroke, who was very warm in support of my opinion, went down with me and Jackson to the House on Monday. I mov'd that it was highly reprehensible in any person to advise the Crown to exercise its indisputable prerogative of creating a Peer in favour of a person, &c. vide p. 3; this occasioned a long debate which lasted till near nine; I was most ably supported by the D. of Richmond, Ld Shelburne, Lord Abingdon, and Lord Derby; the principal speakers against the motion were Ld Sackville himself, Ld Walsingham, Lord Stormont, and the Chancellor, who defended his client by not meeting the question so much on its real ground as by combating the sentence itself. Ld Rockingham made but an indifferent figure, he spoke confusedly, said he could not quite agree with the motion, and gave no vote. The D. of Richmond was much hurt at his conduct. We divided, 27 and 1 proxy to 81 and 12 proxy^s; I entered a Protest,[1] which I signed the next morning. Osborne, Rutland, Pembroke, Craven, Chatham, Derby, Egremont, Devonshire, Abingdon. On Wednesday I called upon Lord Shelburne; he was just going to dinner with only Lady Sh. but let me in, and pressed me to stay, but I was engaged to Mr. Purling^s. I told his Lp. I came to thank him for his goodness in having so ably supported me upon Monday. He told me he was much concern'd at finding me so ill supported; that the D^s of Grafton and Richmond, Ld Coventry and Camden, had told him they wished I would give up making the motion; that he told them it would be cruel to abandon me when I was in a manner committed; he said Charles Fox had likewise disapproved it (this I think must be a mistake, as Mr. Fox had expressed himself very differently to me more than once on the subject); he concluded with saying I had done myself much honour with the public by my spirited conduct, and that I had the more merit as I was so ill supported by opposition, many of whom he had censured for it and ask'd them what could be expected from them if they confess'd to the world that they had neither unanimity or spirit; he lamented the conduct of Ld Rockingham on that

[1] The protest ran thus: " Because we cannot look upon the raising to the peerage a person so circumstanced in any other light than as a measure fatal to the interests as well as the glory of the Crown and to the dignity of this House, insulting to the memory of the late sovereign and likewise to every succeeding branch of the illustrious House of Brunswick, repugnant to every principle of military discipline, and directly contrary to the maintenance of that honour which has for ages been the glorious characteristic of the British nation, and which, as far as depends on us, we find ourselves called upon not more by duty than by inclination to transmit pure and unsullied to posterity."—Rogers' *Protests of the Lords*, vol. ii. p. 212.

day, who he said was browbeat by a meaning look from Ld Sackville; he was likewise severe upon Ld Southampton, who he said ought by all means to have spoke fully upon the subject, and have done justice to Prince Ferdinand.

On Sunday night, Feb. 24, Lord Fitzwilliam told me at Brookes' he was very sorry he had not known of my motion time enough to have come up and given it his hearty concurrence; he said I must know from particular reasons [1] Ld Rockingham was prevented from voting himself upon the subject,* and that therefore he should have thought it a reason the more for his L^d F^s who was not so circumstanced supporting me.

The next morning going to Lord Godolphin^s I met the Prince of Wales on horseback; he stopped and called to me; when I came up his R. H. gave me a hearty shake by the hand and said, Carmarthen, I give you joy of our division [2] the other night.†

A similar question by way of resolution was moved by Genl. Conway [3] on Wednesday the 28th. The Attorney-Genl. moved to

* Lord Rockingham voted with me on the first motion on Thursday the 7th.

† 193 to 194, against continuing the war in America on a motion of Genl Conway's for an address, Fryday the 22^d.

[1] As Lord North's Ministry was now in the agonies of dissolution, it became important to know who were to succeed them. Lord Shelburne and Lord Rockingham, both Whigs, but leaders of different sections, disagreed principally on the question of recognising the independence of America.

[2] General Conway's motion for putting an end to the American war was lost only by one vote, 193 to 194. Pitt and Fox both spoke in favour of it. Fox immediately gave notice that the question would be raised again, which was done on Feb. 27.

[3] Horace Walpole says of this, March 1, 1762 (vol. viii. p. 171): "On Wednesday last General Conway renewed his motion for an address of pacification with America, and carried the question by a majority of nineteen. His speech was full of wit, spirit, and severity. After the debate Mr. Fox complimented him publicly on this second triumph, he also having been the mover of the repeal of the Stamp A t. In short he stands in the highest light, and all his fame is unsullied by the slightest suspicion of interested or factions motives in his conduct."

adjourn: the adjournment was however negatived by a majority of 19,* and ministers did not afterwards chuse to oppose the address, which was presented by the House to the K. on Fryday, March 1.

On Sunday, March 3, I called at Ld Rockinghams. I found several people with him; they were talking tho' in a loose manner of taking notice of the K^s answer[1] in the House, as it by no means appeared satisfactory I advised them to be prudent, and not throw away the advantage they had so recently acquired, and owned if there had been anything unpleasant in the answer it must have been more in the manner than the matter of it. I paid a few other visits, and then went to Lord Shelburne'*, with whom I had a long and interesting conversation. He reminded me how ministers had on every occasion in the H. of Lords avoided saying anything on the subject of America, and told how he had meant to have proposed a question which might have forced an explanation from them on that subject. We joined in expressing our dislike of any formal avowal of the independency of America, particularly in a rash and hasty manner, without well considering and weighing the natural consequences of so very important a measure. I told him I thought the idea absurd, unless we chose at the same time to beg France would guaranty their independence. I added that considering how apt people in this country were to run into extremes I thought it very probable that those who had been the most violent for unconditional submission would now be equally eager for inde-

---

* 234 to 215.

[1] The King's answer to the address was expressed as follows: " Gentlemen of the House of Commons: There are no objects nearer to my heart than the ease, happiness, and prosperity of my people. You may be assured that in pursuance of your advice I shall take such measures as shall appear to me to be most conducive to the restoration of harmony between Great Britain and the revolted colonies so essential to the prosperity of both, and that my efforts shall be directed in the most effectual manner against our European enemies until such a peace can be obtained as shall consist with the interests and permanent welfare of my kingdoms."

pendence. He said he thought it likely, and that would be strong ground indeed to attack ministers for giving up the interests of their country because they, from their own absurd conduct, had not been able to preserve them. He said it would require the greatest exertions to carry on the war with any prospect of success, and could not conceive how a peace could be made at present except of the most humiliating sort to this country, that he understood there was some communication with France but that it was conducted by means of very low and inconsiderable people, and that he had heard a strong language was held by some Scotch runners[1] employ'd by the administration, viz. that Philosophy[2] had made so great a change in the national character of the French that they would shew moderation in treaties of peace, and would allow us the most equitable terms; neither his Lp. or myself agreed by any means to this representation of the disposition of France. His Lordship observed that there could be but two descriptions of persons who wished for an avowal of the independence of America, those who have all along been for that measure as Ld Coventry, the Dean of Gloucester, &c., or those who, feeling the immediate impressions of the expenses of the war, were for sacrificing every future consideration to the immediate relief which they expect from procuring peace at any rate.

My friend Jackson told me on Tuesday, March 5, that Mr. Brooks had desired him to inform me in confidence that Lord Sackville had wrote to Lord Hampden[3] to desire his Lordship (as having long been acquainted) to be one of his introductors into the House of Peers, but Lord H. had desired to be excused. Jackson

---

[1] Spies employed by the Government to run the blockade between France and England, then at war.

[2] A curious recognition of the power of Voltaire and Rousseau, which was afterwards to show itself so prominently in the Revolution. As a matter a fact, Louis XVI. and his Ministers were strongly disposed to peace and amity with England.

[3] First Viscount Hampden and fourth Lord Trevor. He was a man of great distinction, a fellow of the Royal Society; his later poems were printed by Bodoni. He died in the following year.

attributed this matter to the impression made by something I had either wrote or spoke on the subject, but I could not presume to think so.

On Wednesday, March 6, in a committee of the whole House, the D. of Chandos moved, that from the papers on the table it appeared that the immediate cause of the loss of the K's army in Virginia was the inferiority of the fleet ; this occasioned a long debate, but was carried in the negative by 72 to 39 ; during the debate the Chancellor was sitting on the Duke[s] bench and asked me to sit by him ; we had a good deal of conversation. I asked why he did not give the decided blow to L[d] North, who after what had passed could not go on with any effect as first minister. He said, Who could we put in his place? I said anybody, that I thought the first Hackney Coachman in the street would do near as well at present. He said, I suppose by way of odd man, but, however, if you are serious I think as you do. I told him I thought some arrangement must be made, that things could not go on as they were ; he perfectly agreed with me. During the course of the next week there were frequent reports of changes, and that Lord North was out ; this idea was very current on Thursday the 14 ; that day I met Mr. Byng, who asked me if I had seen L[d] Rockingham,[1] I told him not that day. He seem'd to wish I would call upon his Lordship, which I did about three, and found the Dukes of Richmond and Man-

[1] An account of the negociations between Lord Thurlow and Lord Rockingham is to be found in Albemarle's *Life of Rockingham*, vol. ii. p. 451, following. It began on March 11, in the House of Lords, much as the conversation with Carmarthen reported above. He asked R. to suggest a *plan of arrangement* and form an administration (as he expressed it) on a broad bottom. On Thursday, March 14, Rockingham proposed the following scheme, "American independence, no veto; Establishment Bill; great part of Contractors Bill; Custom House and Excise, &c.; peace in general if possible; economy in every branch." The negociations broke for the moment, because the King wished to form his Ministry first and discuss measures afterwards, whereas Lord Rockingham said to Lord Thurlow (March 16). "I must confess that I do not think it an advisable measure first to attempt to form a Ministry by arrangement of office and afterwards to decide upon what principle or measures they are to act." It was still going on, March 18.

chester, Admiral Keppel, and Mr. Townshend with him. L^d R told me there was a sort of negotiation on foot, and that he had been that morning with the Chancellor by appointment; he said he had given in his terms for his M^{ts} consideration, and shewed me a copy of them, which were nearly as follows. "no absolute veto to American independence, a general peace if possible, some of the establishment bill, the contractors bill, and the excise and custom-house officers bill." Ld Pembroke came in, and when the others were gone, we three conversed some time. L^d R^m said the D. of R^d was apprehensive Lord Shelburne might not be contented with the plan as not thinking it went far enough. We hoped, however, that would not be the case, as we conceived it was fully sufficient to every necessary degree of reformation in the State. The next day Sr John Rouse moved a resolution that ministers had lost the public confidence. This was negatived by only a majority of nine.*

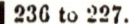

236 to 227.

MARCH 20, 1782—FEBRUARY 28, 1783.

POLITICAL MEMORANDUMS.

No. 5.

On Wednesday, March 20,[1] a motion similar to those already made by Lord John Cavendish and Sir John Rous was to have been made in the H. of Commons by Lord Surry, but was pre-

[1] The House of Commons met at 4·15. Lord North rose at once to say that His Majesty's Ministry "were no more." Lord North tendered his resignation on the 19th, but it was not accepted. On the 20th, after the levée, Lord North had an interview with the King of three hours, after which he told "several persons" "the game is up." The King had agreed to all Lord Rockingham's propositions except the reform of the household. Lord North apparently came straight from the King to the House. Walpole (*Journal*, vol. ii. p. 521) says that the King parted with him rudely without thanking him, "Remember, my lord, that it is you who desert me, not I you."
On March 21 the King sent for Lord Shelburne. His account of it is (*Life*, vol. iii. p. 131), "The King proposed to me to take the administration with the Chancellor, Lord Gower, Lord Weymouth, Lord Camden, the Duke of Grafton, Lord Rockingham, &c. if the latter would agree to state their pretensions of what they meant by a broad bottom for the King's consideration. I declined this as utterly impracticable. The other features of this conversation were, the state of his health, his agitation of mind; his determination to do anything rather than risk an act of meanness; the cruel usage of all the powers of Europe; the bad opinion of Lord Rockingham's understanding; his horror of C. Fox; his preference of me compared with the rest of the opposition; that it was unbecoming to speak to many; that the general wish was for a broad bottom. The King after this sent for Lord Gower. On Sunday 24, Lord Shelburne communicated with Rockingham, who replied at 6 p.m. stipulating for the same conditions which he had mentioned to the Chancellor, and sending a sketch of the Ministry similar to the one given by Lord Carmarthen in its main outlines. Lord Shelburne replied giving his approval at 8·30 the same evening.

vented by Lord North informing the House that the K's ministers were to be changed, and only remained in till their successors could be appointed, and therefore moved the House to adjourn till Monday, when he in a manner assured them a new ministry would be formed.

Nothing appeared settled for some days, tho' the Chancellor had seen Ld Rockingham¹ by the K's order, and Ld Shelburne had been to His Majesty. On Tuesday L^d Sh. came to L^d R^m from the K. to desire him to make an arrangement; this proceeding was certainly meant to create a difference between those two noblemen. However, this expedient failed and a list of the proposed cabinet was agreed upon,* to which his Majesty made no objection. On Tues-

Lord Rockingham—1st Lord of the Treasury.
Lord Shelburne } Secretaries of State.
Mr. Fox
Lord Camden—President of the Council.
Duke of Grafton—Lord Privy Seal.
Admiral Keppel—First Lord of the Admiralty.
General Conway—Commander in Chief.
Duke of Richmond—Master Gen. of the Ordinance.
Lord J. Cavendish—Chancellor of the Exchequer.
D. of Portland—Ld Lieut^t of Ireland.
Ld Ashburton—Chanc. of Duchy of Lancaster.
Mr. Burke—Paymaster.
Col. Barré—Treasurer of the Navy.
Mr. T. Townshend—Secretary at War.

¹ Not since the interview described above. On Saturday 23, the Chancellor told Shelburne that the King would not see Lord Rockingham. Shelburne replied that he could not act with the Rockingham party. The King agreed to negociate with Rockingham through Shelburne, which gave rise to Shelburne's letter to which Rockingham's of Sunday evening is a reply. Lord Shelburne saw the King again. In consequence of this interview Thurlow remained Lord Chancellor, Denning was created Lord Ashburton. Pitt was to have had high office, but Rockingham objected. He refused the Vice-Treasurership of Ireland. The arrangements were probably concluded on Monday 25th.

day morning Lord Rockingham and Lord Shelburne both sent for me; they received me most kindly and asked me if there was any particular employment I had any desire to have. I told them I really had none, that my only object was to serve their Gov^t and should be happy to be useful to them either with or without employment, that I would freely own I wished much for a Prebend of Westminster for my friend Jackson. In the course of my conversation with Lord Shelburne he made use of these words, " I have made great sacrifices to the Rockinghams,[1] I hope I am acting with honest men." The last thing I mentioned was how anxiously I wished to see him and Lord Rockingham act cordially together, as I was convinced the salvation of the country demanded the closest unanimity between them. The next day, March 27, having received a summons to the Privy Council, I went to St James's; Lord Shelburne took me aside and said how much he wished I would take something; he proposed removing Lord Barrington to make me joint post master General in his room. I objected to that tho' I expressed myself highly sensible of his kindness to me in offering it, that I should prefer being employed abroad, if consistently with the K^s Service, and said I should like extremely to be sent to Holland when an opportunity offerd ; he seemed to approve of the foreign line for me, and said he fancied there would soon be an opening. Lord R^m came out from the K. and told me with great joy I was to be restored to the Lieutenancy of the E. Riding of Yorkshire, and Lord Pembroke to that of Wiltshire ; he told me the Lieutenancy of Buckinghamshire was to be taken from Lord Chesterfield and given to Lord Temple. I own I think this a violent and improper measure, though I knew Lord Ch. had behaved very improperly to Ld T. in his official character.*

On speaking to Mr. Fox (who had just received the seals as Secretary of State) on the important event of the day, he said

[1] Dunning and Pitt.

The Wednesday afterwards, viz., April 3, I kissed the King's hand for the Lieutenancy of the East Riding of Yorkshire, and the next day kissed the Queen's hand; her M. was remarkably cool; I found indeed she by no means approved of the change in administration, and the P. of Wales had told me she had cried all dinner time the day the new ministers were presented. In consequence of proposals being made by Russia to Holland for a treaty with England, Mr. Fox told me at a ball at Devonshire House on the 10, he fancyed they would be soon ready for me to set out for Holland. Sr Joseph Yorke had told me I might have his house at the Hague. I assured him I wished to see him return thither, he told me that was impossible, but said he should be very happy to give me every information in his power. I had an application from the Bp. of Durham[1] to let his son Major Egerton go with me as Secretary, with which I complyed, and was assured the Bp. would be happy to do something handsome for my friend Jackson. On Fryday, April 18, there was a chapter of the Garter, when P. William[2] the Dukes of Richmond and Devonshire, and Lord Shelburne were elected Knights companions. Mr. Fox told me at St. James's that the last accounts from Holland were very bad, that they had entered into such positive engagements with France for the ensuing campaign that all thoughts of peace for some time must be given up. That same evening at the masquerade at the Pantheon, Lord Temple begged to speak to me on something of consequence. When we were retired out of the crowd he told me that, knowing the footing I was upon both with Lord Rockingham and Lord Shelburne, he wanted to mention his apprehensions to me of the latter nobleman's conduct toward the former; he said he much feared he wanted to play him false, and told me for certain L^d Sh. had spoke to a

— — — ..

certainly things look very well, but he, meaning the K., will dye soon, and that will be best of all.

[1] John Egerton, since 1771.   [2] Afterwards William IV., then aged 17.

person¹ wishing them to be Secretary of State in case of a vacancy, which his Lp. concluded was owing to some secret plan of removing Mr. Fox and of course L^d R^m and his friends; he said he wished L^d R^m should know it. I advised him not to mention it yet, as I feared it would inevitably create confusion and totally prevent what I had much at heart and thought necessary for the public good, a sincere and cordial connection between them. I said I would endeavour if possible to know more of the matter, as I thought it of the utmost importance. On the first of May there was a long debate in the House of Lords on the motion for the committment of the Bill for excluding contractors from the H. of Commons. The Chllor. opposed it with violence, and his speech was look'd upon as extremely hostile to the new ministers. Ld Gower opposed it likewise, but assured the ministers of his good wishes and support; on the division the motion was carried 70 to 45, including Proxies; two days afterwards the Ch. and the D. of Richmond had high words² on the Cricklade bill. I cannot account for my friend the Ch: behaviour, as he certainly might have opposed those particular bills in a more friendly manner. May the 4th I met Ld Bulkeley³ in the street, he told me he feared the ministers were going on too fast, he said he had been sent for to a meeting of several members of the H. of commons at the D. of Richmonds on the Tuesday before, relative to some alteration in the representation of the Commons, in which Mr. W. Pitt⁴ was to take the lead; he did not seem to approve of the

¹ Could this be William Pitt?
² "The Duke of Richmond replied with some heat, charging the learned lord on the woolsack with opposing indiscriminately every measure of regulation or improvement which was laid before the House. The Lord Chancellor complained of the asperity with which he had been treated by the noble duke, and said that he thought it a peculiar hardship that his manner, that of a plain man who studied nothing but to convey his sentiments clearly and intelligibly, should be imputed to him as if arising from motives of indiscriminate opposition or to intentional rudeness."—(*Parl. Hist.* xxii. 1386.)
³ Lord Bulkeley was made an English peer in 1784.
⁴ This motion was made on May 7. The division was 161 against 141. Thomas Pitt spoke strongly against the motion.

idea, and said Lord Temple and Sr James Lowther were averse to it. I told him I could by no means approve of alterations in the constitution, that as far as the two bills relative to contractors and revenue officers went I thought we were right. Mr. Pitt's motion for appointing a committee to take into con-ideration the state of the representation of the people was negatived in the H. of Commons.

About this time a plan was in agitation for arming the great towns in order to increase the general defence of the country, and a circular letter was sent from Lord Shelburne to all the Lord Lieutenants and chief magistrates of the principal towns throughout the Kingdom inclosing a plan for their consideration; this occasioned a great alarm; the example of Ireland struck many people with serious apprehensions of the mischief likely to ensue from putting arms into the hands of the multitude; a meeting was held at the St. Albans Tavern of the Lord Lieutenants, and it seemed their unanimous opinion that the plan as stated in the circular letter was liable to many weighty objections; they agreed with me in thinking something of the sort might be of great service in the maritime counties under proper regulations; a bill soon after pass'd the H. of Commons relative to the disciplining such corps of volunteers as might be raised, and soon after it came into the H. of Lords. Sr Geo. Savile came to me to shew me a letter he had received from the principal dissenters of Leeds, Wakefield, &c. signed by forty of them, expressing their being willing to serve in defence of their king and country, provided it was not necessary for them to take the sacrament according to the rites of the established church. Sr Geo. said something might perhaps be done for their relief in this point in the House of Lords, and Ld Rockingham and he desired me to take the papers and ask of the Chancellor whether I thought the law obliged them to take the sacrament previous to their receiving commissions; L^d R^m wrote to me to desire me to act as I judgd best in this matter as he was too ill to attend the House of Lords; on Monday the 24th of June I went to the House and ask'd the Chancellor if by law a dissenter in order to receive a commission in the volunteer corps would be obliged to take the sacrament, he said certainly; I observed it would make a difficulty; he said that if that objection prevented them from taking commissions he thought it would be a very fortunate thing. Ld Shelburne not being in the H. I told Lord Ashburton[1] what had passed between the Ch. and me, and added what I had before said to Ld Rockingham and Sr Geo. Savile, that I thought we had much better let the matter sleep, that I thought the bill would at any rate be opposed in the H. of Lords, and that if the matter of the dissenters was introduced it would increase the opposition to it; his Lp. perfectly agreed with me, as did Lord Shelburne, whom I saw that evening at his return from Wyccombe, and who surprized me (tho agreeably) with observing that it was necessary to be cautious in any business relating to tests, &c. and that in all time the Church of England were the people to be stood by.

Poor Lord Rockingham continued extremely ill all the week, and at length expired on Monday, July the 1st, between twelve and one, to my real grief both on the score of private affection and public regard. I cannot but consider him as a very great national loss at this time, as he was a check upon the extravagant ideas of innovation which others entertained.

On Tuesday morning I wrote to Ld Shelburne to renew my solicitation in behalf of Jackson, and on Wednesday received a letter from his Lordship merely to say he forgot nothing I said to him. That day I went to the K^s Levee; Mr. Fox lamented to me the confusion likely to ensue from L^d R^{ms} death; he said he wish'd that party would act strictly together whether in or out of place, that for himself he would spare no trouble to act as their leader, and expressed himself as extremely anxious to have the Duke of Portland at the Head of the Treasury.

Lord Shelburne was closetted a considerable time with the K.

[1] Dunning.

and when he came out proposed we should go together to the House of Lords. Mr. Fox desiring to speak to him they retired to another room, and I waited till the conference was over. The instant we were got into his coach, his Lp. began on the present situation of affairs; he told me the K. had press'd him to go to the Treasury; that Mr. Fox had spoke fairly and candidly to him of his wish for the D. of Portland; he added no one wish'd more than himself for a real independent ministry, but he could by no means think of canvassing for votes to succeed to an office; he agreed with me on the improbability of the great Families who form'd the Whig party submitting to become the mere creatures of Mr Fox, however highly they might think of his abilities. I return'd from the House of L^{ds} soon after seven; Glover din'd with me; my friend Langlois called upon me after dinner, and we had a deal of conversation; he said he look'd upon Lord R^{ms} death, particularly at this time, as a very great loss to the public, as he regarded him as a barrier to protect the constitution against any mischievous innovation; talking of the K. he said he took for granted his M's coldness to me which I had mentioned to him must proceed from my motions upon the affair of Ld Sackville having been totally misrepresented to or misunderstood by him and considered as meant personally disrespectful to him. Lord Shelburne in the morning having express'd a desire to see me again soon, I went to him between ten and eleven at night; he told me Sir James Lowther had just been with him and said he and his connections should withdraw their support from Gov^t unless his Lp. took the direction of affairs and went to the Treasury. He told me he could not bear the idea of a *round robin* administration, where the whole Cabinet must be consulted for the disposal of the most trifling employments; he said the Ch. was friendly to him and he reposed confidence in him, though the others had told him the Ch. would deceive him. The D. of Richmond he said was to come to him the next morning at eight, and he fancy'd things would be soon finally settled.

The next morning I went with Glover down to Mims, and

returned with him and Jackson at night. On Fryday morning, July 5, to my greatest surprize, I found Mr. Fox had resigned the seals[1] the day before. Jackson, on his return from walking, said he had seen Lord E. Bentinck, who had informed him of the transaction, and had added that I was to be offerd the Lieutenancy of Ireland. This conduct of Mr. Fox struck me as the most ill-judged and ill-timed measure I ever heard of. I went to the H. of Lords, and was happy to find it universally condemned by people of all parties whom I conversed with on the subject. Lord Temple told me Ld Egremont * (Mr. Fox^s personal and intimate friend) highly disapproved it, as did likewise Lord Spencer; that even the D. of Richmond disapproved of it; he said he had tried to dissuade him from it, and that he thought he must have been put upon it by Stare and Fitzpatrick, the only person of real weight he had been told approved the measure was Lord Fitzwilliam.

L^d Sh. having informed me he wished to see me I went to him

☐This idea of Lord Egremont I believe was a mistake.

[1] The grounds of Fox's resignation are now known; it proceeded from fundamental differences of opinion with Shelburne. Fox was in favour of the *unconditional* independence of America; Shelburne was against it. The general conduct of foreign affairs was in Fox's department as Secretary; but that of American affairs was in Shelburne's; both worked to negociate the treaty. Shelburne sent Mr. Oswald to Paris, who communicated with Franklin, while Shelburne did not also communicate to his colleagues what he heard from Franklin. Fox sent Greville to treat with Vergennes. After Rockingham's death Fox would have been willing to have served with Shelburne under a neutral person like the Duke of Portland, or with Lord John Cavendish as brother Secretary. The King however determined to give the Treasury to Shelburne, "who had declined it in favour of Rockingham" on a previous occasion. Upon this Fox resigned. He writes to Greville, July 5, 1782: "I am sure my staying would have been a means of deceiving the public and betraying my party; and there are things not to be done for the sake of any supposed temporary good." Col. Fitzpatrick said of his resignation (*Life of C. J. Fox*, by Lord J. Russell, p. 329), "All persons who have any understanding and no office are of opinion that Charles has done right. All persons who have little understanding are frightened; and all persons who have offices, with some very brilliant exceptions, think he has been hasty." Lord Carmarthen was not one of the brilliant exceptions.

at night; he told me there was some difficulty in the way of Jackson's having the Prebend as Mr Fox has askd it as a deathbed request of Lord R^m for Mr Zouch; L^d Sh. said he would give no answer till he had seen me, and expressed himself to serve Jackson at all events even if the present object was unattainable; he did not mention a word of Ireland, tho Mr Fitzpatrick was waiting in the other room; he told me Mr Pitt was very willing to come forward in a responsible office; that he believed the D. of Richmond would remain in office, but if he went out meant to be friendly, and not oppose; that Gen. Conway and Mr. T. Townshend continued in office, and meant to cooperate cordially with him; he said he had no quarrel on public grounds that he knew of with Mr. Fox; that upon being asked by him if he was to go to the Treasury and answering in the affirmative Mr Fox replied, then I go out, and immediately went into the closet and resign'd the seals. L^d Sh. said he, Mr. Fox, spoke to the K. rather in a strong way, and seemed surprized to find His M. dare have any opinion of his own.

On Sunday morning, in consequence of a report of my going to Ireland, I received several applications for aids de camps, &c. &c.; in the evening Mr. Fox called upon me desiring me to recommend his friend Dickson, Dean of Downe, to me. I assured him I had not heard a word from Gov^t of my being thought of for Ireland. We then entered upon the subject of his late resignation, for which I told him I was sincerely sorry, and feared the abrupt manner in which it had been done might prejudice him materially in the opinion of the world; he owned he thought it would, that it was impossible for any one to form a true opinion on the case who had not been in the cabinet; he said he did not wonder if people were displeased with him, but that he acted from conviction, and would never hesitate to sacrifice popularity where it could not be preserved but at the expense of his character. He said he looked upon Lord Shelburne to be as much a tool of the King^s as ever Jenkinson had been, that the D. of Richmond was much hurt at the step he had taken, and yet, says he, when I ask'd the D. of

Richmond before thirty or forty people on Saturday at a meeting at Lord Fitzwilliam's if he could trust to one single word of Ld Shelburne's his Grace answered in the negative. I ask'd him how the K. behaved to him when he resigned, he told me very obligingly The next day I met the D. of Richmond at the House of Lords; I told him how sorry I was for what had happened, that I had seen Mr. Fox who had called upon me last night, and spoke openly to him on the subject. The D. said he believed Mr. F. had called upon every body, that for his part he was very sorry, and thought those who had come in on the present system ought to remain so long as it was adopted. Mr. Dudley Long being below the bar, I went and conversed with him on our present political situation; he told me from what he learnt Sr Geo. Savile had in a great measure been the cause of Mr. Fox's resignation, for that a few days before upon the discussion of some bill in which America was concerned, Sr G. having observed that it was necessary to be very cautious how any Legislative regulations were mentioned in regard to America, Mr. F. made an open avowal of his inclination to allow independence to America and spoke of it as a measure agreeable to the ministry; that upon the question being proposed in the Cabinet it was carried against him, and that he thought himself so far pledg'd on that subject as to render his continuance in office totally improper.

On Wednesday,* July 10, I went to the K.'s Levee which was remarkably full; previous to the K. calling, Lord Temple took me

---

The alterations in the Ministry were as follow:—
Ld Shelburne—1st L^d of the Treasury.
Mr. W. Pitt—Chanc. of the Excheq^r.
Mr. T. Townshend, } Secretaries of State.
Lord Grantham,
Lord Temple—Lord Lieut. of Ireland.
Col. Barré—Paymaster.
Lord Advocate—Treasurer of the Navy.
Sr George Yonge—Secretary at War.

aside in the Privy Chamber and began with saying he wanted to speak to me on a very delicate subject, that he understood "We had been smelling to the same nosegay." I told him I did not quite comprehend his meaning, but that if Ireland was the nosegay alluded to I was most extremely happy, as tho' I had heard nothing from Gov^t on the subject, still the repeated applications I had received, the numerous reports I had heard had alarmed me very much, as I had some very strong reasons tho' not of a public nature to render that very high and honourable post extremely irksome to me: his Lp. behaved in the most polite and friendly manner on the business, and relieved me from a load of anxiety which the apprehension of its being offer'd me had for some days thrown upon me and very much affected my health. Ld Shelburne was appointed 1st L^d of the Treasury, Mr. W. Pitt, Chanc. of the Excheq^r, and Mr. T. Townshend, Secretary of State. After the Levee and Council I had an audience of the King; I told his Majesty I wish'd not to take up a moment of his time but only came to assure him of my hearty zeal for his service and anxious desire to support his Gov^t at a time when I thought the late abrupt revolution in the Cabinet might be productive of very bad consequences, and that I thought it was every man's duty to prevent the confusion which might arise from it; he seem'd much pleas'd with what I said, and added he was very glad to hear me say so. His M. expressed himself much surprized at the sudden step Mr. Fox had taken, and that even when Ld Shelburne told him on the Thursday before that Mr. F. meant, he understood, to give up, he did not think he had then the seals in his pocket to resign; he told me it was Mr. F.'s wish to have an inactive 1st Lord of the Treasury,[1] but one whom he himself could answer for clearly in order that he might govern in his name.

On Tuesday, July 16, soon after six in the evening, I receiv'd an express from my friend Mr. Burges (on the circuit), dated Lincoln, July 15, to inform an account was received there of the

---

[1] The Duke of Portland.

Dutch being off Hull with 15 sail, and that the Dragoons were marchd from Lincoln for Malton; I immediately communicated this intelligence to L⁴ Shelburne, Mr. Sec. Townshend and Gen. Conway, and remarked that I flatterd it might only arise from some of the Dutch Fleet being drove by the easterly wind within sight of the coast and having been seen off the Humber, which people's fears had interpreted off Hull; they all agreed with me in the idea which I dare say was the case, as no accounts came that night or all the next day. When I was with Lord Shelburne that evening he was as usual extremely civil and wished to know if I should object to go for a short time to Berlin, where he thought there might soon be some important business to be transacted; I excused myself to him, at the same time thanking him for the proposal, but told him the present state of my Father's health[1] would alone be a strong objection in my mind to so remote a commission.

On Saturday, July 27, I received a letter from Lord Shelburne to inform me that my friend Jackson was appointed a Prebendary of Westminster. On Wednesday, the 31, he kissed the K⁸ hand on his appointment. The same day I was at Council, and L⁴ Temple was declared Lord Lieutenant of Ireland.

On my arrival in Town for the winter I went to court Nov. 7; after the Drawing room L⁴ Shelburne took me aside, and after saying a great many civil things told me the K⁸ speech at the opening the Sessions would be a very important one, and that he much wished I would move the address; that he wishd to have it moved by me as he knew he could open himself freely and without reserve to me on the plans of Government. I told him I certainly was much flatterd by the manner in which he proposed it to me, and could have no objection to moving the address; he said it was not yet determind who should second me, but thought it should be some Lord who had been in opposition with us, and fancyd I should think that most proper, to which I answerd certainly. On

[1] The Duke of Leeds died March 23rd, 1789.

Monday, Nov. 11, my friend Lord Pembroke (who was come to town to attend Genl Murray's[1] Court Martial) called upon me; he told me Ld Spencer[2] was by no means violent, that he meant not to oppose Gov^t, and was only apprehensive that Ld Shelburne might have promised the K. too much. The Wednesday after I dind at Lord Shelburne' with the Chancellor, Ld Grantham, Ld Ashburton, Mr. Sec. Townshend, Mr. Pitt and Mr. Pratt; before dinner L^d Sh. took me aside and said things were still in so uncertain a situation that until he had fresh intelligence both from France and America he could give me little information with regard to any likelihood of Peace; that M. de Vergennes had sent to him upon the idea of his dislike of American independence, which he owned he disapproved of; he told me he knew we agreed about America, and declard that if he was forc'd to acknowledge her independent it should not be for nothing, but upon condition of a Federal union between the two countrys. I reply'd I thought *that* the only measure which could justify such a step; he added the Chancellor acted cordially with him, that he should have the support of almost all the property of the Country, and that he did not believe his opponents in the H. of Commons would exceed 60, a circumstance he added which he had reason to be assurd of tho it appear'd scarce credible. On Thursday, Dec. 5, the Parliament met. The K. in a speech much longer than usual among other important matters informed us of his having offerd independence to America, and thereby having

---

[1] The Hon. James Murray was Governor of Minorca when it was besieged by the Spaniards under the Duc de Crillon. The Duke tried to bribe him to surrender the fortress, but he indignantly refused. The court-martial was promoted by Sir William Draper. Walpole says (*Letters*, viii. 326): "The sentence was a strange one, yet I imagine calculated to prevent very desperate consequences between a madman and a very hot-headed one. Of twenty-nine charges they pronounced twenty-seven trifling; and on the two others, that seem not very grave, reprimanded Murray, and then ordered the accuser and accused to make mutual apologies to each other. Draper, though the greater Bedlamite, obeyed. Murray would not utter all that was enjoined, and was put under arrest."

[2] The first Earl, born 1734, died 1783.

sacrificed his own opinion in compliance with the wishes of his people. I moved the address (Lord Hawke[1] seconded me), and found myself in a very delicate predicament. Lord Sh. had given me little or no information whereby I could proceed, so that I kept my speech as general as possible; the address passed without a division in both Houses; during the debate Ld Grantham and I sitting near each other his Lp. told they must look out for an Ambassador for France, and wished to know who would like to go there;* this he repeated so pointedly that I told him I should think myself much honoured by such a commission if I was thought a proper person; he said he was glad to hear me say so; represented it as the most agreeable as well as honourable commission of the sort, and said if the negotiation seemed likely to succeed we must have some further conversation on the subject. On the Saturday I went with M. Rayneval, who was here to negotiate on the part of France, and M. le Vicomte de Vergennes, son of the French Minister for foreign affairs, to shew them Westminster Abbey, the Tower, &c. On Sunday they dind with me, as did Lord Grantham, the D. of Dorset, Ld Pembroke, Ld Herbert and Lord Southampton. Nothing very material happen'd previous to the recess.[2] One day in the House of Lords a conversation took place relative to the avowal of American Independence, which occasioned some warm language between the L^{ds} Shelburne and Fitzwilliam.

I went down to Bath as usual at Christmas, and returnd a day or two before the Queen's birthday.[3] The preliminaries between England, France, and Spain, were signed at Versailles, Jan. the

---

* Upon my mentioning Ld Carlisle he did not seem to approve that nomination.

[1] He had succeeded his father the great admiral in October, 1781.
[2] The House did not meet between December 19 and January 22.
[3] Queen Charlotte was born May 14. Her birthday was generally kept on January 18.

20th, and the courier arrived with them on the 24th. I was at dinner that day at Lord Shelburne's when Lord Grantham brought us the news. It was settled that I should go Ambassador Extraordinary and Plenipotentiary to France, which L⁴ Grantham informed me of the next day, tho I was not formally appointed by his Majesty till Feby the 9th, and had the honour to kiss his hand the 10, as did Mr Fawkener, appointed secretary to the embassy. I appointed Mr Chas Jackson, jun^r, of the Post Office, my confidential private secretary, and Mr F. Moore, son of Dr Moore, as an assistant for transcribing, &c. Mr. Fawkener and I daily attended the office for foreign affairs, where we were permitted to read former correspondence, as well as those down to the present time.

On Monday, Feb. 17, the debate took place in both Houses on the Preliminary Articles. Ministry had a small majority[1] of 13 in the House of Lords,* and were beat by 16 in the House of Commons. The common language of opposition was that they did not mean to break the peace, to the performance of which they looked upon the public faith as plighted, but that their great object was the removal of Lord Shelburne. Both Houses sat remarkably late, the Lords till ½ past four, the Commons till ½ past seven the next morning. I went with Fawkener the next day to L⁴ Grantham; he join'd with us in thinking the vote, however qualified, might affect the Peace. On Tuesday night I wrote a letter to his

---

* The amendment to the Address was moved by L⁴ Carlisle, who had a few days before resigned the Steward's staff, which was given to the D. of Rutland, who was likewise appointed a Cabinet Minister.

[1] The numbers were 72 against 59. There were in the House at one time of the day 145 peers, a greater number than had been known on any question during the reign. The numbers in the Commons were 208 to 224. Ministers in a minority of 16. The line taken by the Opposition was not so much against the peace as against Ministers. North in the Lords and Fox and Sheridan in the Commons were equally bitter.

Lp., which I shewed him the next day at Court, as likewise to Ld Shelburne and Mountstuart (who was to go Ambassador to Spain), expressive of my gratitude to the King for the high honour he had conferred upon me in appointing me his Ambassador to France, but at the same informing Ld G. of my desire to resign in case the Ministry were changed, as I should feel myself in a very awkward situation at Versailles (supposing the new ministers continued me in office) receiving my instructions from people whose sentiments on the peace were so different from the opinions of those by whom I was first appointed. On the Fryday following[1] the Ministry were again beat in the H. of Commons on a motion of Ld J. Cavendish[a] that the terms of peace were inadequate to what G. Brit. had a right to expect, considering the relative situations of the belligerent powers. This second defeat and the declared coalition of Mr. Fox and Ld North convinced Ld Shelburne that it was impossible to go on, and accordingly he had a meeting of his friends at Shelburne House on Sunday night, the 23,[2] when he declared his determination to resign. On the Wednesday Ld Grantham was so obliging as to communicate to His M^y the sentiments I had expressed in my letter to his Lp.; but added, at my desire, that if his Majesty's service required it I should think it my duty to continue till the negotiation was completed. Ld G. assured me the K. seem'd to be pleased with my conduct on this occasion.

---

[1] February 21. The division was 207 to 190. Pitt made a magnificent speech; and during it he said of Fox, "he has declared, with that sort of consistency that marks his conduct. 'Because he is prevented from prosecuting the noble lord in the blue ribbon to the satisfaction of public justice he will heartily embrace him as his friend,' so readily does he reconcile extremes and love the man whom he wishes to persecute; with the same spirit, so I suppose, he will cherish this peace too, because he abhors it." A good account of the formation of the Coalition is to be found in Fitzmaurice's *Life of Lord Shelburne*, iii. 339 foll. The Coalition was formed in the afternoon of February 14.

[2] Shelburne resigned the next day. He persuaded the King to send for Pitt, who however refused to take office, as he was not certain of a majority in Parliament, The King used every argument, but to no purpose.

CARMARTHEN, 1783.

This short fragment is probably an exercise in French written by Carmarthen in the view of being English Ambassador in Paris.

Le 10 de Fevrier j'ai eu l'honneur d'être presenté au Roi en qualité de son Ambassadeur Extraordinaire et Plenipotentiaire pres sa Majesté tres Chretienne, le meme jour Monsieur Fawkener fut nommé secretaire d'Ambassade, nous allâmes deja depuis quelque tems tous les jours au bureau de Milord Grantham (secretaire d'Etat aiant le departement des affaires etrangeres) pour lire les differentes correspondances qui pouvoient nous etres utiles en nous fournissant les instructions necessaires pour la commission dont nous vinmes d'etre chargés. J'ai commencé par celle de M. Grenville, qui fut envoié en France pendant le ministere de M. Fox, le printems passé pour entamer une negociation avec la cour de Versailles et generalement avec toutes les puissances belligerantes.

M. Le Comte de Vergennes Ministre d'Etat aiant le departement des affaires etrangeres, etoit le ministre avec lequel M. Grenville devoit naturellement avoir affaire, ce seigneur paroit avoir beaucoup des talens necessaires pour former un grand politique; sous un dehors froid il possede une grande etendue de connoissances, avec une certaine façon de parler extremment mesurée, quoique toujours remplie de professions de franchise et de la sinceritè. Les premieres conferences ne donnoient pas lieu de se flatter que l'affaire pût se terminer bientôt, un certain hauteur de la part du Ministre Français sembluit au contraire annoncer des difficultés presque impossibles à vaincre. M. Grenville ne s'en rebutoit point pourtant mais le changement qui arrivait dans le ministere Britannique à l'occasion de la mort du Marquis de Rockingham et la retraite de M. Fox, en lui fournissant un pretexte pour demander son rappel jetterent la conduite de la negociation entre les mains de M. Fitzherbert, qui etoit deja ministre du Roi à Bruxelles, qui fut nommé à remplacer M. Grenville en France. M. Fitzherbert s'est conduit pendant le cours de la negotiation d'une façon à se procurer la reputation d'un ministre habile, tres applique aux affaires, dont il etait chargé il a scu s'accomoder au differens characteres des differens ministres avec lesquels il avoit affaire, et enfin apres une longue et penible negotiation qui avoit dure pendant six moix il a signé conjointement avec les ministres de France et d'Espagne les articles preliminaires le 20 Janvier, 1783.

This fragment, contained in another MS. book in the British Museum, gives a fuller account of the same transaction.

On Monday, Feb. 17, on the question relative to the Prelim.^{ry} ministry carried it only by 13 votes, including proxys, in the H. of L^{ds}, and were beat in the H. of comm^s 224 to 208. On the Fryday following they were again beat in the H. of Comm^s 207 to 190. On the Wednesday evig., Feb. 19, I shewed the draught of a letter I proposed sending to Ld Grantham to his Lp. and Ld Shelburne relative to my wish to resign the Embassy to France in case of a change of Ministers. L^d Sh. desired I would not make up my mind yet, and begged I would trust him in the course of my determination on the present very delicate situation of public affairs. The next day I dined at his house. I could not help expressing my surprize to Ld Grantham at the conduct of Lord Shelburne, which appeared to me totally devoid of spirit and inconsistent with the opinion I had entertained of his Lp^s activity of mind, particularly on occasions that called for vigorous measures. Ld G. perfectly agreed with me, as did the D. of Rutland, with whom I had some conversation on the same subject. I afterwards just mentioned confidentially to L^d Sh. that I had my doubts a certain person might not be acting a fair part towards him. He appeared struck at my suggestion, and only answered, " You know him."

On Saturday morn., the 22^d, I met Ld Grantham at the office; he told me L^d Sh. had mentioned nothing to him of what steps he meant to pursue in consequence of their second defeat. I could not help observing I wished the King had received the City address on the Fryday, instead of appointing the Wednesday following for that purpose. Ld G. strongly agreed with me, and said L^d Sh. had either not known, or had chosen to conceal, his knowledge of the City address. These circumstances, joined to what dropped from the Ch. in the debate in the H. of Lords,* I own induce me to suspect some secret influence which L^d Sh. is combating, particularly as he told me Lord N.'s party were willing to join with him, which coalition not taking place, but, on the contrary, a union between Ld N. and Mr. F. seems to indicate L^d Sh. having refused the terms on which Ld N.'s support was offered.

Feb. 23.

In case the resignation of the present Ministers is not determined upon, the only means of support must be derived from some one or other of the following measures being adopted:

1. A strict union with the Bedford party at all events.†
2. A coalition with one or other of the opposing parties, if not too late. Mr. F^s, for many reasons, to be preferred, though I apprehend extremely difficult, if not totally impossible to be formed at this juncture.‡

---

* In the course of his reply to Ld Loughborough he observed the violent expressions made use of agt. the peace could only be calculated for mischievous purposes, and that he thought there was some dark design meditated, which so far broke forth as to give rise to that violence which had appeared in the language of those who had spoke on the other side.

Endorsed: Mem. Feby 22, 1783.
Secret.

† By these are understood the Ch: Ld Gower, Ld Weymouth, Mr Rigby, and their connections. The Duke of Marlborough and his friends to be prevailed upon if possible to give a firm and open support.

‡ Attention paid to the Dukes of Northumberland, Montagu, and Newcastle, by the second it may be learnt perhaps what degree of support may be expected from a higher quarter.

3. A dissolution of the present Parliament, which may to a great degree be looked upon as dependant on Ld N., and consequently ought to have been dissolved, unless Gov. had been certain of his support in the business of the Peace.

4. The landed and commercial interests to be consulted on the proposed plans of Gov^t, as far at least as time will permit.

Endorsed: Mem. Feb. 23, 1783.
          Secret.
Recommended to Lord Shelburne.

The King press'd Mr. Pitt to take the lead in a new arrangement to be formed. Mr. P. humbly represented his apprehensions at the idea of so arduous an undertaking, and wished to decline it; but the King renewing his solicitation, Mr. P. said he would look about to find what support he had to expect from such as were not exceptionable (for reasons which must prevent his acting with them), and endeavour, if possible, to obey his M^{rs} commands.

Endorsed: Mem. Feb. 26, 1783.

March 14, 1783.

I had an audience of the K. and thanked his M. for the honour he had done me in appointing me his Amb. to Fr. but begged to represent the very unpleasant situation I should find myself in at Versailles, being sent by those who had so strongly reprobated the preliminary Artic^s upon which the Defin. Tr. must be founded. H. M. saw the awkward situation I should be in, and only desired me to wait till something was settled, which he assured me was far from being the case; that he had wished to have a neutral person at the head of the Treasury, but however, having at length consented to the D. of P.'s nomination, he had desired Ld N. would bring him an answer in two days, but that as yet he had received no answer. H. M. observed he thought neither Lord N. or Mr. Fox had done themselves much honour by the coalition.

Endorsed: Secret Mem.
March 14, 1783.
Confer^e with the K.

On Wednesday, March 26th, I went to the K.'s Levee. I was told the D. of Portland was there (but did not see him) tho H. M. spoke but little to him, and his Grace retired soon. Ld Shelburne had a long conference with the K. and soon after he came out of the closet informed me he had resigned, that he had postponed actually taking that step in order to give the K. time if possible to form an administration, and to see if the Debate in the H. of C.^{s} would produce any new lights on that subject. Mr. Pitt had a short conference, and on coming out of the closet told me he had thought himself obliged to decline His M^{js} proposal of his taking the place of First Minister, as he could not see a probability of a firm support, or at present any appearance of a want of union among the coalescing parties; that he had in the debate on Monday[1] in the H. of C. purposely endeavoured to collect the real wishes of the independent part of

[1] Lord Shelburne's Ministry was beaten in the House of Commons on February 21, in consequence of which he resigned on Feb. 24, recommending the King to send for Mr. Pitt. The next day the King employed every argument to persuade Pitt to take the seals, but without effect. The King then used every effort to form a Ministry without calling on the Coalition of Lord North and Fox, who had upset Lord Shelburne, but without effect, and the country remained practically without a government. On March 18 Mr. Coke gave notice of an address to his Majesty, asking him to form a Ministry entitled to the confidence of the people. The motion was not brought on till Monday, March 24, and it was this debate to which Pitt refers. The King did not lose all hope of persuading Pitt to come forward till March 31, when he announced to the House of Commons that he had resigned the Chancellorship of the Exchequer.

the House, but not finding any reason to expect a substantial support from thence he should think it inconsistent with his duty to the King or to the public service, as well as highly detrimental to his own character as well as his future views, to undertake under the present aspect of affairs so weighty a charge as the Gov^t of the country.

Endorsed: Mem. March 26th 1783.

April 2nd, 1783.

Having been informed in the morning by Sir Charlton Leighton that matters were finally adjusted with the D. of P., Ld N., and Mr. F., and that they were to kiss hands on this day, I immediately dressed and went to Court. The new Ministers[1] were there. I waited in another room while the *Council* met, and immediately afterwards had the honour of an audience. His M. received me in the most gracious manner, and before I could say a word began by assuring me how sorry he was for what he had been obliged to do the preceding evening,[2] but which he thought a measure of absolute necessity as the H. of Commons had not taken any steps to prevent it. On the Monday before he told me he was determined to stay till that Debate was over. That last night (Tuesday 1st) he sent at seven to Ld N. to come at half past 10, for, says His M. though you

---

[1] The Duke of Portland became First Lord of the Treasury, Lord North and Mr. Fox Secretaries of State, Lord Stormont President of the Council, Lord Carlisle Privy Seal, Lord Keppel First Lord of the Admiralty, Lord John Cavendish Chancellor of the Exchequer. The Great Seal was put into commission, to the disappointment of Lord Loughborough.

[2] The Ministers were appointed on Tuesday, April 1, the day after Lord Surrey's motion in the House of Commons. The truth was that the treasury was entirely exhausted; and the King, writing to Lord Temple on April 1, said that nothing would have compelled him to submit to the new situation " but the supposition that no other means remained of preventing the public finances from being materially affected."

know I do not love late visits I was determined to shew I was in no hurry to receive him, that upon Ld N.^{s} producing the list of the Cabinet the K. asked if those were the persons the D. and he had agreed to name. Ld N. answered to *recommend*, Sir, but the K. insisted upon the term to name. H. M. told his Lp. there were two other places of importance they must provide for, Ireland[1] and France, for, my Lord, continued the K. I can inform you Ld Temple will not stay, and Lord Carmarthen will not go.

H. M. did me the honour to express his approbation of my conduct, and appeared fully convinced of the propriety of my wishing to resign my embassy under the present circumstances of affairs. He said he thought things would come right e'er long, and when I took my leave did me the honour to say he should be always happy to see me, and hoped I should soon be restored to his service.

Endorsed: Secret Mem.
April 2, 1783.
Confer. with the K.

June 15, 1783.

Conversation with Ld Temple.

I went up to Town from Mims on Fryday, June 13, and the next morning called upon Ld Temple, who returned the Thursday before from Ireland. His Lp. was not at home, but the next morning, Sunday the 15, he called upon me about one and stayed till near three; he told me he had found Ireland in a most extraordinary situation on his arrival there, scarcely any appearance of Government, the D. of Portland, his predecessor, having thrown everything into the hands of the volunteers,[2] that Mr. O'Birne governed

[1] Lord Temple's administration lasted from September, 1782, to June 3, 1783.
[2] Companies of volunteers had been raised in Ireland to defend the island, at a time when England was at war with America, France, and Holland. They were officered by the noblemen and gentlemen of Ireland, and obtained large political influence, which they used principally in favour of the independence of Ireland.

the Duke by means of the Duchess, and that he Ld T. found it a very difficult task to prevent many serious consequences arising to Gov^t from the state in which that country had been left at the end of the Portland administration.

Upon the last change in the Ministry the D. of P. wrote a very polite letter to Ld T. hoping he would remain in Ireland, and assuring him the executive part of Gov^t would be wholly placed in the hands of those generally known by the appellation of the Friends of their much lamented Friend the late Marquis of Rockingham. Ld T. was not a little surprized, immediately almost after the receipt of this letter, at receiving one from Ld North informing him that he was appointed sec. of state, and was to have the honour of corresponding confidentially with him upon the business of Ireland; his Lp. mentioned two very particular circumstances relative to Mr. Scott, the late, and Mr. Yelverton, the present attorney-general of Ireland, the former abusing the D. of Portland to Lord North in the most gross and unguarded manner, and the latter, though in England lately upon some personal business, refusing to have anything to say to Ld North or even going near him, though his Lp. was the Minister to whose department the affairs of Ireland were immediately entrusted, and he himself the first crown officer in the H. of Commons in Ireland; he added the Duke of Leinster [1] being particularly hostile to the new administration, that he had asked his relation Mr. Fox to be a vice-treasurer, but that Mr. F. had excused himself by informing him that place was promised to Mr. Eden,[2] who had been personally offensive to the Duke during his residence in Ireland as Secretary to Ld Carlisle. Ld Temple told me both his successor Ld Northington[3] and his Secretary Mr. Windham appeared totally uninformed as to the state of Ireland on their arrival there;

The Duke of Portland had exerted his efforts to conciliate the National Party. The volunteers, gradually falling into the power of a lower class in the community, were suppressed in 1785.

[1] Second Duke, born March 13, 1749.   [2] Afterwards Lord Auckland.
[3] Second Earl, died 1786.

that Gov^t at home seemed to have given them little or no lights, but referred them to him, and that he had accordingly given them every information in his power, and that they appeared much struck with the many difficulties they found they should have to encounter in the carrying on the Government of that country, with any prospect of essential service to the state.

His Lp. declared his surprize at the marks of respect he had met from the volunteers, as far from paying any servile court to them he had on many occasions strongly and effectually opposed several of their measures and even been obliged to order them to be fired upon when some lives were lost in a dispute with the military.

He joined with me in amazement at Ld Shelburnes imprudent conduct with regard both to making and preserving friends; he said his head seemed to have been turned by his high situation, that he did not sufficiently communicate his ideas to his brother Ministers but assumed a dictatorial tone too frequently, and that he Ld T. had been obliged to enter into an explanation with him by letter on that very subject, after which L^d Sh. corrected himself in that particular with him during the remainder of his administration.

Endorsed: June 15, 1783.

Minutes of Conversation with Lord Temple.

CABINET MEMORANDUMS, 1784.

Lord Carmarthen only spoke once in Parliament during the Coalition Ministry, and that was on April 14, on the Irish Judicature Bill.

1784.

Late at night on Thursday Dec. 18, 1783, His Majesty sent for the Seals of both the Departments, with orders for them to be delivered up to him by the Under Secretaries, which was immediately done; the next morning Mr. Pitt was appointed First Commissioner of the Treasury, Earl Temple Secretary of State (holding both departments till some one should be named to that of Foreign Affairs), and Earl Gower[1] President of the Council; Lord Hertford resigned the Chamberlain's staff the same day. On Saturday, the 20, I dined at Lord Temple's; the company was numerous; Ld Gower, Ld Thurlow, Mr. Pitt, the Duke of Dorset, Duke of Bridgewater, Lord Grantley, Duke of Richmond, and several others were there: the principal characters seemed remarkably thoughtful,[2] and

---

[1] According to Lord Stanhope (*Life of Pitt*, i. 156) he offered his services.

[2] In fact Lord Temple resigned next day. There can be little doubt, since the publication by the Duke of Buckingham of Lord Temple's letter to Pitt, December 29, 1783, that Temple's real reason for resigning was that suggested by Lord Stanhope (*Life of Pitt*, i. 164), namely, that Temple had applied for "a dukedom or some other personal object of ambition. Finding that the King refused him and that Mr. Pitt was not willing to make that personal object a *sine quâ non* condition in so anxious a state of public affairs, he flung down the seals in anger and set off to Stowe."

I apprehended something unpleasant had happened but could by no means devine what it was; the Duke of Dorset remarked to me before we sat down to table that he feared a want of resolution in the new Ministers. On Monday, the 22^d, I went to the House of Lords, where to my astonishment I heard Lord Temple had resigned; the lately discarded Ministers concluded all was over and expected to be sent for back upon their own terms; the consternation this spread among the friends of Mr. Pitt is easily conceived. The next morning, Tuesday the 23, I received a note from Mr. Pitt informing me he was orderd to attend the King that day at two o'clock[1] at the Queen^s House, and desiring me earnestly to come to him at Lord Chatham^s in Berkeley Sq^r before he went to the Q^s House. I immediately went to him; he opened the business upon which he had sent for me, by stating the absolute necessity of supporting the constitution against the encroachments which had been attempted by the late Ministers, particularly in their India Bill, which had been the immediate cause of their dismission; that some arrangement must be made immediately to prevent the return of the old Ministers upon their own terms, which the King had declared he *would not submit to*, and that the consequences of that resolution being carryed into effect must be dreadful indeed for the country: after many very flattering expressions to me personally he expressed to me an earnest wish that I would take the seals for the department of foreign affairs. I thanked him for this very strong and unequivocal mark of his good opinion of me, but begged to decline accepting the offer as by no means thinking myself equal to the undertaking an employment of such great importance; he answered the King desired it of me as an essential service at this juncture when a moment's unnecessary delay might throw every thing into the utmost confusion. He desired me to reflect on the necessity of forming a Cabinet immediately, and then said he hoped

---

[1] Pitt, in his letter to the Duke of Rutland, written at eleven a.m. the same day, says that he is to see the King at one.

I should be ready to testify my duty to the King and Public by accepting the employment in question. I then told him that in the way he had represented the King's situation I must sacrifice my own ease and comfort to His Maj^s service; that if my accepting the office could any ways contribute to that end I would submit, but begged him to do me the justice to be convinc'd that my acceptance was a matter of Duty, not of choice; he thank'd me in the warmest manner for my conforming to his wishes, and desired me to come to the Queen's House at two o'clock. He shewed me a letter from the King, in which His Majesty express'd his willingness to entrust his affairs to Mr. Pitt, Ld Gower and the Duke of Richmond, whom he wished to form an administration; His Majesty express'd the very disagreeable situation he was in and compared it to that of a person in danger of drowning, who would gladly catch at every twig. I went home to dress, and then went to the Queen's House, where I met the Dukes of Richmond and Rutland, the Lords Gower, Howe, Thurlow, and Sydney, and Mr. Pitt; we had all separate audiences. The King received me in the kindest and most gracious manner, and testifyed in the warmest terms how much he felt himself obliged to me for coming into his service at so critical a moment; I repeated to His Majesty my unfeigned desire of evincing upon every occasion my Duty and Loyalty to him, and repeated to him what I had already mentioned to Mr. Pitt on the subject of receiving the office proposed. His Majesty delivered me the seals, those of the Home department were given to Ld Sydney, and, the Duke of Rutland having received the Privy Seal, we three were sworn into our offices in Council immediately; the Lords Commissioners for the custody of the Great Seal being ordered to attend His Majesty with the Seal at the Queen's House that evening at seven, came accordingly and delivered it up; and at eight o'clock that evening a Council was held there when His Maj. delivered the Great Seal to Lord Thurlow, who was immediately sworn in Ld Chancellor. The Cabinet was now formed, and consisted of the following persons: Ld Thurlow, Lord Chancellor; Earl Gower,

Lord President; Duke of Rutland, Lord Pr'vy Seal; Lord Vis. Howe, First Lord of ye Admir.

Lord Carmarthen, } Secretarys of State.
Lord Sydney,

Mr. Pitt, First Lord of the Treasury.

That night I received a very polite letter from the Duke of Manchester expressing his desire to resign the embassy to France. The Duke of Dorset was appointed to succeed him; soon after Lord Mountstuart resigned the embassy to Spain. It was offered to Lord Harcourt who begged to decline accepting it, but appeard much pleased with the offer being made him, and came to Court, where he had never been since the death of his Father.[1] Lord Chesterfield was appointed to Spain.

The Duke of Chandos and Lord Salisbury kissed hands for the Stewards and Chamberlain^s staves. The Majority of the H. of Commons at the disposal of Mr. Fox presented an address[2] to the King praying His Majesty not to interrupt their deliberations by any exertion of his Prerogative till the very important affairs then under discussion had been determined upon. They were answered they should not be prevented meeting again after the recess. They had forbid the issuing of public money[3] for several weeks, and adjourned to the 12th of January;[4] little hopes appeard of obtaining a majority in that House, and the resolutions they had taken in regard to the issuing public money renderd a dissolution very difficult. The First Cabinet met at my office on Dec. 28; nothing more passed than conversation on the present temper and probable future conduct of the House of Commons, and, as we were naturally taken up with the business of our respective offices[5] in

[1] His father had been accidentally drowned in an old well in his park at Nuneham, September 16, 1777.
[2] Received by the King on December 24.
[3] This referred to the acceptance by the Treasury of bills from India amounting to about two millions and a half.
[4] This was about a week earlier than the ordinary time of meeting.
[5] Stanhope (i. 169) says: " The finances at the close of an unprosperous war were

order to get *au courant des affaires*, we had little else to do at those meetings for some days. On Jan. 12 the House of Commons met in the same ill humour they had seperated for the recess. The next day the Cabinet dined at the Duke of Rutlands; there was also present the D. of Richmond, Lord Weymouth (G^r of the Stole), Mr. Dundas (Treasurer of the Navy), and Mr. Arden (Solicitor General). Mr. Rose, Sec. to the Treasury, came to us after dinner; we endeavoured to find out some method to surmount the obstacles [1] thrown in the way of a dissolution by the opposite party; this however seemd extremely difficult, and at the same time it appeared impossible to go on with the public business with the H. of Commons against us, no matter by what means. Mr. Pitt even hinted at giving the thing up;[2] this however was represented to him by us all as betraying both the Crown and People, as well as highly disgraceful to ourselves personally, unless we could obtain such conditions for the Crown and People as should prevent their being trampld upon by the late Ministers on their return to Power. A cool but spirited line of conduct appeard necessary to us all, and the Duke of Richmond in the handsomest manner told Mr. Pitt that though he had declined his offer of being of the Cabinet at first, now he perceived there was some difficulty and perhaps might

in the utmost disorder. The commercial system with the now independent colonies was as yet undetermined, and required prompt and final regulation. Our foreign relations, which at last had left us almost without a single ally, called for vigilant foresight and conciliating care. But as claiming precedence above all others was the East India question. It was necessary for the new Cabinet, without the loss of a single hour, to frame a new measure in place of that which the House of Lords had rejected. By incessant labour Mr. Pitt and his colleagues effected this object. Their draft Bill was not only prepared, but was approved by both sections of the East India body, previous to the meeting of the House of Commons on January 12.

[1] On January 12 Fox had moved and carried three resolutions: 1. That any person issuing money for the public service without the sanction of an Appropriation Act would be guilty of a high crime and misdemeanour. 2. That an account should be rendered of all sums of money issued since December 19 for services voted but not appropriated by Act of Parliament; and 3. To postpone the Second Reading of the Mutiny Bill to February 23.

[2] There is no trace of this hesitation elsewhere.

be danger in the supporting the constitution, he would willingly
and chearfully share both and contribute every assistance in his
power to promote so good a cause, and was ready from that moment
to be of the Cabinet; the offer was, of course, gratefully received,
and the next morning obtained the K.'s consent, and indeed a great
acquisition to the Cabinet the Duke was.

The Mutiny Bill being to expire on the 25 of March, threw a
fresh obstacle in the way of getting rid of the present Parliament.
We had a Cabinet at my office several times. Mr. Pitt feared he
was bound by an assertion of his friend Mr. Bankes [1] not to dissolve;
this however in fact engaged no more than to suffering the House
to meet again after the recess, which it had accordingly done. On
Sunday the 25 we met at my office, where we remained near five
hours in discussing the question of Dissolution Lord Gower and
myself were decidedly for it, provided the difficulty of the Mutiny
Bill could be got over. The Duke of Richmond thought we could
do with this H. of Commons, and seemed to have changed his
opinion. The Chancellor seemed perplexed. Mr. Pitt and the
Duke of Rutland were still apprehensive of an engagement being
understood to have been given not to dissolve. Lord Howe would
give no opinion, but was ready to abide by the decision of the
meeting Lord Sidney for the dissolution. At last we agreed to
advise the measure, and the Duke of Richmond rather that prevent
unanimity assented. We all dined at a great dinner at Lord
Salisburys,[2] and afterwards the Cabinet adjourned to the Duke of
Rutland's, where we resumed the subject of our morning's delibera-

[1] Mr. Bankes had assured the House, on behalf of Pitt, on December 19, "that
he was authorised by his right hon. friend to assure the Committee that he had no
intention whatever to advocate either a dissolution or a prorogation of Parliament,
and that he would not be one of those who should advise any such measure. This
he quotes from authority, and he stated it as an assertion to which his right hon.
friend would most readily pledge himself." Mr. Pitt's scruples seem more justified
than Lord Carmarthen's explanations. It does not appear in the ordinary histories
that Pitt was so strongly opposed to a dissolution.

[2] His house and the Duke of Rutland's were both in Arlington Street.

tion, and sat near six hours. It appeared plainly upon reconsidering the whole state of the case, that, although it was just possible for the new Parliament to meet and pass the Mutiny Bill within the appointed time, yet to obtain the dispatch necessary for that purpose it would require some of the established and most essential forms of the House of Commons to be dispens'd with; for instance, the voting of money for the payment of the Army without going into a Committee of Supplies. This appeared to me so irregular that I made no difficulty in saying that I thought it a sufficient objection to the carrying a measure I had so much at heart even as the Dissolution into execution; that my support of the measure in the morning had been conditional, and that finding a fresh difficulty, and that according to my conception of such magnitude, I was equally ready now to give my sentiments against taking a step which must be productive of so irregular a proceeding at the opening of the new Parliament. This seemed to be the opinion of all my colleagues. We lamented the circumstance, but thought it insurmountable, and accordingly resolved not to dissolve in the present situation of things. We communicated this our opinion to the King by Mr. Pitt. The K. received it with more coolness than might have been expected, as it was well known His Majesty was much bent on getting rid of this Parliament. He commanded us all to attend him the next morning at eleven o'clock at the Queen's House. We humbly represented in the most Dutiful manner to His Majesty that our attending him at that Place and Hour might have an appearance highly prejudicial to His Service, and be represented by the emissaries of opposition as a general resignation, which might produce very unpleasant consequences, and therefore submitted to His Majesty whether it would not be far more advisable to attend His Majesty in a less conspicuous manner at St. James' after the Levee. The King saw the force of the objection, and accordingly commanded us to attend him at St. James' after the Levee, which accordingly we all did, and not without great anxiety, to receive His Pleasure. His Majesty in a well conceived speech of some length, and in different parts of which he appeared much agitated, expressd his wish upon all occasions to observe the true principles of the Constitution as the sole rules of his conduct; he lamented the misconstructions put upon his Government, which he alone wished to enjoy for the good of His People, and declared a fix'd and unalterable resolution on no account to be put bound hand and foot into the hands of Mr. Fox, that rather than submit to that he would quit the Kingdom for ever! at the same time he was perfectly ready to make every arrangement which might be conducive to the welfare of his People, and was too sensible of the blessings of Freedom ever to submit to see either his subjects or himself enslav'd.

We made him (by Mr. Pitt) our most dutiful acknowledgments for the communication of His Royal sentiments at this very serious and important period, and, after assuring His Majesty of our firm persuasion of his parental regard for his people, assured him we would by no means desert him in his gracious endeavour to preserve our constitution inviolate. It is scarcely possible, I think, to conceive a more interesting scene than that which presented itself in His Majesty's closet during the few minutes this conference lasted on Monday, Jan. 26th, 1784.

Present:

The King.

Lord Chancellor.	Lord President.
Lord Privy Seal.	D. of Richmond.
Lord Howe.	Mr. Pitt.
Lord Sydney.	Lord Carmarthen.

The attention of the Cabinet was now and for a considerable time engrossed by a project set on foot by a considerable number of members of the House of Commons, among whom were several of the most respectable, for the professed purpose of effecting a union of partys upon principle and thereby healing the present distractions and forming an able and permanent administration. The utmost fairness and candour was to be observed by these Gentlemen in pursuit of their object; they met at the St. Alban's Tavern,[1] and deputed some of their body to wait upon the Duke of Portland and Mr. Pitt, to communicate their wishes to them. Many letters passed upon the occasion between the society and the leaders of the opposite partys, but it very soon appearing that far from impartiality profess'd by them at the outset of the business being observed in the conducting of it, the most barefaced predilection for the late Ministers was manifest, the greater number of those who really meant well and fairly by both partys chose to decline attending; a Preliminary insisted upon by Mr. Fox' Friends was that Mr. Pitt should resign previous to any negotiation being entered upon for a future arrangement, as they look'd upon themselves as pledg'd to support the honour of the House which had by a resolution expressd its disapprobation of many circumstances which attended his coming into Power. This proposal was of course too absurd to be complyed with; the negotiation, if it deserved the name, seemed at an end more than once and was afterwards resumed merely, as it should appear, for the purpose of delay. The K. himself even condescended so far as to authorise Lord Sidney to write to the Duke of Portland to manifest his readiness to comply with an union upon fair and honourable principles; the answer was respectful to the King and perfectly absurd in every other particular. About the middle of February the Duke of Rutland was appointed Lord Lieutenant of Ireland in the room of the Earl of Northington[2] who had desired to resign. His Grace, of course, gave up the Privy Seal, which was some time afterwards put into commission, and the custody of it delivered to Messrs Fraser, Nepean, and Cottrell.

Two very strong addresses[3] were presented to the King by the

[1] Probably in St. Alban's Street, Pall Mall, a small street removed to make way for the enlargement of Waterloo Place and Regent Street. The party was called the *Independents*. They met to the number of 53, and put Mr. Thomas Grosvenor in the chair. (Stanhope's *Pitt*, i. 184 foll.)

[2] Son of the Lord Chancellor; he died 1786.

[3] On February 2 Mr. Coke moved against the continuance of the present Ministry

House of Commons for the removal of the Ministers, though without alledging any specific charge against them. They were however drawn up in respectful terms towards his Majesty, and were answered in cool but firm language, setting forth the impropriety of a compliance with them. Ever since the change in the Govern[t] addresses had been pouring in from all parts the Kingdom thanking his Majesty for the removal of the late Ministers, and many of them of a later date reprehending in the strongest terms the conduct of their representatives, who were obstructing the public business for factious purposes, and praying His Majesty to have recourse to His People by a speedy dissolution of the Parliament. So strong was the tide without doors against Mr. Fox and his majority that they thought prudent to pass the Mutiny Bill in compliance with the wishes of the Public, though at the same time they thought or pretended to think a Dissolution would not take place as no Appropriation Act had yet passed; that measure however was now finally determined upon. We met at the Lord Chancellor[a] (who was indispos'd) on Sunday, March 21st, and agreed to advise His Majesty to prorogue the Parliament in Person, and to make a speech setting forth the reasons of the measure on the Wednesday following, and declaring his intentions of having recourse forthwith to the sense of His People. The Duke of Richmond wished something might be said in the speech on the subject of Parliamentary reform. Mr. Pitt seemed to approve this idea. The Chancellor, Lord Gower, Lord Sidney, and myself, however, could not help thinking it in many respects liable to very great objections, and after some conversation they agreed to its being omitted. We met again at the Chancellor's and settled everything relating to the Speech, List of Scotch Peers,

in office. This was carried by 223 to 204. Next day Mr. Coke moved to lay this resolution before the King. This was carried by a majority of 24—211 to 187. On February 20 Mr. Powys moved, "That the House relies on the King's readiness to form a united and efficient administration." This was carried by a majority of 20—197 to 177. A motion to present an address was carried by 177 to 156. On March 1 Mr. Fox moved for an address to the King to remove his Ministers. This was carried by a majority of 12—201 to 189.

&c. Lord Stormont[1] was in at first; it was said the King wished him to be chosen. His Majesty one day did me the honour to converse with me upon the subject, and said that if Lord St. would be quiet he had no objection to his being in the Government list, but if he interfered with and canvassed for other opposition Lords the case was widely different. The Duke of Argyle had said his friend Lord Roseberry would willingly consent to be left out of the list to accommodate Gov^t, who meant to recommend some new Peers; in the first list his Lp^s name was omitted, and Ld Stormont remained; the Duke of Richmond however objected to recommend him, and his name was then omitted and Lord Roseberrys again inserted. It seemed however to be the general opinion that unless we were sure of keeping Ld Stormont out it would be advisable to let his name remain; the experiment, however, was tryed, and failed, for His Lordship and Lord Elphinstone were afterwards chosen to the exclusion of two of the Government list, viz., the Earls of Marchmont and Roseberry.

Early on Wednesday morning, March the 24, the Chancellor^s House was broke open and the Great Seal stolen, and though some candlesticks, a sword, and some money were at the same time taken, yet it being so near the time when the Great Seal would necessarily be wanted for sealing the writs for the new Parliament, much speculation arose concerning the real motive which occasiond such a theft at such a very particular time. Previous to the King going to the House on Wednesday to prorogue Parliament a new Great Seal was in Council orderd to be prepared with the utmost dispatch, and being cast by the next day a Council was summond to meet at the Queen^s House on Thursday evening, March the 25, at which I attended, when the King signed the Proclamation for dissolving the Parliament, and issuing the writs for calling a new one, the writs to bear date the next day the 26, and to be returnable on

---

[1] Lord Stormont held many places of importance both at home and abroad. He was buried in Westminster Abbey 1796. He was a representative peer of Scotland from 1756 to 1790.

Tuesday the 18th of May next ensuing. Thus was an end put to one of the most extraordinary Parliaments that had ever existed, and which, from every motive of Prudence and sound Policy, ought to have been dissolved much sooner.

During the interval between the two Parliaments nothing very material occurred; the Cabinet met for the new settlement of the Province of Nova Scotia[1] which was to be divided, and for other ordinary affairs; I found I could not prevail upon them to give that attention to Foreign affairs that I thought necessary, and consequently afterwards gave them little trouble on the subject. Mr. Pitt however for some time applied himself to the correspondence with great assiduity, and during a day I stayed with him at Wimbledon we had a great deal of conversation on the general subject of European Politics; this happen'd in May, and I was very happy to find our ideas were similar on the great object of separating if possible the House of Austria from France,[2] as likewise a degree of desire to form some system on the continent in order to counterbalance the House of Bourbon, though at the same time the strongest conviction of the necessity of avoiding, if possible, the entering into any engagements likely to embroil us in a new war.[3] The Parliament met on the 18 of May; the Elections[4] went far more favourably

---

[1] In 1784 New Brunswick and Cape Breton were separated from Nova Scotia and made independent governments. In 1819 Cape Breton was united with Nova Scotia again. At this time this colony was especially important as being the place of refuge of loyalists escaping from America. The town of Shelburne rapidly developed in this way, but was afterwards nearly deserted.

[2] The key-note of the English foreign policy at this time was jealousy of France, and connected with this was a strong desire to separate her from Austria. Carmarthen's letters are full of this, to the derision of more experienced statesmen, such as Kaunitz. It can scarcely be believed that Pitt shared this ungenerous distrust of France. Certainly things became much better after the conclusion of the commercial treaty.

[3] There can be little doubt that Pitt's predominant desire was for peace at this time.

[4] About 160 supporters of the Coalition Ministry lost their seats, and went by the name of "Fox's Martyrs."

for Government than its most sanguine Friends could have imagined. On the 24th there was a great Breakfast at Carlton House,[1] the Duke of Richmond and myself were the only two of the K's Ministers invited. I had a long conversation with his Grace in the Gardens on the present situation of affairs; he could not help lamenting to me a want of confidential communication in the Cabinet, and of the dilatory proceedings in some of the departments; he told me in confidence that Pitt has express'd a wish of his (the Duke's) taking the Seals of the Home department, and of giving the Privy Seal to Lord Sydney, but that he had declined the arrangement.

The administration had a very considerable majority[2] in the new House of Commons, and carried all the measures[3] they proposed. The Parliament sat till August.[4] After the Prorogation the rest of the Ministers had more time for attending to foreign Politics. The Revolution[5] brought about by the Prince Royal of Denmark having

[1] The Prince of Wales had begun to reside there in 1783.
[2] The address was carried by a majority of 282 to 114.
[3] The principal measures carried were Pitt's India Bill and certain financial reforms.
[4] The King closed the session on August 20.
[5] Previously to the French Revolution the word was not used in a bad signification; it only implied a serious and important change of government. The change which Carmarthen here alludes to happened as follows: Frederick V. of Denmark had married as his second wife Julia Maria, of Brunswick-Wolfenbüttel. Her stepson Christian V. married the unfortunate sister of George III., Caroline Matilda. Caroline Matilda was exiled to Celle, in consequence of an intrigue with the minister, Struensee. The King, Christian, was unfit to govern, and everything was left in the hands of Queen Julia. She placed herself in the power of Guldberg, a Minister of the most narrow and retrograde type. When the Crown Prince Frederick was fourteen years of age he ought to have been confirmed and taken his place at the council table; but the Queen, Julia, contrived to defer this event for two years. He received confirmation on March 28, 1784, and was admitted to the Council on April 14 of the same year. He persuaded the King to sign papers appointing a new Council, and summoned Count Bernstorff to the direction of affairs. Bernstorff, who was the nephew of his more illustrious predecessor of the same name, had been dismissed in 1780. He developed commerce, industry, and education in the most enlightened manner. A full account of this is given in the Appendix.

restored Count Bernstoff to power, appeared a most flattering circumstance tow^d forwarding our object of a more close connection with Denmark and Russia. The hostile designs of Sweden towards Denmark which I had communicated to Russia the last winter had waken'd the jealousy of that power, and this appear'd considerably augmented by a convention lately made between France and Sweden, whereby the former was to have the free use of the Port of Gottenburg,[1] in exchange for which she was to cede the small Island of St. Barthelemi in the W. Indies to Sweden. This idea of France acquiring such a footing in the Baltic naturally occasioned

[1] Carmarthen probably made more of this Gothenburg business than it deserved. He was actuated, as I have before said, principally by jealousy of France and desire to separate France and Austria. Sweden was at this time closely attached to France. There is in the English Record Office a *Project of Instructions for Mr. FitzHerbert*, dated about the second week in October, which gives a clear account of our position. It appears to me to show the hand of Pitt : "A joint representation on the part of the Courts of London, Petersburg, and Copenhagen, to that of Stockholm, to require an explanation of the treaty by which Sweden allows France a depôt in the port of Gothenburg, and to be informed to what extent the privileges allowed to the French by this arrangement are *bonâ fide* meant to be carried out.

" The answer probably may be an assurance of its being by no means calculated to occasion the jealousy of other powers, being merely a renewal of the privileges granted to the French at Wismar by the treaty of 1741. It will be necessary however for Sweden to be explicit on the subject; that in case the answer may be satisfactory for the present, and any advantage may be taken at a future period of the French establishment at Gothenburg, to the prejudice of the three above-mentioned powers, or either of them, they may be enabled to produce the friendly assurance of Sweden in addition to the other motives which may call for action and effectual interference, in order to defeat such a dangerous and hostile design. And if it shall appear that the convention shall have no other than its professed object in view it may be fully worth the consideration of the three Courts how far that arrangement may be consistent with the interests (both commercial and political) of their respective dominions.

" But, on the contrary, should a total silence be observed, and a direct refusal on the part of Sweden be the result of this application, it will then behove the three powers to take (in concert) such measures as may effectually tend to protect their mutual and reciprocal rights from the ambitions projects of those at whose instigation or by whose connivance the public tranquillity as well as the particular concerns of individual nations shall have been endangered. The very suggestion of

some degree of alarm in the Courts of Petersburg, London, and Copenhagen, and Mr. Simolin was directed by his Court to communicate to me the contents of a note setting forth the Empress's desire of knowing the King' sentiments upon so alarming a circumstance, and the measures his Majesty would wish to adopt in consequence of it. I had long regarded M. Simolin as unworthy of confidence, and therefore sent the answer by a messenger to Mr. Fitzherbert without communicating the particulars of it to the Russian Minister in England. It contained expressions of His Majesty's satisfaction at the confidential communication made to him by the Empress; and the proposal of an application from the three Courts of England, Russia, and Denmark, and that of Sweden, for a bonâ fide explanation of the extent of the advantages both present and future to be obtain'd by France in virtue of the late convention; at the same time recommending a firm and permanent system of cooperation to be adopted by the three Courts to prevent any mischievous consequences resulting from it let the answer be what it would. On the 15 of October I received a long confidential letter from Mr. Pitt, in which after many flattering expressions in respect to myself, and apologizing for the nature of the subject, which he said he never would have mentioned but from the firmest persuasion of my Friendship, and that I would see the matter in question in the true light in which he meant it, and stating at the same time that my wishes would decide his conduct; he suggested the great acquisition Lord Camden would be to the Cabinet, but that having sounded his Lordship on the subject he found him not desirous of entering into the administration unless in conjunction with his Friend the Duke of Grafton ; that such being the case Mr. Pitt suggested that this arrangement should by no means be listened to without my full and sincere concurrence, as he saw no

such an idea taking place must be an additional though an unnecessary motive to prove the expediency (not to say necessity) of a cordial, firm, and permanent system of alliance between the three Courts." It is obvious that Pitt did not rate the danger as highly as Carmarthen.

other way of bringing it about but by my taking some other situation suitable to my Rank, &c. &c. and leaving the Seals for the Duke of Grafton, not immediately but at a future period; he again repeated many encomiums upon my conduct in my present office, and assured me that this idea had been communicated to nobody, and would go no further till my sentiments were known.

I answered him immediately by thanking him for the very friendly as well as flattering manner in which he had made this confidential communication to me, assuring him that no one could wish more than I did for the addition of Lord Camden's weight and abilities to the administration. That my only surprize was at the possibility of the Duke of Grafton wishing again to enter into an office of great Labour and Fatigue; this merely from an idea of his preferring a retired life, though I thought him well calculated both from personal character and abilities to be of great service to any Government he wished to support. I added that I was convinc'd Mr. Pitt would do me the justice to recollect the motives which induced me to accept my present office; that it was by no means a matter of choice or inclination but merely with a view of being of service to the King and to the Public; that the same principles still remaining in full force (as I trusted they ever would) in my mind I should be equally ready to resign my office from the same motives, and therefore was ready so to do either immediately or some time hence, though I owned I could wish to remain till the answer from Russia could be received, as I was extremely anxious for the success of our system with regard to Foreign Politics. A day or two afterwards Mr. Pitt came to me at the office, and expressed himself under the greatest obligations to me for the manner in which I had received his communication, and after giving much more praise to my behaviour upon this business than it was I think entitled to, assured me he could by no means think of proceeding in it, and begged me to look upon it as entirely dropped. In a few weeks afterwards Lord Gower accepted the Privy Seal (which ever since the Duke of Rutland's appointment to

Ireland had remained in Commission), and Lord Camden was appointed President of the Council on this vacancy.

This memorandum contains a sketch of the system of foreign alliances which Lord Carmarthen tried to adopt at his entrance into office. A short account of the situation of England at this time will be found in the Introduction.

St. James's, June 11, 1784.

The most desirable object without doubt would be an alliance (defensive at least) with Austria and Russia. I wish to look upon Denmark as a sure Friend, unless neglect on our part drives her from motives of necessity rather than choice into the hands of our enemies.

If either the impracticability or even difficulty attending our forming any solid and substantial connection with the Emperor[1] should render it advisable to turn our attention to another Power (in order to avoid any delay which might be dangerous in respect to the necessary measure of a Continental alliance), Prussia[2] is naturally the Point to which our views must be directed; it will be necessary however at all events to consider the connection of these two Powers, I mean Austria and Prussia, so far as they are likely to be affected by them, in the course of any negotiation which may be undertaken on the part of England with a view to securing their Friendship, or in case of necessity their assistance. Russia must at all events be esteemed well worthy the attention of England, not only on account of her own importance in the scale of Europe, but from the weight and influence which she possesses in the respective Cabinets of Vienna and Berlin, and without the

---

[1] Joseph II., Emperor of Austria.

[2] Frederick the Great still occupied the throne of Prussia. Denmark was the natural rival of Sweden; and, that country being at this time friendly to France, it was natural for Carmarthen to make overtures to Denmark.

cordial co-operation on the part of the Court of Petersburg there is little probability of seeing any essential stop put to the influence of French councils or at least to the impression of the system established by Prince Kaunitz,[1] in any important line of conduct likely to be *soon* adopted by the Emperor, and unless some arrangement can *speedily* be made I much fear the wisest and best concerted plans which are only to be adopted at a remote period would come too late to be productive of any salutary consequences to Great Britain. For the attainment of this desirable end (I mean the putting an end to the connection which at present subsists between Austria and France) the degree of intimacy which now reigns between the two Imperial Courts might if properly managed be of the utmost service to us, but on the contrary may be equally prejudicial if not directed to its proper channel, as, if not likely to secure us the Friendship of the Emperor, it may perhaps operate with equal force in preventing the Empress of Russia from adopting a friendly line of conduct towards England for fearing of offending the Court of France, with whom the Emperor is so strongly connected.

On the other hand the Empress of Russia may find some difficulty in entering into any alliance of which the King of Prussia is a party, as that monarch is at all times the rival, not to say the most inveterate opponent, of the Emperor's power and interest in Germany. Whichever alternative therefore may be preferred in respect to our future connections it is evident Russia ought to be gained unless we should think it adviseable to risque offending both the Imperial Courts by confining our views to the two Courts of Berlin and Copenhagen.

Endorsed: June 11, 1784.
Memorandums.
Foreign Alliance.

[1] Kaunitz, the Prime Minister of Maria Theresa and Joseph II., had established the alliance between Austria and France against Prussia at the opening of the Seven Years War in 1756.

No appearance of the two Northern Crowns going to war after the Swedish plan being detected, and the consequent declaration of Russia in favour of Denmark.

In case, however, this event should soon take place, Russia might fully answer every purpose of defensive alliance in support of Denmark, unless France should think proper to join Sweden, and in that case, independent of any new connection, could England suffer a French fleet on the Baltic, without sending a strong force there likewise?

The suffering Denmark to be in any case overpowered by Sweden would be in fact sacrificing the *North to the Views of France*. Only general assurances of the Friendly Disposition of England towards Denmark. That wee flatter ourselves the Hostile Designs of Sweden are laid aside, which, had they been carried into execution, could not by any means have been looked upon with indifference by this Court. The Friendly declaration of Russia towards Denmark has given great pleasure to the King; the respectable assistance of that Power would doubtless have been infinitely more than sufficient to have defeated the ambitious projects of Sweden. At all events, however, Denmark might have been sure of meeting a sincere disposition in this country to have afforded such assistance as her circumstances would have admitted of.

Endorsed :—Memorandums,[1]
June 25, 1784,
(Concerning Denmark)
In Cabinet.

Reasons for a Danish Alliance.

If Denmark is attacked by Sweden we must defend Denmark, for we cannot see Norway in the hands of Sweden.

[1] This memorandum refers to some passing misunderstanding between Sweden and Denmark, owing to the connection between Sweden and France and the accession of Count Bernstorff to power in Denmark.

Copenhagen is the entrance and key of the Baltick, thro' which all naval stores must pass—of great importance, therefore, whether we want them for ourselves, or wish to keep them from our Enemys.

The Danes have the best regulated Marine of any of the Northern Powers.

They have no other *natural* Enemy than Sweden—with Sweden they are able to cope by themselves, and would, if attacked from that Quarter, prefer our pecuniary to our effective assistance.

Russia also would join them, and we run no risk of embarking in a war for Denmark if she is attacked by Sweden alone; if France seconds Sweden we must in that case be engaged in it whether we have or have not an alliance with Denmark.

Proposals for this Alliance should be made under great Secrecy, and no communication of the intended connection made to any Power whatever till it is too far advanced to be broken off.

Denmark (and particularly under the ministry of Mous^r de Bernsdorff) is jealous of being thought an independent and respectable state, of sufficient consequence to be of weight by itself,— besides this secrecy would prevent the intrigues of other Courts, who all, either from good or bad reasons, seem adverse to suffer us ever again to hold to the continent even by the slightest thread.

If in Hatred to this Connection, Prussia becomes an enemy to Denmark, Austria becomes her friend, and vice versâ; and if by forming it we should be fortunate enough to force any one of the great European Powers to declare themselves, we shall then be able to see our road, and a system on which G. Britain must take a leading part will in a manner trace itself out.[1]

---

[1] This appears to refer to a design of Sweden for the conquest of Norway from Denmark, of which no trace is to be found in the ordinary histories.

April 20. 1785.

The strongest Reason to believe the Emperor and France act in concert both with respect to the difference with Holland[1] and the projected Bavarian Exchange.[2]

Q.

How far a direct explanation with the Emperor Himself may be expedient, in order to ascertain what probability there may be of deriving any advantage from a professed acquiescence in any future views of that Prince.

Appearances of a very important change in Holland,[3] Ger. likely to be brought over. Necessary to assure the leading Patriots that England is above harbouring any personal resentment against V. B—l.[4]

The Prussian Plan[5] to endeavour to effect a union between The Stadtholders and the Patriotic Party and to crush the French Interest in the Republic.

Q.

How far the K. of Prussia can be trusted in his opposition to the Views of France?

Supposing the Principles of the Treaty of 1756[6] to remain in full

---

[1] This refers to Joseph's design of opening the Scheldt to commerce and demanding the cession or the ransom of the town of Maestricht from the Dutch.

[2] Joseph proposed to give the Austrian Netherlands in exchange for Bavaria and to make them into a kingdom of Burgundy under the Elector of Bavaria. France opposed this ambitious scheme, whilst she made peace between Austria and Holland.

[3] Sir James Harris was now in England and was having personal communication with members of the Cabinet. *Ger.* is Gyslaer, the pensionary of Dort.

[4] *V. B—l* is Von Berkel, the leader of the Patriotic or French Party. He had conducted the communications of Amsterdam with America during the war, which it was thought might rouse the animosity of England.

[5] Frederick tried to persuade his niece, the Princess of Orange, to make a compromise with the Patriots.

[6] The alliance between Prussia and Russia, as opposed to that between France and Austria.

force, which according to all appearances they do, it should seem the K. of P. may be depended upon. It will however be necessary to receive his Successor,[1] which may I believe be done without much difficulty.

As soon as it appears beyond a doubt that France and Austria are agreed to cooperate in one great system, every method must be tryed to diminish the Emperor's influence at Petersburg; this perhaps may be done by representing to the Empress[2] the essential difference between those plans of the Emperor in which she can be any ways interested and the other views of that monarch which can in no shape interest the Russian Empire, and which from their nature must excite general anxiety and alarm.

Denmark no further connected with Russia than in respect to *Northern* Politics.

Q.

How far a war in Germany, unconnected with the immediate interests of the three Northern Crowns, may commit Denmark in consequence of her *present* engagements?

Endorsed: Memorandum,
April 20, 1785.

To state the situation of Europe as it appears from the Correspondence. It is such as claims equally the attention of England and Prussia.

Austria and France are united for views of mutual aggrandizement. Russia is closely connected with Austria, Spain with France. The Consequences of this formidable League are evident. They would be felt by all Europe in general, but more particularly by England and Prussia. It behoves therefore these two Courts to

[1] Frederick William II., the nephew of Frederick the Great, who was now very old and infirm.
[2] Catherine of Russia.

concert Measures for their reciprocal Safety. To compare their Information. To communicate their respective Ideas; and to examine how far it will be advisable for them to go to prevent the dangerous effects of this Confederacy.

It will be necessary, if England means to obtain a clear and explicit Answer from Prussia, that England should, on her side, be clear and explicit; and if after a fair Discussion of the present State of Affairs it should come out that their Apprehensions are grounded, to say to what extent she is ready to go. Whether she means to confine her cooperations with Prussia merely to Negotiations and a confidential intercourse between their Ministers at the different Courts; whether she will advance a step farther and enter into eventual Engagements; or whether instead of adopting this uncertain and inefficacious Conduct, which appears unequal to the Importance of the Crisis, she will declare herself ready to meet the King of Prussia half way; and to enter immediately into an actual Alliance with Him, to oppose, under any Circumstances, the Effects of this Union between their natural Enemies.

It may be very natural on a retrospect of the King of Prussia's Conduct to question his sincerity; but besides his Interests being so deeply concerned, he is, on this Occasion, so circumstanced that he cannot betray England, unless France betrays Austria; and, in that case, the League is broken up of itself, and England will get, in Austria, as powerful an Ally as she loses in Prussia.

The object of a Prussian connection being to counteract that between the Houses of Bourbon and Austria, we must endeavour to strengthen it as much as possible. To increase and consolidate a confederacy in the Empire. To separate Russia from the Emperor. To preserve Denmark. To neutralize Sweden, either by Fear or Bribery; and what is still more essential to reclaim Holland. These different objects, all very important in themselves, should be fairly and candidly discussed with the King of Prussia, who is better able to give us Advice, Intelligence and Assistance than any Prince in Europe.

It must be understood on both sides that it is not to drive a Bargain that the Negotiation is opened. It is a Union of Defence and Security, not one of Attack and Ambition, that is proposed. All past Transactions must be forgotten. All future Contingencies overlook'd. The Importance of the Moment alone attended to. Each Power must declare what she can do and what she will do. Prussia must say what kind of support she expects from England; whether subsidiary or otherwise; and, if subsidiary, how much. This support, of whatever kind it is, must be so directed as to operate against the Common Enemy; and any increase of the Power of France as much attended to, in the Application of it, as an Increase of the Power of Austria. France must on no account have the Low Countries. If Prussia will bonâ fide exert itself to prevent that, England will use similar exertions to prevent Austria obtaining Bavaria. On these Grounds the Alliance is to be formed. Anything short of this would defeat the great end of the Connection.

Endorsed: May 9, 1785.
   Memorandums for Cabinet.[1]
   Sr James Harris.

May 26, 1785.

M. de Kazeneck[2] by order of his Court assured me for His Majesty's information that the reports industriously circulated not only throughout the Empire but in every Court of Europe, of the Emperor's ambitious projects, of forcible exchanges[3] of Territory, Secularizations of Bishoprics, &c. &c., were totally destitute of

[1] This memorandum is dated May 9, 1785. The Cabinet met on the morning of May 10 (*Malmesbury's Diaries*, ii. 125). At this time the English Government were particularly anxious to obtain the co-operation of Prussia in their efforts to detach Holland from France. The King (*loc. cit.*) was in favour of sending Sir James Harris to Potsdam. The paper was written by Sir James Harris for the information of the Cabinet.

[2] Count Kazeneck was Minister of the Emperor at the Court of London.

[3] This is a reference to the proposed Bavarian exchange, as *the league* below refers to the league of princes, or Fürstenbund.

foundation, and that he had the Emperor's commands to disavow any intention of such a nature, that the liberties of every individual as well as the general interest of the Empire were too much the object of H. I. M." constant attention to permit his ever harboring an idea of making use of *Force* in order to the carrying any exchange or other views of arrangement into execution; that on the contrary the E. was willing himself to come into any league which might be thought necessary to protect the rights of individuals as well as the general interests of the Germanic Body against any encroachments.

I of course received this communication with respect, and a compliment to the declaration of the Emperor, but added that if so many Powers had taken the alarm at the idea of the exchange I conceived its being effected tho' with the consent of the Elector and even of his heir, however free from the least idea of *force* or constraint, would still leave the same impressions on those who had manifested so great a degree of apprehension on the subject that it appeared to me the thing itself occasioned the alarm and not the particular mode either of *force* or free consent by which it was to be carried into execution; upon this he said he had no instructions.

He added the Courier du bas Rhin (under the influence he was sure of M. Hertzberg) had dared to insert the K.'s name [1] as being (in his electoral capacity) one of the chief promoters of the German League. To this I answered I was not much influenced by newspaper information. That I made no doubt H. M. in his electoral capacity would ever prove himself a zealous asserter of the liberties and rights of the Empire, and that if there was no design of infringing them I thought no measures of a defensive nature in favour of them could give offence anywhere.

He said he thought an equitable exchange agreed to by both parties could not create alarm any more than if he and I were to exchange our watches. I said I thought the value of both watches

---

[1] The King of England, Elector of Hanover.

should be ascertained, in short that what was to be given in exchange should be well known. He answered the House of Austria acquired too much from the possession of the Low Countries to think of bartering them against Bavaria; my only answer was the alienating the Low Countries would be a very serious object indeed.

He then talked upon other subjects. He appeared perfectly good humoured throughout our whole conversation, and withdrew.

Endorsed: Gros^r Square, May 26, 1785.

Minute of a conversation with Count Kazeneck.

June 14, 1785.

After some few remarks upon the reciprocal advantages which must ever ensue from the most close and friendly connection between Russia and England, the Count entered upon the subject of the Emperor's situation in respect to France; he said he was convinced the two Courts of Versailles and Vienna, however friendly to outward appearance, entertained the strongest jealousy of each other. That the Emperor flatterd himself with ultimately overreaching France, in which he (the Count) lamented the certainty of his being mistaken, and ultimately proving the Dupe of that opinion. That France was making every preparation for a Land War, and according to his sincere and firm persuasion would infallibly in the course of another twelvemonth throw off the masque and fall upon the Emperor. He then showed me a letter from Count Romanzov, containing a piece of intelligence which he said gave him the utmost concern, viz., a Report of the Court of Hanover having entered into a Treaty with Prussia to oppose the Emperor's views upon Bavaria, and that the Hanoverian Troops were actually in march. A step of this nature he observed would unavoidably throw the Emperor into the arms of France, and would be directly accomplishing the joint views of France and Prussia, in effectually preventing any probability of a friendly understanding between Austria and England. This he repeated several times during our conversation, adding the Inveteracy of the King of Prussia towards this country ever since the Peace of 1763, and his constant connection with France, mentioning at the same time that the French and Prussian Ministers were holding precisely the same language in regard to the Emperor in almost every Court in Germany.

Considering England as inseparable from Hanover, he thought this a most fatal circumstance, and lamented our not having remained quiet some time longer, instead of coming to so hasty and (as he feared) so unfortunate a decision.

I stated to him the perpetual silence of the Court of Vienna towards England, the coldness with which every opening towards anything like a Friendly intercourse had been received, and how much the system of the Austrian Cabinet seemed to be adverse to what I owned to be my favourite Plan — an alliance between England and the two Imperial Courts; that on the contrary the uniform conduct of the Court of Vienna seemed to imply a desire of either seeing England totally unconnected with the Continent (which was likewise the object of France), or else obliging her to connect herself with Prussia, a connection which I at least would never recommend unless *forced* to it by the conduct of the Emperor. That as to Hanover I could easily conceive the Bavarian Exchange to have occasioned a considerable degree of jealousy in the Empire, but that as an English Minister my only concern in the business was the eventual alienation of the Low Countrys, either directly or indirectly to France, which would indeed be a very serious event for this country. That I knew nothing but from public rumour of the Hanoverian Councils, but flattered myself they would not justify his apprehensions.

Endorsed: June 14, 1785.
  Minutes of a Conversation with
    Count Woronzow.[1]

[1] Count Woronzow was Russian Ambassador at the Court of St. James. George III. joined the Fürstenbund as Elector of Hanover. The Empress of Russia was opposed to it as the close ally of Austria.

Jan. 1787

Lord Carmarthen begs leave with all humility to submit to your Majesty, whether it might not be proper (in consequence of the very material information received from Holland) to express to the Prince and Princess of Orange the sense your Majesty entertains of the very dignifyed and becoming conduct their Royal and Serene Highnesses have manifested upon the subject of the terms of accommodation proposed to them as worthy their acceptance, not only by the Court of Versailles but even by that of Berlin. The King of Prussia appears to be as little disposed to support, as in truth able to advise, any future measures which the Princess his sister might find it advantageous to pursue in conformity with Her Royal Highness' noble and truly becoming sentiments, on indeed consistently present critical situation not only of Her own Family but of the Republic itself, and eventually (as far as appearances may justify the opinion) of every part of Europe.

Lord Carmarthen thinks it his indispensible Duty to submit to your Majesty his most serious and confirmed opinion that your Majesty's service necessarily calls for some decisive measure with respect to Holland with the smallest delay circumstances may admit of, for the determining of which, however, it may be expedient to wait for the Dispatches which Sir James Harris proposes sending to your Majesty by Mr. Bouverie. The present situation of France, which implies an extraordinary *Convocation des Notables* as necessary to be convened in the course of the present month at Versailles, renders a proper degree of exertion on the part of England in respect to the affairs of Holland less liable to any objection than at another period a prudent and apprehensive degree of caution might have thought it liable to.

Lord Carmarthen wishes by no means to hazard in the smallest degree the continuance of the public tranquillity, but cannot help thinking that the surest method of contributing to the continuance of so invaluable a Blessing is by preventing France (whatever her inclinations may be) fin ling herself in such a situation as to make it her interest to disturb it.[1]

Endorsed: Hendon, Jany 9, 1787.
To the King.

Whitehall, Sepr 19th, 1787.
Present:

The Lord President. | Duke of Richmond.
Lord Visc^t Howe. | Lord Sydney.
R^t Ho^{ble} Wm Pitt. | Marquis of Carmarthen.

It appearing by Mr. Eden's Dispatch of the 11th Inst. and by the communication made by Monsr Barthelemy, that the French Court have determined to assist in opposing the command of the Duke of Brunswick, And there being every Reason to suppose that measures will be taken for that Purpose immediately on receiving the accounts of the Prussian Troops advancing towards the Province of Holland,

It is humbly recommended to your Majesty that immediate orders should be given for arming your Majesty's Fleet with the utmost expedition, and for augmenting the army.

[1] A letter from Lord Carmarthen to the King, the proper date of which is evidently January 7, 1787, as appears from a letter of Lord Carmarthen in the *Malmesbury Correspondence* (vol. ii. p. 267), dated January 8, 1787. He says: "The person whom you do not venture to answer for is *not* of the Cabinet. We are at present *sine pulvere*, and, from what I can judge from a letter I received to-day from *Windsor*, are likely to remain equally *sine palmâ*. I own I am equally hurt and (if I might say it) angry at the answer I received from thence to my letter of yesterday." The disgraceful conduct of this country with regard to America is quoted, the *supposed* idea of being the Drawcansir of Europe *properly* reprobated; a future hope by means of some years peace, held out as likely to restore the country to its former situation, suggested; and the event (not barely the attempt) of acting and indeed realising that part regarded as *destructive* at present. So much for the sublime! It is interesting to see that up to this time the King was with Pitt in favour of peace.

POLITICAL MEMORANDUMS.   119

And that Mr. Eden should be directed to give immediate notice to the French Government that your Majesty cannot remain an indifferent spectator of the armed interference of France. That consequently your Majesty can no longer consent to a suspension of naval preparations. But that at the same time your Majesty is still willing to carry on the Negociation and to concur in every proper measure for bringing the Disputes in the United Provinces to an amicable settlement on the Principles already stated to the Court of France.[1]

R^d H. Nov. 26, 1788.

The great object appeared to be the Establishment being only Temporary and of course determinable whenever the K^g was in a state capable of resuming the Gov^t.

The Ch. beggd all private or partie animosity^s to be suspended as it might happen that to give the intermediate Gov^t effect arrangements might be prepared which, if consonant to the above Principle, might be admissible. Mr. P. thought that any alteration which might make it impossible for the K. to resume the Gov^t in such a state as he had left it would be an insuperable objection to any alteration of that nature. This was observed as far as the executive

[1] This paper relates to a time when we were within an ace of going to war with France. The Princess of Orange, the sister of the new King of Prussia, had been arrested on her journey from Nymwegen to the Hague; and when the States General refused the satisfaction demanded, the Duke of Brunswick marched into Holland at the head of the Prussian troops. Mr. Eden's despatch of the 11th is not published, but there is in the *Auckland Correspondence* (vol. i. p. 193) a letter of September 13, which contains the following words: "M. de Montmorris informed me that in the opinion of His Most Christian Majesty's Ministers it would be deemed necessary to offer to Holland support in whatever manner might be most efficacious if His Prussian Majesty should advance his army into the Provinces." Mr. Pitt, writing to Mr. Eden on September 14, says of the French: "They must, as things stand, give up in effect their predominant influence in the Republic, or they must be determined *to fight for it.*"

power was concerned might be pleaded in defence of such arrangement, as the P. might say the same motives might induce him to name particular persons in whom he had confidence to places in Gov^t during his Regency, as the K. might have in continuing the servants of his nomination in power.

The Ch. is to go to Windsor to-morrow. The Que^n is to see him, and he thinks he shall see the K. on Fryday. H. M. is to be removed to Kew, probably either Fryday or Saturday.[1]

---

[1] This is probably an account of a Cabinet Council held at Richmond House to decide the question of the regency arising from the King's illness. It was important to know how long the King was likely to remain ill, and on that subject doctors were uncertain. Mr. W. Grenville, writing on the same day to the Marquis of Buckingham, says: "Warren told Pitt yesterday that the physicians could now have no hesitation in pronouncing that the actual disorder was that of lunacy; that no man could pretend to say that this was or was not incurable; that he saw no immediate symptoms of recovery; that the King might never recover, or, on the other hand, that he might recover at any one moment."

1788-9.

On Thursday, Nov. 27th, I received a letter from Mr. Pitt, dated the preceding day, to Lord Sydney,[1] sent me by the latter agreeable to Mr. P.'s desire, stating that a message had been received late the night before from the Prince of Wales desiring the attendance of the King's confidential servants the next day at two o'clock at Windsor Castle.

I arrived at Windsor a few minutes before two, and walked up from the Inn to the Castle, where I met Lord Sydney,[2] and we went together to the Prince of Wales' apartment; there we found the Duke of York and the Lord Chancellor. The Duke of Richmond, Lord Stafford, Lord Chatham, and Mr. Pitt, arrived soon afterwards. The Duke of York left us, and a few minutes afterwards Col. Gwyn (Equerry to the King) came and said he would show us to the Council Chamber. He conducted us from the Prince's to the Duke of York's apartment. The Duke came to us with a paper in his hand which he said the P. of Wales had desired

[1] W. Grenville writes to the Marquis of Buckingham (*Courts and Cabinets*, ii. 20): "The Prince of Wales has sent a letter to the Chancellor, desiring that all the members of the Cabinet may attend at Windsor to-day:' but this I imagine (and indeed his letter conveys it) has no relation to any other subject but to an idea of moving the King to Kew, where he can take the air without being overlooked, as is the case at Windsor."

[2] Lord Sydney was Secretary of State with Lord Carmarthen.

him to deliver to us, that he would leave it with us for our consideration, and should remain in the Castle in order to receive the result of our deliberations upon the subject contained in it.

The Paper was written in the P.'s own hand, and signed by H. R. H., and stated that not chusing to act from his own *authority* he had thought it necessary to convene the K.'s confidential servants that they might inform themselves from the Physicians respecting the melancholy situation of the King, and how far it might be proper to remove H. M. to Kew, agreeable to a proposal laid before the Prince by H. M.'s Physicians for that purpose.

The manner in which we were convened and the style of the Paper referr'd to us rendered it necessary for us to proceed with caution in framing our answer to it. The object of it was to avoid taking notice of the word *authority*, made use of by the Prince, and at the same time not to express that we could go any further than merely stating our opinion in regard to the propriety of removing H. M. to Kew, and to this particular point only we look'd upon ourselves as called upon to reply.

We examin'd the K.'s Physicians, viz., Dr. Warren, Sir George Baker, Sr Lucas Pepys, Dr. Addington, and Dr. Reynolds. They were unanimous in thinking His M.'s recovery a probable event, although by no means certain, the length of time necessary they could by no means even guess at, tho' Dr. Addington thought it not impossible but that so desirable an event might take place in a much shorter time than H. M.'s most sanguine Friends at present hop'd for. Dr. W. and Sr G. B. did not seem to entertain so much favourable expectation on this part of Dr A.'s reasoning as both Sr Lucas Pepys and Dr Reynolds appear'd to do. They all thought the King's removal to Kew highly desirable, and on the D. of Richmond and Mr. Pitt expressing the concurrence as conditionally depending on H. M.'s consent, they said he certainly had expressed a wish for such removal himself, but that their principal difficulty was how to act in case the K. should object to it when the time of removal came, and when they might think it absolutely necessary to be effected. On the D. of Richmond, Ld Chatham, and Mr. Pitt's deprecating the idea of anything like compulsion being used, the Physicians declared they did not mean force to be employed however necessary they thought the removal to be. They all concurred in Restraint being necessary, and that the degree in which they thought it expedient could be much better observed at Kew than at Windsor, in addition to the other material advantages of air and gentle exercise which the K. might profit of at the former of those places. Having examined the Physicians for a considerable time we desired them to withdraw and prepare a paper to be signed by them, and delivered to us respecting their opinion of the expediency or necessity of H. M.^s removal to Kew. Some time afterwards Dr Warren returned with a paper signed by himself and the four other Physicians stating shortly their opinion that the removal to Kew was desirable as change of air and objects was likely to prove beneficial towards the King's recovery.

Dr. Warren being withdrawn, the D. of R^d, Lord Chatham, and Mr. Pitt seemed to object to the manner in which the paper was drawn, as there was nothing in it which seemd to imply the K.^s own consent as necessary, and that were we to give a sanction to that paper we might be instrumental in any act of violence or force which might be employed upon the person of the King. The Chancellor, Lord Stafford, and myself thought it highly necessary to leave that degree of discretion to the Physicians which could alone render their attendance in any degree beneficial. That with regard to actual force if unfortunately necessary from the nature of the Disorder could we take upon ourselves to forbid it. That to the point at present under discussion the Physicians had declared they should not think of what could be looked upon in any degree as force or violence. This occasioned a conversation of some length between us, as it was proposed that in our answer to the P. we should object to any force being used or even the removal attempted without the K.^s consent previously obtained. At last, however, we agreed to an answer founded upon the paper delivered by the

Physicians, which we annexed to it, as well as upon the conversation we had with them in consequence of the P.'s message delivered to us by the Duke of York on our arrival at Windsor, where we had come in consequence of the intimation made to us thro' the Lord Chancellor that it was the pleasure of the Prince of Wales and the *Royal Family* that we should repair to Windsor the next day.

The Duke of York being informed that our answer was prepared (it having been shown to the Physicians and approved of by them), returnd, and we deliverd it to him to be communicated to the Prince of Wales. The Prince did not honour us with his presence either at his own or at the Duke of York's apartments.

The Chancellor saw him in the morning, and again in the evening after we had separated.

We did not leave the Duke of York's apartments till past six. I went with Lord Sydney to Salt Hill,[1] where we dined and passed the evening with the D. of Richmond, Lord Stafford, Lord Chatham, and Mr. Pitt. The next morning, in conversing with Mr. Pitt about the Chancellor, he told me that he understood Mr. Fox had been with the Chancellor the evening after we had dined at Richmond House.[2] I returned by Windsor (in order to enquire of the Groom of the Bedchamber in waiting after the K.'s health) to town, and after dining with the Master of the Rolls[3] attended the Cabinet at my office, the Lord President[4] the only Minister absent. We all seemed perfectly agreed as to the Prince being sole regent; certain points of limitation would deserve much consideration, such as the creating Peers, issuing Grants, Dissolution of Parliaments, &c. The D. of Richmond thought it not unlikely but some proposal might be made for a coalition, which he thought would be a

---

[1] Probably Botham's famous hotel. W. Grenville writes to the Duke of Buckingham on Nov. 28: "The Ministers were all sent for to Windsor yesterday by the Prince, in order to give advice with respect to moving the King. They were detained so late that Pitt went to Salt Hill to sleep there."

[2] See Mem. p. 118, which evidently refers to this dinner.

[3] Pepper Arden had been appointed to the office in June 1788

[4] Lord Camden.

fortunate circumstance, as by rejecting any junction with men who were personally obnoxious to the King we should do ourselves honour, as H. M. servants, as well as to our own characters, by not sharing the Gov' with those whose former conduct and principles we had so much reprobated. Lord Stafford observed that he should certainly be no object of difficulty, as, independently of other considerations, he was too old a man[1] as well as a Politician to think of embarking in any *new* system. The next day, Sat. Nov. 29, I dined at Mr. Pitt's. The company consisted of Lord Chatham, the Chancellor, Lord Stafford, the Duke of Richmond, Lord Weymouth, Lord Sydney, Lord Hawkesbury, Lord Kenyon, and myself. Mr. Pitt came to us after we had dined, having been at Windsor, seen the King, and seen His Majesty set off for Kew (where he arrived at half-past five), and been there to enquire after him.

It seemed to be the general wish of the company to avoid if possible the coming to business on Thursday next,[2] at the same time the difficulty of remaining totally inactive without we were able to hold out a probability of a speedy amendment of the King's health seem'd evident. I could not help stating the propriety of summoning the Privy Council before we met in Parliament. This seem'd to meet the sense of the other Lords, but under the uncertainty whether we might not adjourn again on Thursday they thought it not pressing. The Ch. said he believed that in case the Prince of Wales declined the Regency on account of any limitations, the Duke of York and the other Princes would follow his example. The Duke of Richmond thought that such refusal would rather prejudice their R. H.[s] in the public opinion than be at all hurtful to those who might either propose or enact such limitations.

The next day, Sunday, 30th, I went to Kew to enquire after the K. I met the Lord Chancellor on the road returning from thence.

[1] The Marquis of Stafford, born in 1721, was now sixty-seven years old.

[2] December 4, the day to which both Houses of Parliament had been adjourned from the time of their meeting on November 20.

I found he had seen H. M. and Dr. Warren said the Chancellor had been extremely affected by the interview. The King had borne his journey tolerably well, but was very violent after his arrival and during a great part of the night, particularly at not being suffered to see the Queen, having expected before he left Windsor to have that satisfaction when he came to Kew, and being in some measure reconciled to his removal by the expectation of seeing Her Maj. When he arrived there he was very angry with his Physicians for coming to him at Kew, saying he expected they would have been discharged on his leaving Windsor.

Dec. 1st.—The whole Cabinet, with Lords Weymouth, Hawkesbury, and Kenyon, dined at Ld Staffords.* Soon after we had entered on the subject of the K.^{s} Health and the mode of Treatment Ld Sydney, with the utmost emotion, enter'd upon that subject : he asserted the K. had actually been struck by one of his Pages, and with great agitation said it was impossible such treatment could be suffered, as the King had not only been shamefully treated but actually betrayed. The Ch. observed that if anything of the nature mentioned had occurred, the person ought not to be suffered about the King's person ; that in a paroxysm he knew the King had hurt one of the Pages *extremely*. Ld S. replied that was not the Page alluded to. We all were sensibly affected by these circumstances, though fully persuaded H. M. in his present unhappy condition ought to be effectually restrained.

We were all of opinion that some person should be thought of as proper to inspect the arrangements of the King's attendance,

---

* The Chancellor, who had met me yesterday on the road, asked me privately if I had seen the Prince at Kew. I told him I had not. He said he wished I had. I told him I had just received a letter from Mr. Payne written by the Prince's commands, but it was only desiring a messenger might be sent to the South of France with letters to Prince Augustus from H. R. H. I shewed Mr. Payne's letter to the L^d Ch.

and after much conversation whether the Privy Council was necessary to give the first idea on the subject, unanimously agreed to sign a paper recommending it as our individual opinions that the Queen should superintend H. M.'s attendance, &c. I stated the propriety of the Privy Council being convened on the General State of the K.'s situation, more especially as the Parliament was to meet on next Thursday. I thought it might better have been consulted earlier, that a Prayer for the K.'s recovery had been ordered by their authority many days back, and that we the K.'s confidential Serv^{ts} could not be supposed to be in ignorance of H. M.'s unfortunate present situation after the Note communicated to us by way of message from the P. of Wales, and the proceedings held in consequence of that note. The Ch. stated that all which had hitherto passed could only be regarded as the arrangements adopted in a domestic light. I said that however serviceable domestic care might be I thought the case of the King must be considered as a public concern, and again recurred to the necessity, if not in substance at least in appearance, of assembling the Privy Council. Ld Chatham recommended the whole being conducted as privately as possible. The Duke of Richmond expressed himself as strongly of my opinion, and we afterwards agreed that the Privy Council *Generally*[1] should be summoned on Wednesday, and the K.'s Physicians orderd to attend.

Tuesday, Dec. 2. I was invited to dinner at Ld Sydney's, but, being engaged to the Archbishop of York,[2] did not go there till the evening, about eight o'clock. I found with Lord Sydny the Chancellor, Lord Stafford, Lord Chatham, Lord Hawkesbury and Lord Kenyon. The Ch. told me he had been at Kew in the morning, and had seen the Queen. That Her Majesty had accepted our proposal of taking care of the K.'s person, tho' with evident

---

[1] W. Grenville to Lord Buckingham, December 2, 1788: "A Privy Council is summoned for to-morrow, to which *all* the Privy Councillors are summoned, those of the royal family by letters from the Lord President."

[2] William Markham, since 1776.

marks of diffidence and apprehension respecting so important a charge, that he had not thought it necessary or even expedient to deliver H. M. the paper signed by us yesterday, but had thought it more adviseable to recommend it to Her by argument in conversation. She appeared much afflicted, but seemd strongly and agreeably affected by his observing to Her M. that the whole nation wished to see the care of the K.ˢ Person, under the present circumstances, entrusted to her management; he added suspicions of many people about her being likely to shake her determination, and even to represent him as too likely to be influenced by the P. of Wales, and that under such probable impressions he thought it necessary for him to see the Queen again tomorrow as soon as the Privy Council would be over. Ld Camden and Mr. Pitt came to us soon after. Mr. P. mentioned that in consequence of the wishes expressed to him to day by several good Friends in the House of Commons, he thought it might be highly expedient to have a meeting tomorrow evening at the Cockpit, just to state the general subject of the K.ˢ indisposition, and the steps likely to be proposed in Parliament the next day; on his explanation of the circumstance it was agreed to, and a similar communication to the Friends of Gov^t in the House of Lords likewise agreed to, to be made at Ld Sydnys tomorrow evening at nine; we likewise thought it right to have a meeting at my office tomorrow morning previous to that of the Privy Council, in order to settle the questions proper to be put to the Physicians, and which we desired the Lord President might arrange, in order to our taking them into consideration previous to the Council. We were unanimously of opinion that the first step to propose to Parl^t upon the Indisposition of the K. being laid before them would be for each House to appoint a Committee to examine and report Precedents of such Proceedings as may have been had in cases where the personal exercise of the Royal Authority has been prevented or interrupted by Infancy, Sickness, Infirmity or otherwise.

Previous to our breaking up the Chancellor received a note from the Queen expressing her wish that the *Privy Council* (meaning the Ministers) might approve of Dr. Willis being sent for.

Wednesday, Dec. 3ᵈ. We had a meeting at my office. The Lord President had prepard some general questions to be put to the K.ˢ Physicians by the Privy Council, where went as soon as the Chancellor came to us; there was a numerous meeting. The Principal Members of Opposition, except Mr. Fox, who was confind by illness, were there. The Questions proposed by the Lᵈ President were agreed to be put, and the Five Physicians were separately examin'd upon Oath. Dr. Warren appeared under much confusion, and his answers both in respect to matter and language were very unlike what one naturally expected from him. The others were clear and distinct in their answers, all five agreeing That the King was at present totally incapable of attending to business; that there certainly from their experience in similar cases appeared a probability of his recovery, but the time which would be necessary to effect his cure was not possibly to be ascertained.

Having heard the Physicians deliver their opinions (which they did upon oath), the Council orderd the examination to be communicated by the Lord Presᵗ to the House of Lords, and by the Chancellor of The Exchequer to the House of Commons. The business being over, Mr. Pitt, by way of conversation, wished to know the wishes of the members present respecting the mode of proceeding, and after a short time it was understood to be agreed on by all parties that after the examination was communicated to Parliament, both Houses should appoint it to be taken into consideration on Monday next and adjourn to that day. The meeting then broke up. Before we left the Room Lᵈ Camden said he had a word for my private ear, and then whisper'd me *Dr. Warren is a damn'd scoundrel, tho' I believe him to be a very able Physician, and I dare say you will agree with me in both.* I said the latter I was persuaded of, and hop'd *he* was not so of the other.

The Ministers after the Council returned to my office. We agreed on the propriety of the Lord President communicating by letter to the Prince of Wales what had pass'd at the Council. The Lord Chancellor went to Kew, and, the other Ministers being gone, Mr. Pitt, the Duke of Richmond, and myself remained together. The Duke observed we *must* have an explanation from the Chancellor of what he meant to do. Mr. P. said such an explanation was absolutely necessary, as the Chancellor's conduct seemed very extraordinary indeed. The last night at Lord Sydny's he had again reverted to the idea of a Council of Regency, altho' it had apparently been for a considerable time agreed by us all that a sole Regent should be appointed under certain, and those only absolutely necessary, restrictions in the Person of the Prince of Wales. They both seemed to think that the Chancellor was acting a double part, and that provided he was sufferd to keep his place he could easily be prevailed upon to accede to such mode of Gov^t as the strongest interest might chuse to establish. I said I wished him to be more explicit than he appeard to be, and mentioned the circumstance of his having stated at L^d S^ys last night before Mr. Pitt came (the Duke was not there) his own suspicions of being misrepresented to the Queen, and among other false surmises as not deserving Her M^s confidence from his *partiality* to the Prince.

We afterwards talkd upon several subjects respecting the present crisis, and the D. of Richmond, observing the apparent disposition of Opposition to remain quiet for a few days, ad-led, smiling, he fancied Lord Loughborough had no intention of bringing forward his doctrine concerning *Devolution*.[1] To-morrow, Mr. Pitt answered in the same manner, if he does the natural mode of proceeding will be to have his words taken down by the Clerk, and if they are not satisfactorily explained by His Lp., to send him to the Tower. He then said that tho seriously speaking it might not be necessary to proceed to so violent a measure, yet should he advance the Doctrine

---

[1] Lord Loughborough held the opinion that the regency passed of right to the Prince of Wales, in opposition to those who held that a regent must be appointed by the Legislature. Lord Loughborough reasserted these principles in the debate of December 11. Fox expressed the same opinion.

imputed to him it must be directly met by a resolution declaring it totally repugnant to every principle of the constitution, the assertion of the Executive power devolving to any one person (during a casual incapacity in the Person of the Sovereign) without the consent and authority of Parliament.

Many members of the House of Commons attach'd to Gov^t having wish^d Mr. Pitt to have a meeting at the Cockpit this evening in order to know the Plan of Gov^t in their House for to-morrow on the meeting, with which he complyed. There was a similar meeting for the Lords at Ld Sydney's, where the whole business consisted in stating the examination taken this day before the Privy Council, being to be communicated to Parliament to-morrow, and to be taken into consideration on Monday. Nothing material occurred to me at this meeting, tho it appeared somewhat singular that Lord Denbigh should privately express to me his satisfaction at seeing *two Lords there in particular*, which, when I asked him to name (by no means guessing who he alluded to), he immediately answered, *The Ld Chancellor and The Lord Privy Seal.*[1]

Thursday, Dec. 4. Both Houses of Parliament met. The Examination of the Physicians taken by the Privy Council was laid before them, and ordered to be taken into consideration on the Monday following. Ld Winchilsea carried me from the House to Lord Sydny's, where we dined; he conversed with me on the subject of the present situation with great good sense and judgment; thought many restrictions necessary, and much care to be taken respecting the improper use that might be made of the sort of double influence the Prince might possess if both the King's Household and his own were equally in his power, as well as the general powers of the Executive Government.

Fryday, 5. Nothing material occurred.

Sat. 6. There was a Cabinet at my office in the forenoon, where the several general topics were discuss'd, and we agreed to meet the next evening.

[1] The Marquis of Stafford.

Sunday, 7. I put down some memorandums founded upon my own ideas of the necessary restrictions to be put upon the temporary exercise of the Regent' delegated authority. Mr. Pitt, to whom I shewed them in the evening at the Cabinet, thought them perfectly right. The L.ᵈ President was prevented attending by a violent cold. The Chancellor in his conversation appeared perfectly fair, and seem'd to think the Prince of Wales did not wish to have anything like confidential communication with any of the King' servants; that in the several conversations H.R.H. had had with him there never had been anything of a political or ministerial nature introduced.

Monday, 8 There was a Cabinet at my office, finally to settle the mode of proceeding that day in the two Houses. The Lord President being still indisposed, it was agreed that the Lord Privy Seal should open the business and make the necessary motions. The Chancellor stayed a short time after the others were gone, and I had some conversation with him. I told him I wished much to see the paper the D. of Richmond had drawn, with a view to communicate to the P. of Wales the sentiments of the King' Servants respecting the necessity of substituting a Temporary Gov' to be constructed by H.R.H., and which paper His Lp. had the preceding evening described as a manifesto. He said the paper would not do either for our own sakes or other peoples. He then mentioned the difficulty of imposing restrictions, and that foolish one respecting the Peerage, adding, *I should not call it a foolish one, as you have argued in favour of it in the paper you showed me just now.* He said the *Solicitor Gen*^{l1} thought it could not be adopted. I said I should not then upon the merits of this or that particular resolution, but thought some must be necessary. He said they might, but he did not suppose they were thought necessary with a view to weaken the Gov', so that we might pelt it with more advantage. I answered not. The Chancellor agreed with me in thinking there was no

---

¹ Since June, 1788, Sir John Scott, afterwards Lord Eldon. For his conduct in this crisis see his life by Twiss, i. 189 foll.

probability of the K.'s recovery, and that for the quiet of the country the melancholy circumstance of his Death might not be a very unfortunate event.

The House met, and we agreed to have a select Committee to examine the Physicians: we settled a List consisting of several of the Opposition Lords as well as friends of Gov^t at the Cab., and after the House agreed with the Duke of Portland, L^{ds} Carlisle, Stormont, Loughborough, &c., about the List, and put an end to the individual Lords of both sides preparing theirs without consultation. I brought the Duke of Richmond home from the House, who had before told me Mr. Fox was with the Chancellor in his room. In the carriage His Grace remarked he thought the Ch. had appeared pleased with his conference, and then said he thought it shameful for the Ch. to be making his terms with Opposition at the same time that he was present at all our Cabinet meetings ; that he ought to communicate to us what passed, or tell us at once that he had separated from us. The Duke of Richmond gave me his paper above-mentioned to read, which on perusal after I got home, I thought had great merit, and I own I think might be laid before the Prince without any impropriety.

Tuesday, the 9. The Committee for examining the Physicians was appointed and orderd to meet the next day for that purpose.

Wednesday, the 10. The Committee, which was of 21 Lords, sat, only three were absent, viz. Lord Bathurst, Ld Weymouth, and Lord Kenyon. On the same day in the H. of Commons Mr. Fox thought proper to state the P. of Wales having a right to execute the Regal Power immediately H. M. being incapable of attending to public business. This assertion was directly contradicted by Mr. Pitt, and a very spirited conversation took place between them upon the subject. After dining at Ld Sydney's I went with his Lp. to Lord Stafford's, where we found the Chancellor and Att.-Genl. Mr. Pitt came soon after for a short time. He gave us an account of what had passed in the H. of Comm^s, and seem'd to think it expedient that such a doctrine having been advised there an early opportunity should be taken of noticing it in the House of Lords, for fear our silence might be misconstrued into acquiescence.

Thursday, the 11. Lord Camden laid the report of our committee before the House, which being read, H. Lp. moved for a committee to search precedents of cases where the personal exercise of the Royal Authority had been prevented or interrupted. In introducing this motion H. Lp. took care to mention the strange position which it was reported had been laid down elsewhere respecting the P. of Wales' *right* to assume the exercise of the royal authority. This brought on a warm discussion, in which Lord Loughborough and Lord Stormont took leading part, but without making any apparent impression on the House, and these arguments were completely defeated by the Chancellor.

Fryday, 12. Mr. Fox endeavoured to explain away in some measure the bold assertion he had made in the House of Co⁵ on Wednesday. Mr. Pitt however insisted on having the subject brought to an issue, and for that reason moved for a committee of the whole House for Tuesday next on the state of Parties with a view to coming to some resolution upon the subject then at issue between them.

S. 13. Our Committee for searching Precedents met. None of the opposition Lords, except Lord Dartmouth, were present.

M. 15. While we were at the Committee we received notice that business of consequence was expected to come on that day in the House, and that the Chancellor had been *desired* not to adjourn directly. The House being met and very numerous, Ld Fitzwilliam rose and stated that he had no motion to propose, but that his object in addressing their Lordships was solely for the purpose of deprecating the agitation of any question respecting the right of the P. of Wales to the Regency, which he understood was to be discussed the next day in another place; and the principal reason for wishing to avoid the subject was the difference of opinion which might arise and produce consequences of a disagreeable if not dangerous nature. In answer to this the Lord President observed that although in form the present conversation was irregular, yet he should, from respect to the noble Lord, give his reasons for thinking it impossible to comply with his request of dropping a subject of so much importance, which had been introduced and absolutely required to be determined one way or another. The Chancellor was of the same opinion, at the same time agreeing with Lord Fitzwilliam in his general wish to avoid all *unnecessary* points of an abstract nature, or even such as were purely theoretic, neither of which descriptions, however, he thought, were applicable to the present subject. The Dukes of York and Gloucester both supported Ld Fitzwilliam, the former assuring us that the P. of Wales was too sensible of as well as too much attached to the principles on which the House of Brunswick was called to the throne ever to take an important step without the advice and consent of Parliament, and adding the Princes not having made any claim on the subject. The Duke of Gloucester appeared apprehensive of mischievous consequences arising from the discussion, but declared himself as a single person totally unconnected with any party. No question but for adjournment being proposed, the House rose.

T. 16. In the Committee in the H. of Commons on the state of the nation Mr. Pitt proposed three resolutions, the first declaratory of the King's situation, the second of the right and duty of Parliament to provide for the exigency, and the third particularly recommending the giving a power to some one to pronounce the Royal Assent to such an Act as the Parl^t might agree to for that purpose; a long debate took place and much altercation both personal and political arose between Mr. Pitt and Mr. Fox. At three the next morning the Committee divided on Ld North's motion for the Chairman to leave the Chair, Ayes 204, Noes 268, M. 22. The report was brought up from the Committee, and after a long debate the House divided: for the Resolution 251, against 178. The next day, 23^d, The Commons at a conference, manag'd by the Marquis of Worcester and others, communicated to us their resolutions, which we afterwards referred to the Committee of the whole House appointed to sit on the Fryday following.

Fr. 26. In the Committee, Lord Rawdon moved an amendment, by way of addition to the First resolution (which declared the state of the K.'s Health rendering him incapable of business), viz. to address the Prince of Wales to take upon himself the executive Gov' during the K.'s illness. After a long debate, in which all the resolutions were argued at large, the Committee divided on L.ᵈ R.'s amendment, Contents 66, Not Contents 99. The Duke of Queensbury, Lord Lothian and Lord Malmesbury ! ! !¹ voted in the minority. On the Monday following the Question being put in the House to agree to the Resolution there was a short debate but no Division. A Protest was however enterd sign'd by 47 Lords with the Dukes of York and Cumberland at their head, and L.ᵈ Malmesbury also thought proper to sign the Protest.

T. 30. Mr. Pitt wrote a Letter² to the Prince of Wales laying before H.R.H. the outline of the Plan to be laid before Parliament respecting the P.'s appointment to be sole Regent during the K.'s illness, the restrictions to be proposed, &c. &c. The Speaker being too ill to attend, no business was done in the House of Commons.

1789.

Th. Jan. 1ˢᵗ. Lord Grantley³ dyed.

Fr. 2ᵈ. The Speaker dyed. We had a Cabinet at noon in consequence of this event, where it was agreed that Mr. Wᵐ Grenville

---

[1] Lord Malmesbury had always been a supporter of the Opposition. When he accepted the embassy to the Hague it was understood that he was not expected to change his party. There is a letter from Fox to him (*Diaries*, ii. 434), dated November 27, 1788, asking him to return from Switzerland to support the Opposition. Lord Carmarthen was so extremely intimate with him that it is strange that he should have been surprised at his action.

[2] This letter is printed at p. 143, from a copy in the Leeds MSS.

[3] Better known as Sir Fletcher Norton, Speaker of the House of Commons.

should be proposed to the House of Commons on Monday to succeed Mr. Cornwall as Speaker. During the Cabinet The Chancellor received a letter from the Queen, the contents of which she wished to be communicated to the rest of the King's Ministers; it was to complain of the Disputes between the K.'s Physicians, and particularly complaining of Dr. Warren, whom Her Majesty declared she would never see again; it was evidently written under the impression of passionate resentment. The Ch. wrote word he would wait upon Her Majesty the next morning at Kew. After the Ch. was gone the D. of Richmond observed that the Ch. was not perfectly agreed with other Ministers respecting the question of the Restrictions upon the Regent being permanent.

S. 3. The Chancellor having received late the preceding evening a Paper sealed from the Prince of Wales to be communicated to the K.'s Ministers, and being obliged to go to Kew this morning sent it to Ld Stafford, who opened it and read it to us at the Cabinet; it consisted of three sheets of Quarto Paper, and was signed by the Prince of Wales; it contained observations on the Plan laid before H.R.H. in Mr. Pitt's letter, and in some parts was strongly expressive of displeasure towards Mr. Pitt, complaining of the nature as well as some of the probable motives of the proposed restrictions, though holding out an intention to accept the Regency rather than leave the Country in its present state, trusting to the Loyalty and Generosity of the Country to enable him to undertake the task, and to perform it with comfort to himself and advantage to the Public. It was upon the whole a strange performance, and by no means an able one; now and then there appeared something of Sheridan's language, and still more of Lord Loughboroughs, tho very far from being in either of their best manners.

Su. 4. There was a Cabinet at which all the Members (except the Chancellor) attended, as did likewise Ld Hawkesbury, Lord Kenyon, Mr. Grenville and Mr. Dundas. It seemed the universal opinion that the Queen should have a Council to advise and assist Her M. in the care and management of the K.'s person during his illness. The Chancellor we found was out of Town, which appeared very singular to the D. of Richmond, L⁴ Chatham, Mr. Pitt, and myself, considering his having proposed going to Kew yesterday morning to wait upon the Queen in consequence of the Letter received from Her M. on Fryday, and still more so as he had seen the Prince of Wales on Fryday night, from whom he had received the Sealed Paper delivered by L⁴ Stafford to the Cabinet yesterday morning.

M. 5. There was a full Cabinet at my office, where also were present Lord Hawkesbury and Lord Kenyon. All present except the Chancellor seemed to think some answer in writing ought to be returned to the Paper sent by the Prince of Wales. The Ch. himself put down some words which he thought might do, supposing the propriety of sending an answer was resolved on. He told us that on Fryday night he was sent for by the Prince; that on arriving at Carlton House a note was deliverd him in the Hall desiring him to go to Mr. Fox* in South Street (Mr. F. for more quiet was removed to Mrs. Armisteds), who was not well enough to come out, and that there the Prince would meet him. His Lordship went, and found L⁴ Robert Spencer and two other members of the House of Commons, whose names he did not recollect : they conversed with him a short time upon indifferent subjects, and when Mr. Fox came withdrew. Shortly afterward the Prince arrived; I think the Ch. said H. R. H. received the paper afterwards, and offered to read it to the Chancellor, but his Lp. declining giving him that trouble, the Prince signed it, sealed it up, and gave it to the Chancellor, desiring him to communicate it to the Cabinet.

Both Houses met to day. Mr. Grenville was proposed for Speaker by L⁴ Euston, seconded by Mr. Pulteney ; Sʳ Gilbert Elliott was proposed by Mr. Ellis, seconded by Mr. F. Montague. On the question being put, Mr. Grenville was chosen by a considerable Majority, viz. 215 to 144. We had a conference with the Commons to inform them of our having agreed to the resolutions communicated to us by them at the last conference, which done, our House adjourned to Monday next. Previous to our going to the conference, Lord Camden and I had some conversation in the House of Lords about the Chancellor. He said repeatedly, *he* is an odd man; adding, he has got himself into the Queen's confidence (probably by having formerly flattered the King about Power, and recommending corruption as necessary to carry on Government), and will be employed to reconcile the Queen and Prince, no matter at whose expence. As soon as the House adjourned Lord Camden went away. Mr. Pitt and the rest of the Cabinet retired to the Chancellor's room. Mr. Pitt read the proposed answer to the Prince. The Chancellor, however, disapproved sending any. We were all for sending that, and endeavoured to prevail upon the Ch. to agree with us. He asked why so large a majority of the Cabinet as seven to one (Ld Camden having agreed to the measure in the morning) could not carry it into effect. We tryed to convince him of the mischievous effect anything like divisions amongst us must produce in the public at so critical a period as the present, and how much the King's Interest might suffer from such a situation of the Cabinet. Lord Stafford particularly urged this, and throughout the whole conference endeavoured to bring the Chancellor to agree with us; he, however, continued sulky, and complained of having been misrepresented as differing from other Ministers upon certain points now in agitation without any foundation. We observed the newspapers were full of falsehoods of every sort, and particularly such as might misrepresent the real state of the Gov^t, with a view, if possible, to prejudice the cause we were all so cordially embarked in. After a long time an expedient was thought of which might meet the opinion of every one of us, viz. that the Chancellor should take our answer with him to the Prince, and ask H. R. H. whether it was his wish or expectation to receive any answer to the paper he had sent us; and, in case of his answering in the affirmative, then to deliver our Paper, but not otherwise. To this the Chancellor, though not with a very good grace, consented, and indeed it was not easy for him to avoid consenting to a proposal so stated, as his chief objection had been not to the particular answer in question, but to any being sent, as he thought the Prince did not mean that *any answer should be* returnd. I set the D. of Richmond down at his House, and in talking of the Ch. and his behaviour to-day he could not help saying *That man will ruin us all yet.*

T. 6. There was a Cabinet at my office: Lord Camden came there before the rest, and we had a good deal of conversation; I told him what had passed after we parted yesterday, he repeated a good deal of what he had before said to me about the Chancellor, adding that his wonderful Parliamentary Talents were the cause of his being so much courted, that in other particulars he was not without superiors, and that he had little judgment and no decision, which latter failing was much felt in the Court of Chancery. Ld Stafford and Lord Weymouth were the only two people who had weight with him, and of both those persons he was afraid. He was well with the King because he had supported the American War, and had never forfeited His Majestys esteem by joining Mr. Fox and his party as Lord North and others had done. His Lp. observed that the reason of the K.^{s} dislike to Eden and Dundas was, the latter having deserted Ld North before the coalition took place, and the former having been the instrument of continuing that Coalition; that the only people for whom the King had any regard were those who had formerly supported Ld North to the end of his administration, and who had not joined the Coalition; that as for any of *us*, His Majesty cared not a farthing. He again expressed his concern at the Chancellor's having obtained the Queen^s confidence, as he would certainly bring about a reconciliation with the Prince, though at the expence of sacrificing the King and every body else; in short, my Lord, *he is a bad man.*

The Cabinet was attended by all the members of it, as likewise by Lord Hawkesbury, Lord Kenyon, Mr. Dundas, and the Attorney and Sollicitor Genl; our chief business was talking over the business of the restrictions to be proposed with respect to the Regent' Power, and which were meant to have been opened this day in the House of Commons, but which were postponed on account of a second examination (before a Committee) of the K.ˢ Physicians being ordered.

The Duke of Richmond privately asked the Chancellor at the Cabinet whether he had seen the Prince in consequence of what had been agreed to the preceding evening at our meeting in his L.pˢ room at the House of Lords. I learnt from his Grace and Lord Stafford that the Chancellor had written to the Prince from Lᵈ Stafford's that night expressing a wish to wait upon H. R. H.; that he had soon after received a note from H. R. H. dated Piccadilly (the P. dining at the Duke of Queensberry's) desiring him to come to him at nine to South Street. The Ch. went, and found the Prince and Mr. Fox. The Ch. held the answer of the Cabinet in his hand at the time he asked the Prince whether H. R. H. expected or wished for any answer to the paper he had sent, to which the Prince answered in the negative, but on Mr. Fox observing that as there was an answer prepared it might as well be look'd at, the Ch. delivered the answer to His Royal Highness.

[Here follow five folios blank. The MSS. then proceeds as under, without any notification as to the *year* in which it is written.]

Tuesday, March 3ᵈ.[1]

Having the preceding evening received a letter from Mr. Pitt informing me of the K.ˢ pleasure to see Lord Sydney and myself the next day at Kew at two o'clock, I arrived there at the time appointed. His Majesty had walked to Richmond, and did not return till four. Five minutes after I was introduced by Col. Digby, and remained alone with H. Majesty till a quarter before five.

[1] In the interval the King had quite recovered from his illness, and all likelihood of the advent of a Whig Ministry to power under the influence of the Prince of Wales had passed away.

The moment the door was shut the King embrac'd me, put his cheek to mine, and with tears in his eyes thank'd me for my affectionate behaviour during his illness. I found him grown very thin and his voice hoarse in consequence of an accidental cold. His head, however, appeared perfectly clear, his memory correct, and his conversation less hurried and more connected than in general it used to be. His Majesty expressed himself most grateful for the support he had met with both from Parliament and the nation at large, and particularly expressed himself obliged to my Father and Ld Romney for their anxious concern for him. He desired me to thank my Father in his name, and at the same time desire him to communicate to Lord Romney his obligations to him, adding they could not be conveyed to that worthy nobleman in so agreeable a manner as thro' the channel of his old friend the Duke of Leeds. The K. said it was no small comfort to him to reflect on the small number of those who had deserted him, and still more so as they were persons whose conduct he was not surprised at, and for whom he had not that degree of regard which could cause him a moment's uneasiness for their defection.

Ld Malmesbury' conduct was no surprise (I own I thought there was much delicacy towards myself in H^s Majesty' enlarging no more upon Ld M.^{s} behaviour considering how much I had been attached to him, and how *anxious* I had been in procuring him his Peerage), nor did the Duke of Queensbery' nor Lord Lothian' occasion him a moment's uneasiness. It was, however, impossible for them to be continued in his service after what had passed, but in consideration of Ld Lothian' family His Majesty would make an arrangement by offering him a Reg^t of Cavalry in Ireland which he thought must soon be vacant by the death of Genl Fitzwilliam, whom H. M. told he had visited that morning, and whom he thought could not live many weeks.

[Here is another break of eleven blank pages.]

Sir,

The Proceedings in Parliament being now brought to a point which will render it necessary to propose to the House of Commons the particular measures to be taken for supplying the Defect of the Personal Exercise of the Royal Authority during the present interval, and your Royal Highness having some time since signified your Pleasure that any communication on this subject should be in writing, I take the liberty of respectfully entreating your Royal Highness' Permission to submit to your consideration the outlines of the plan which His Majesty's confidential Servants humbly conceive (according to the best judgment which they are able to form) to be proper to be proposed in the present circumstances.

It is their humble opinion that your Royal Highness should be empowered to exercise the Royal Authority in the name and on the Behalf of His Majesty during His Majesty's Illness, and to do all acts which might legally be done by His Majesty, with Provisions nevertheless that the care of His Majesty's Royal Person and the Management of His Majesty's Household and the Direction and appointment of the Officers and Servants therein should be in the Queen under such regulations as may be thought necessary; that the power to be exercised by your Royal Highness should not extend to the Granting the Real or Personal Property of the King (except as far as relates to the renewal of Leases), to the Granting any office in reversion, or to the Granting for any other Term than during His Majesty's Pleasure any Pension, or any office whatever, except such as must by Law be granted for Life or during good Behaviour, nor to the Granting any Rank or Dignity of the Peerage of this Realm to any Person except His Majesty's Royal Issue who shall have attained the age of twenty-one years.

These are the chief Points which have occurred to His Majesty's Servants.

I beg leave to add that their Ideas are formed on the supposition that His Majesty's Illness is only temporary, and may be of no long duration. It may be difficult to fix beforehand the precise Period for which these Provisions ought to last; but if unfortunately His Majesty's Recovery should be protracted to a more distant period than there is at present reason to imagine, it will be open hereafter to the wisdom of Parliament to reconsider these Provisions whenever the circumstances appear to call for it.

If your Royal Highness should be pleased to require any farther explanation on the subject, and should condescend to signify your orders that I should have the honour of attending your Royal Highness for that purpose or to intimate any other mode in which your Royal Highness may wish to receive such explanation, I shall respectfully wait your Royal Highness's Commands.

I have the honour to be with the utmost deference and submission, Sir,
  Your Royal Highness
    Most Dutiful and Devoted Servant,
        W. PITT.

Downing Street,
 Tuesday night, Dec. 30, 1788.

Endorsed: Dec. 30, 1788.
  Copy of a Letter
   from
 The Right Honble Wm Pitt
    to
 His Royal Highness
 The Prince of Wales.

[This is the letter referred to in the Memorandums under Dec. 30.]

The Duke of Leeds begs leave to inform your Majesty that the Duke of Orleans[1] came to him this morning.

The Duke of Orleans began the Conversation with a Repetition of the French King's wishes, " to continue and even to improve the system of Friendship and good understanding which so happily subsisted at present between the two Kingdoms of Great Britain and France, that it never could be the Interest of them to quarrel, and that by coming to a fixed and determined system, not only of Peace but of intimate and substantial Union and Friendship, the two Kingdoms would not alone derive advantage, but all Europe must gain by such a Connection as it would be in the Power of the two Crowns to maintain the general tranquillity."

The Duke of Leeds in answer to the Duke of Orleans ventured to assert that your Majesty wished upon all occasions to promote the general Tranquillity and to render it permanent and secure; the Duke of Orleans then mentioning the alarm which must arise in France should the Emperor march an army into the Austrian Netherlands for the purpose of putting an end to the Disturbances in those Provinces. The Duke of Leeds, after stating your Majesty's Friendship and Regard for the French King, expressed an earnest desire to learn the Sentiments of that Monarch on the event of such a step on the part of the Emperor taking place, in order that your Majesty might form a just Idea of the apprehensions entertained in France upon the subject, and of course be enabled to communicate directly with His Most Christian Majesty upon the subject whenever it became necessary to be discussed.

The Duke of Orleans replied the King of France wished immediately to sound your Majesty upon so important an event, and

[1] The Duke of Orleans left Paris for England at 3 o'clock p.m. on October 14. When he asked for his passports Count Montmorin wrote to say that the King had given him a commission of the highest importance. Huber writes to Lord Auckland (*Auckland Correspondence*, ii. 364) that in reality he had been driven away by Lafayette for plotting against the King. The Duke of Leeds had succeeded his father on March 23, 1789.

which was so likely to arise in a short time. The Duke of Leeds in answer observed that upon general principles it was natural the Emperor might exert himself in order to suppress the spirit of Discontent and Revolt now so prevalent in His Flemish Dominions; that England was certainly under no particular consternation from any efforts which the Court of Vienna might employ for that Purpose; and that the most Friendly advice he could give the Duke of Orleans, as a Friend and Relation as well as to a certain degree a Minister of the King of France (whose situation as well as that of His Kingdom your Majesty and every Person in your Dominions possessed of common Humanity must Deplore), was, not to look to Foreign Countries either with Hope or Apprehension, but to employ his whole Thoughts and attention, and to engage others to do the same towards the means of restoring good order and Tranquillity at Home, without which France could have no Government of her own, and of course could not expect any favourable estimation on the Part of other Nations.

Whitehall,
   Oct. 30th, 1789.

Endorsed: Whitehall, 30th Oct^r, 1789.
  To the King.
    (Copy.)

          Whitehall, Nov. 30, 1789.
    Present :—

The Lord Chancellor.	The Lord President.
The Earl of Chatham.	Right Honble Wm Pitt.
Mr. Secretary Grenville.	The Duke of Leeds.

Your Majesty's Servants, having taken into their most serious consideration the several Dispatches lately received from Berlin and the Hague, as well as the various Intelligence respecting the actual Situation of things in the Austrian Netherlands, humbly beg leave to submit the result of their opinion to your Majesty's consideration.

The main object which the Allies ought to pursue appears to be the preventing the result of the present Troubles in the Netherlands from raising up in that quarter a Power formidable to our system, which might arise to the Emperor, supposing that Prince to succeed in overturning the constitution, or to France, in case the Independence of the Provinces was established in any mode which should connect them with that Kingdom.

That the uncertain state of this business in the present moment does not seem to call upon any of the Allies for immediate interference by Force, or by acknowledgement of the Independence of the Provinces: Because it is probable that whatever turn the events in that country may take, we shall be able to secure the main object of our Policy as above stated, and that with more advantage, by our not having pledged ourselves beforehand.

That in the mean time the two Principal Points to which our attention should be directed are: First, to place ourselves in such a situation with respect to the Insurgents as may incline them to look up to us for Protection in the case of their being unsuccessful, and that for this purpose it is advisable to hold out to them assurances that we consider ourselves interested as guarantees in preserving their present Constitution, and shall be very desirous of contributing to that object, if the circumstances afford an opening for our Interference. Secondly, to use our Influence with them immediately and without a moment's delay, to induce them to take steps for preventing the prevalence of Democratical Principles, in the event of the Emperor's being unsuccessful; because this seems to be a point of absolute necessity in order to prevent such an event from producing an immediate connection with France.

Endorsed: 30th Nov. 1789.
Minute of Cabinet.[1]

---

[1] This minute has reference to the rising in the Austrian Netherlands against Joseph II. caused by his military reforms. The allies referred to are Holland, Prussia, and England, who had formed the Triple Alliance in 1788.

1791.

On Fryday, March 4th, Burges[1] called upon me in the evening, and mention'd a report, which he had heard from Nepean, that besides Dundas being appointed Secretary of State for India it was supposed to be in contemplation to make Lord Auckland Secretary of State for the Home Department: Ld Grenville to take that for Foreign Affairs; that Mr. Pitt, Lord Grenville, the D. of Montrose and Dundas were daily closetted together for hours at a time. Nothing had transpired respecting the mode in which the foreign department was to be vacated, whether I was to be dismissed, driven to resign, or any arrangement proposed to me.

Wednesday, March 9th, Burges wrote me word of a conversation he had had with Mr. Smith, Mr. Pitt's private Secretary, in which the latter seemed much hurt at his mentioning how long it had been since I had been honored with any conversation by Mr. Pitt. Mr. S. said there must be some mistake somewhere, and begged he would not mention a word to me on the subject till he (Mr. S.) had seen him again.

The next day, March 10th, I went to the House of Lords, which met early in the Committee of Privileges on the election of the Scotch Peers, and not being able to get any private conversation with the Chancellor I put down upon paper the report above mentioned, desiring to know if he had heard anything of it. I sealed

[1] Burges was Under-Secretary in the Foreign Office.

up this in form of a letter and gave it to him, desiring him to put it in his pocket. On Fryday 11th I went to the House of Lords. Mr. Cowper told me he had just sent a letter from the Ch.[1] to my house. I had but little conversation with the Ch., as there was a cause before the house. He told me however that he had heard reports similar to those contained in my letter, but that the Duke of Montrose had been mentioned to him as likely to succeed to the Foreign department. On my return home I found his letter, in which he observed that he himself was in a situation similar to if not worse than mine, as to a want of communication on the part of other ministers; that he hardly knew whom he could look upon as his colleagues, unless those who with him happened to attend the Hanging Cabinets.[2]

Early on Saturday morning, March 12, I awaked very feverish, and was when I got up so much indisposed that I meant to have stayed at home all day. Receiving however a letter from the Ch. expressing his wish to call upon me at the office about three, I went there and we had a long conversation. He told me he was convinced they meant to get rid of him when their minds should be made up respecting his successor. He talked of a want of confidence between members of the same administration as not only unpleasant to individuals but injurious to the general interests of the Gov.t. Mentioning those who were the bosom friends of Mr. Pitt, he could not help observing that Dundas was the most impudent fellow he ever knew; that he had proposed a dinner to the Chancellor at the house of the latter, at which Mr. Pitt and L.d Grenville were to be present, for the avowed purpose of knowing the Ch.s opinion respecting the complicated business of the Election of the 16 Peers,[3] now actually before the House of Lords. The Ch. told

[1] Lord Thurlow.

[2] Cabinet Councils held for the purpose of determining who of the numerous prisoners condemned to death should be actually hung.

[3] This had reference to a petition presented to the House of Lords on March 1, regarding certain informalities in the next preceding election of representative Peers for Scotland.

him he would very readily give him a dinner, but no opinion, and would ask L.ᵈ Kenyon to meet them, when they would know whether his Lp. would be at all more disposed to communicate his opinion upon a matter still *coram judice*. He then returned to the subject of the Reports I had communicated to him, and seemed pleased with yᵉ confidence I had shewn him. He mentioned L.ᵈ Loughborough as the person who had told him of the Duke of Montrose being supposed to be thought of for the new Sec. of State. He seemed desirous of knowing whether the K. had heard any of these reports, and particularly if I had mentioned anything upon the subject to H.M. I answered I had not, thinking it improper, for various reasons, to start the subject in the closet, till I was better ascertained that such a plan or any part of it was in contemplation. As soon as the Chancellor left me I returned home. My feverish disorder increased that evening, and I was confined to my bed the greater part of Sunday, Monday, and Tuesday, following. I kept my House till the Fryday, and was too much enfeebled by my illness to return to Business that week. During my being confined Mr. Burgess informed me that he again heard from Mr. Nepean that it was reported a new Secretary of State was in contemplation, and that great offers were to be made me to induce me to go to Ireland, it being thought expedient to recall Lord Westmorland.

On Monday, 21ˢ, and Tuesday, 22 March, Cabinets were held at my office, in which the sentiments of the K.'s ministers, with the exception of Lᵈ Grenville, were for sending a Fleet to the Baltic,[1]

---

[1] The Russian armament, as it was called, was undertaken to put pressure upon Russia to make peace with the Porte. The three allied powers, England, Holland, and Prussia, had taken a prominent part in the convention of Reichenbach between Austria and Prussia, by which Austria agreed to make peace with the Porte. This peace was concluded by the mediation of the three powers at Szistova. The war still continued between Russia and Turkey, and great pressure was brought to bear on Russia by Prussia and England to compel her to make peace. The good offices of Denmark were offered for conciliation. After some delay the peace of Jassy was signed between Russia and Turkey on January 9, 1792.

and a squadron to the Black Sea, in order to give weight by active exertion to our principle of establishing peace between Russia and the Porte on the ground of the status quo. L. Grenville thought that an additional armament would produce the best effect, and at all events keep the future direction of the negotiations in our hands by the simple effect of a demonstration so formidable on the part of England, and which, in the event of hostilities, we could no longer answer for short of immediate success. The D. of Richmond at one or other of these meetings, when most of the members were withdrawn, expressed great doubts of coming even to a general determination before the detail of operations was arranged. Ld Chatham very ably observed that to him it appeared more natural to come to some determination upon general grounds, and afterwards discuss the details of executing such measures as might appear expedient to be adopted. We had several communications on the subject, and at length a minute of Cabinet was agreed to stating the necessity of supporting our proposed plan of pacification, of immediately informing the King of Prussia of our intention of sending a fleet of 35 to 40 sail into the Baltic, a squadron of 10 or 12 ships of the line into the Black Sea to assist the Turks, and the hopes that our exertions in the North combined with the march of the Prussian troops on the side of Livonia[1] would produce the desired effect, a joint representation proposed to be delivered by the ministers of the two Crowns at St. Petersburg, stating the necessity of an answer in a reasonable time respecting the Empress' acceptance or refusal of our terms, and the necessity under the latter taking place we should be under of taking a part in the war, was sent at the same time to Berlin to be forwarded if approved of there, two declarations proposed to be signed by the K. of Prussia, the one respecting no further hostilities (in the event of war) were to be undertaken in case the Empress accepted the status quo, but

---

[1] Livonia was a Russian province. Catharine had 54,000 men there, under Ingelstrom, and Frederick William an army of 80,000 on the German frontier.

with the mutual consent of England and Prussia, the other respecting the general grounds on which a commercial treaty with Poland should be formed, and which were both directed to be signed previous to any other of the measures in question being adopted, were sent off to Mr. Jackson by the same messenger, on Sunday, all founded on the above-mentioned minute of Cabinet which I delivered into the K.'s hands on Fryday, the 25th. The messenger set off with the dispatches in the night of Sunday, the 27th March.[1] On the Fryday preceding both Houses of Parl^t were informed that probably a message would be delivered from his Majesty on the Monday following respecting an augmentation of his naval forces. The message was accordingly delivered, and the next day, Tuesday, the 29th, was taken into consideration, when a long debate ensued on the motion for an address to the King. The Opposition members very violent. The address, however, was carried by a great majority[2] in both Houses. Wednesday, the 30th, being in the House of Lords, the D. of Richmond took me into one of the Committee Rooms, and stated his opinion that the numberless difficulties attending the prosecution of our present plan rendered it almost impossible to succeed, that the country would not support it, and that we ought to look out for some expedient to get out of the scrape. I told his Grace my own opinion was precisely the same it had been from the beginning of the business, and that even if it had changed, I should fear we were too late for retreating without hazarding our reputation very materially. That supposing the cautious line he recommended should be approved I could see but one method of succeeding without sacrificing

---

[1] The Duke of Leeds wrote to Lord Whitworth on this date: "It is now determined that preparation should be made without delay for an active interference on the part of Great Britain and Prussia, in order to obtain the terms which have hitherto been repeatedly recommended without effect." He enclosed a representation which was to be delivered in conjunction with the Prussian Minister, and the omission to send an answer within ten days would be considered a refusal.

[2] Ninety-seven to thirty-four in the Lords; 228 to 135 in the Commons

our consistency, viz., a secret but direct negociation with Prince Potemkin (which might indulge in its effects one of his ruling passions, avarice), with a view to obtain the Empress' acquiescence in our terms. He seemed to approve of this, expressing his conviction that to carry on a war against Russia would be impracticable. We went to the Ld Chancellor in his room; Ld Grenville was with him; soon after Mr. Pitt joined us. The Duke of Richmond repeated what he had said to me; the Ch. and Mr. Pitt by no means seemed convinced by his Grace's arguments, which, at all events, however, they thought came somewhat late. Ld Grenville said little on the subject. The House being by this time full and waiting for the Chancellor, it was agreed to discuss the matter no further at that time but to have a meeting of the Cabinet at my office in the evening. When the Ch. and Ld Grenville went out of the Room I remarked to Mr. Pitt the unpleasant circumstance of any hesitation upon a point which had been agreed to, and which had been proceeded upon so far as to render it very difficult to retract with honour or anything like consistency. He perfectly agreed with me, and said his opinion had remained perfectly unchanged as well as mine. In the evening the Cabinet met. The D. of R., Lord Stafford, and Lord Grenville seemed to think it advisable to devise if possible some means of desisting from our present plan. The Ch., Lord Chatham, Mr. Pitt, and myself agreed it might be attended with difficulty but not equal to that which must accompany the change of system proposed. Ld Stafford owned that either part to be adopted in the present circumstance must be liable to great and serious difficulty; if, says he, we are so far committed as to make an honourable retreat impossible we must go on, and I am free to own I had much rather be knocked on the head than survive under the imputation of being either Knave or Fool. We came to no precise determination this evening. The D. of Richmond remained firm in his opinion. Ld Stafford did not appear to have quite made up his mind, tho' evidently leaning to the more cautious line of conduct.

Thursday the 31st.

I was to have been with Mr. Pitt by appointment at half-past twelve. I called at his house, his servant told me was walked out. I returned to my office, and shortly after Mr. Pitt came to me there. We lamented the visible difference in the Cabinet on the subject of our present measures respecting Russia; I told him my opinion was precisely the same as to the expedience of adopting a spirited line of conduct as when the Resolution was agreed to, and instructions in consequence sent to Berlin. He said his own likewise remained the same, at the same time he foresaw difficulties at home that hitherto he by no means apprehended, that several members attached to Gov^t had divided against the address in the House of Commons, and added in confidence that he had just been with the Duke of Grafton, who had expressed himself (tho' in the most friendly manner) decidedly against the risking hostilities with Russia, and that he had been informed by Ld Euston that the Duke had insisted upon his Lp. and his brother Ld Charles Fitzroy not voting upon the question of Tuesday last. I lamented to him that, disagreeable as the difficulties in Parliament, and out of doors, indisputably were, what I own pressed extremely on my mind was the situation of minds in the Cabinet itself, that measures of a pretty decisive nature determined in a Cabinet at which all the members were present, recommended to the King as such, and afterwards acted upon, could not I thought be recalled consistently either with our collective or individual reputations, and that should it so happen that we were compelled by a majority among ourselves to adopt a contrary line, it would be impossible for me to hold the seals any longer. Mr. Pitt assured me in the kindest manner he not only felt *for* me but *with* me, and owned that a measure he so much approved of and which we were in truth committed upon being abruptly counteracted was what he could not feel without serious uneasiness, that he perfectly agreed with me in sentiment upon the subject, even to the point of resignation, but begged me to reflect on the consequences which breaking up the present Gov^t might produce to the country in general, and to the K. in particular, and finished by saying he was convinced I would reflect upon this and temper my feelings, which he could not but approve of as perfectly congenial with his own, by the utmost prudence and discretion. The other members of the Cabinet, being supposed to be near at hand (the Privy Council sitting that day on appeals), were sent for, and they all came. Ld Stafford confessed his anxiety and apprehensions of the event of our measures had considerably increased since he parted with us the preceding evening, and assured us he had scarce closed his eyes all night from the agitation of his mind ; that he thought so many difficulties would occur in the prosecution of our plan that we had nothing left but to get out of our embarrassment as well as we could. The Duke of Richmond strongly supported this idea ; Ld Grenville appeared likewise to approve it (it is but justice to his Lp. to observe that he behaved very honourably through the whole course of this business; at first he opposed singly the proposal of going further than such demonstration as an increase of our naval armament would create, but when he found the sentiments of the rest of the K.'s servants were to employ that armament, he thought we should proceed with alacrity and effect; no part of the Fleet being sailed, or the Prussian Troops yet in motion, his Lp. was certainly at liberty, without a shadow of inconsistency, to take the line he has since done in our subsequent deliberations). The Chancellor said but little, but expressed his surprize and concern that these cautious sentiments had not been sooner declared, instead of coming after the determination upon which the last communication to Prussia was founded ; in this Ld Chatham, Mr. Pitt, and myself agreed with him, and added the consequences wee apprehended would arise from having proceeded so far, and then stopping short without any apparent reason whatever. Ld Camden seemed much agitated, lamented the difficulties he saw were inevitable on both hands, but gave no decisive opinion. We broke up early on account of the House of Lords, and agreed to meet again in the evening. The D. of Richmond and Lord Chatham (only Mr. Pitt and myself being present with them) had a pretty long argument. The latter conducted himself with great coolness and judgement, the former seemed neither convinced nor much pleased with the superiority with which the subject was treated in opposition to his Grace's sentiments.

It seemed understood that something must be decided at our meeting in the evening, and from what had passed in the morning and the preceding Cabinet I had little reason to expect anything short of a direct and abrupt change of system being adopted. Prepared for this event I went to the Cabinet in the evening: Ld Chatham and Mr. Pitt were not come, the rest of the members were present; the Chancellor and Ld Camden in close conference on one side of the chimney, the D. of Richmond and Ld Stafford on the other, Lord Grenville walking up and down the room; I went up to the chimney, and, stirring the fire, observed that as it was probably the last time I should have to do the honours of that Room I thought it particularly incumbent upon me to have a good fire for my company. This produced a considerable effect, the D. of Richmond and Ld Stafford exclaimed, Good God, what d'ye mean? I answered, from what had passed at our late meetings, I took for granted it would be determined at the present to act in a manner directly contrary to what we had communicated as our system to Prussia, in which case I should think myself obliged to *make my bow*. A short silence ensued. The D. of Richmond begged to say a word to me, and we withdrew into my room: he expressed his surprize and concern at what I had mentioned, and in a very kind and friendly manner expressed his hopes that I did not seriously entertain the idea of resigning. I told his Grace that after the opinion I had repeatedly declared and still entertained upon the subject it would be impossible for me to do otherwise should such a change of system as I apprehended was in contemplation be adopted; he went on in the most obliging and friendly manner to state to me how much he regretted the want of more confidence and communication amongst us than had of late prevailed, confessed himself to have been absent frequently and for long intervals, that in truth he was almost tired of business, and had frequently in contemplation to retire. This, I observed, would of course be a much more serious loss to the public than my resignation, and I hoped he would give up any such idea. We conversed with great good humour for ten minutes or a quarter of an hour, and then returned to the Cabinet; by this time Mr. Pitt and Ld Chatham were arrived.

The Discussion in general was similar to what had passed at our previous meetings. Mr. Pitt, Ld Chatham, and myself had to meet the arguments of the D. of Richmond, Ld Stafford, and Ld Grenville. Ld Camden said little, and the Chancellor either actually was or appeared to be asleep the greater part of the time (this I own I thought extraordinary, unless he counterfeited sleep in order to avoid taking any part in the conversation, which was warmly carried on, tho' with good temper, and in which his friend Ld Stafford's sentiments did not appear to coincide with his own). It was proposed to send a messenger without delay to Berlin, to stop if yet in time the representation proposed to be made to Russia on the part of this country and Prussia till further orders. I stated the bad effect this would have at Berlin: the dispatching a messenger merely for the purpose of preventing a measure so lately determined on by this Gov^t, and in consequence not only communicated but recommended to the Court of Berlin to cooperate with us in carrying into effect, would create an impression very unfavourable to the consistency as well as vigour of our councils, and that the hurry in which it would appear we counteracted what we had so recently adopted might bring upon us the imputation of irresolution if not timidity. Should the delay, however, now urged be agreed to, I told them an expedient had occurred to me, which might in some measure soften, if not entirely do away, the bad effects I was apprehensive of: this was the sending a civil answer to the last proposals from Denmark, together with a representation on the subject of their neutrality, and the use of their Ports in case of hostilities between us and Russia, to be communicated to the K. of Prussia previous to their being transmitted to Copenhagen. This might of course justify the dispatching a special messenger to Berlin; and, the proposed delay no longer appearing the sole object of his mission, might in some degree prevent the suspicion I so much dreaded being entertained at Berlin of an anxious timidity on our part. This was agreed to, and Mr. Pitt put down upon paper the substance of a dispatch to be forwarded to Mr. Jackson. This being read was generally approved of. I could not, however, but strongly object to one part of it, namely, the stating the Danish proposition as the specific reason of our wishing for delay: these propositions, evidently approved of, if not actually framed by the Russian Gov^t, were in my judgement little entitled to serious attention as likely to produce any good effect, and by no means of a nature to justify us in a change of system merely out of compliment to the proposals contained in them. I told the meeting fairly that should the Dispatch in its present form be agreed to, Ld Grenville would perhaps have the goodness to sign it, for I could not. This direct disapprobation produced its effect; and Mr. Pitt altered it by stating the delay of a few days as desirable on account of various circumstances which had happened, and which in time would be communicated at Berlin. The delay being now proposed on general grounds I acquiesced. The meeting broke up at near one in the morning, and the messenger set off by three. I accompanied this, and the dispatches to be sent thro' Berlin to Copenhagen, with a short but confidential letter to Jackson, requiring him upon this, as he had done on all occasions, to follow in the most punctual manner the instructions transmitted to him, at the same time assuring him that the delay proposed was submitted to, but not approved of, by me.

Thus ended this interesting, but not very agreeable day, *I might say month!*

Fryday, April 1. A long day in the House of Lords. Ld Fitzwilliam moved a string of Resolutions, the first declaring we were not bound by the Prussian Treaty to offensive measures; the previous question upon this moved by Ld Grenville, and carried in the negative by a great majority.[1]

Sat. 2^d. The Chancellor came to the office for some papers. I happened to be there, and desired him to be shewn into my Room. We had a great deal of conversation upon private Business (Bates, &c.), and afterwards got upon public affairs: he lamented with me our being *gagged* in the debates, and thought as I did that it would be better to come forward in both Houses in respect to the measures we were pursuing in our present discussion with Russia: com-

---

[1] Sixty; 94 to 34, including proxies. An impartial account of these transactions is to be found in Hermann, *Geschichte des Russischen Staats*, vi. 368 foll. He says, p. 406: "On April 5, Jackson in Berlin received intelligence that both Houses had approved of the strengthening of the English fleet, and was ordered at the same time to lay before the Prussian Ministers both the conventions concerning Russia and Poland which had been agreed upon, even to the smallest details. England undertook, (1) to send a fleet into the east sea, in May, upon which Prussia was at the same time to advance with an army of 88,000 men into Livonia, and to march upon Riga; and, (2) as a basis of a commercial treaty between England, Prussia, and Poland, the toll on the Vistula was to be reduced from twelve to three per cent. on the condition that the republic ceded Dantzick to Prussia. Immediately upon the signature of these treaties Jackson was to send a courier to St. Petersburg with a peremptory warning to the Empress that she was either to surrender all her conquests or to prepare for a war with England, Prussia, and their allies.

"Frederick William had already despatched to his generals in command the orders which the urgency of the situation required, and was preparing to depart for Preussen on the 13th to hold a review. To everyone's astonishment, Jackson received on April 7 the ambiguous counter-order to defer the signing of the convention and the despatch of the ultimatum to St. Petersburg for the present.

"This 'temporary delay' was, as was soon apparent, nothing less than the forerunner of an entire abandonment of the great and common interests which Prussia had undertaken to support with its army on the Continent in accordance with the alliance subsisting between it and the sea powers. Just as it was about to draw the sword in defence of their interests Prussia saw itself deserted. Prussia was treated with great injustice. On the contrary, England had been quite justified at Reichenbach in not surrendering the *status quo*. Prussia now saw itself, to the great loss of its prestige in Europe, compelled to give way in all those questions on which, for the sake of her power and position, it was necessary for her to hold her own against the imperial courts. Nothing remained for her but, as Frederick William expressed it, to submit to the imperious law of necessity."

plained as usual of want of communication and concert among the Ministers.

Monday, April 4. Mr. Pitt called upon me at the office, stated his opinion still being the same with mine, lamenting however the prospect of not being supported cordially by Parl^t or People. I told him the support of both, I believed, depended upon having the situation in which we stood in regard to Russia generally at least if not precisely laid open to the public. He said there was great difficulty in doing that in Parl^t, that he had spoke to many individuals his friends upon the subject, and that he found them reluctant in their support beyond any idea he had formed. I told him my mind was made up upon the subject, and after considering it with the utmost attention I felt firmly and decidedly of opinion to give up should the method we had adopted be departed from. He again repeated his sentiments coincided perfectly with mine, that however he felt an inclination to throw up in finding a measure he was convinced was right liable to such difficulties as might render it futile if not impracticable. One consideration strongly impressed his mind. The country he had no doubt (supposing a change of Gov^t to happen) would soon right itself, but what would become of the King? I went to the Prince's Levee to kiss hands for the Garter (having been prevented by illness from attending the former one), and afterwards to the House. The Lords were summoned on a motion of Ld Porchester respecting the War in India; the business however was put off on account of Ld Loughborough's being confined by the gout. Lord Camden took me aside in the House and asked me with great eagerness what I meant by the hints I had dropped at the Cabinet on Thursday night respecting its being probably the last time I should attend there, &c., adding his fears that we are all going out directly. I told him my sentiments were exactly the same they were at the time he alluded to, and that if a change of system was adopted I must give up the seals; he expressed his concern very politely and we parted.

When the Cabinet broke up on the 31st ult. with the professed determination of coming to some specific point in a few days, I own I did expect we should have assembled again sooner. We did not meet however till the 10th, and the preceding evening, Sat. April 9th, I received the draft of a dispatch from Mr. Pitt intended for Berlin; the purport of the Paper throughout was drawn evidently with a view to counteract our former plan, and, in addition to certain parts which I could not approve of, there was a declaration of a difference of opinion in the Empress' mind since the Dispatch of the 27 ult. was sent to Berlin. I took particular notice of this passage in a paper I sent to Mr. Pitt the same evening when I returned him the Dft, being a little surprised how any information of the Empress' disposition could have been received without my knowledge, and the total impossibility of that Princess having known a syllable of the contents of a Dispatch so lately sent off, which, had it been carried directly to Petersburg, could not have reached that place till many days after the time I had received the information; this the next day was explained to me, tho' I cannot say very satisfactorily, by stating that *the language held by opposition in Parliament during our late discussions would probably create a change in the Empress' sentiments, even supposing her to have been previously inclined to accede to the terms of the Allies.*

In the paper I sent Mr. Pitt, after some remarks on different passages contained in it, I concluded in these words:

" I cannot but observe that upon the whole state of the case my
" opinion is unshaken, we ought to proceed upon our First Plan.
" The language of opposition confirms me in the necessity of not
" giving way to their clamour at home or the effects of it abroad.

" What I shall ever look upon as having been wisely determined
" for the interests both Political and Commercial of this Country I
" cannot submit to give up without some motive stronger than any
" I have hitherto heard alleged for sacrificing the Reputation of
" this Gov^t, and in the event establishing a Russian Party in the
" House of Commons."

" Leeds."

Su. April 10. There was a Cabinet. Previous to its meeting Mr. Pitt came to me in Mr. Burges' Room and we had some conversation on the subject of the Dispatches he had sent me the preceding evening, as likewise respecting my observations upon the purport of them; it was in the course of this conversation he explained to me the probable change in the sentiments of the Court of Petersburg mentioned in page 27 (161). He continued that his sentiments still remained the same, but that he felt an absolute necessity of sacrificing his opinion to the difficulties that presented themselves; we went to the Cabinet, when finding how things must now finally go I took little if any share in their deliberations; the D^{ts} were approved of by the rest of the Members. I was not sorry to find the next day they were not to be sent till after an interval of a day or two, in expectation of a messenger from Berlin arriving within that period with despatches that might render some alterations or additions necessary. Although the despatches were not sent the determination of the Cabinet was now manifest, and Mr. Fawkener was fixed upon to be sent first to Berlin and afterwards to Petersburg; the object of his mission was to propose such modifications respecting Oczakow and its district as might be acceptable to the Empress and procure a Peace. I could not but approve of the Person chosen, altho' highly disapproving the timid and unbecoming system upon which his commission proceeded.

Fryday, April 15. I went to St. James' after the Levee, and informed the King how much I regretted that on account of the present measures adopted by the rest of H.M.'s servants in direct contradiction to those we had *all* so recently approved of, recommended to His M. and actually acted upon, I found myself under the necessity of begging His M. to permit me to return him the Seals I had so long held by his indulgence, at the same time expressing the most grateful sense of H.M.'s repeated goodness to me and my unalterable and zealous attachment to his Person and Gov^t. The K. appeared both surprized and concern'd; he said he was sincerely concern'd at hearing my intention, and begged me to

think of it again. I assured H.M. I had given that full consideration to it which the importance of such a step demanded. He
asked when the idea had first occurred. I told him from the time
I found my Colleagues disposed to a change of system which I
disapproved, and which militated so strongly against the advice
submitted to His Majesty on the 22^d of last month, which to me
appeared both wise and honor^{ble}. The King having attentively
listened to my explanation could not but approve my conduct, altho'
he in the kindest manner repeated his concern at the measure I was
about to adopt in consequence of it. I went from St. James' to the
House of Lords; when the House was adjourned, I told the
Chancellor, by whom I was sitting, that I should make my bow
and retire very soon; he thought I was wrong, as it would not
appear from what motives I resigned; he began finding fault with
the mode in which business was transacted in the Cabinet, and
thought I had much better insist upon a different method being
adopted for the future in that particular than give up my office. I
answered I was equally ready to allow that Business both in the
Cabinet and out of it might, in my opinion, be carried on in a
much better manner, both with respect to the Public and indi-
vidually to the Ministers, than for some time back it had been;
but added at the same time that my resolution of quitting my
official situation arose from motives of substance rather than form,
and that when a system I approved of, and which had been adopted
by the Cabinet, came not only to be counteracted but effectively
defeated, and a directly contrary one established, I conceived it
high time for me to withdraw; he did not attempt to contradict or
even observe upon what I had stated, and we parted.

In the evening there was a concert at Lady Holdernesse[1] in
order that their Majesties might hear the Miss Anguishs sing.
The King, Queen, and five of the Princesses were there, all very
gracious to me, and His Majesty never referred at all to what had

[1] Lady Holdernesse was the mother of the first Duchess of Leeds. The Miss
Anguishs were the sisters of the second.

passed in the morning when I had the honour to attend him in his Closet at St. James.

Lord Chatham was at L.^{dy} Holdernesses during the evening; I had more than once an opportunity of some confidential conversation with him. I told him, seeing the turn things were taking, I should probably give up very soon; he said he sincerely hoped I would not, that perhaps things might again change to a situation more agreable to both our opinions, at the same time declaring his sentiments with respect to what *ought* to be done, to remain precisely the same as they were originally.

This day there was a long Debate in the House of Commons on the subject of the armaments, and the probable Rupture with Russia. Gov^t had a majority[1] of ten or twelve more than on the preceding Tuesday.

Sat. April 16.

In the morning I received a letter from Mr. Pitt accompanying several Df^{ts} for Dispatches[2] which he wished me to peruse; I read one for Mr. Jackson at Berlin it was full, and in truth (as I conceived at the time) contained the substance of the others; it had I perceived been drawn mentioning me in the third person, having received his former ones, but had been alter'd by erasing my name and leaving it in the form it would naturally stand for my signature. The contents, however, of this Dispatch and the principle on which it was drawn were so perfectly inconsistent with my way of thinking that I erased the alteration and left it as originally written. I went to the office, a Cabinet was to meet in the forenoon; soon after I arrived Fawkener[3] came into Burgess' room; I wished him joy of

[1] On Tuesday, April 12, the numbers were 253 to 173; on Friday, April 15, 254 to 163.

[2] Any one who has studied the original documents preserved in the English Record Office will know that a large number of the most important foreign despatches, signed by Lord Carmarthen and Lord Grenville, are really the composition of Mr. Pitt.

[3] Mr. Fawkener was being sent to St. Petersburg " in order to conduct in concert with Mr. Whitworth the details of any negociations which may arise there."

his mission; he told me from what he could collect from the correspondence (which he had been allowed to peruse for some days) or from conversation he did not think it would turn out a very pleasant one, that he undertook it merely from motives of duty to Gov^t, and would do his best, at the same time observing to me it appeared but a bad business, *quand on a versé son vin il faut le boire*, he wished our mode had been less liable to the imputation of a disgraceful retreat; however it was his duty and would be his wish to make the retreat as honourable as possible. He left me, and some time afterwards I went into the Great Room where the Cabinets meet; several of the Ministers were come; Fawkener was there talking with Lord Camden; when their conversation was finished he came up to me and repeated in substance the remarks he had made to me in Burgess' room. I told him I could not but allow they were perfectly just, that at the same time I was always happy when he was employed in a situation where he could have an opportunity of displaying his abilities. I was free to own I by no means approved of the measure they were now called forth to support, and as the strongest proof of my opinion upon the subject would tell him in confidence I was *out*, tho' I did not mean to give in my resignation formally till the day of adjournment for the Recess. He appeard both surprised and concern'd, expressed himself in the most friendly manner upon the occasion, and added he thought my conduct truly honourable.

The Cabinet met. The business of the day was taken into consideration, the Papers Mr. Pitt had sent to me in the morning; previous however to the discussion of their contents there passed a pretty long conversation. The Duke of Richmond was anxious to know if it was thought possible the messenger who carried the Dispatch to Berlin urging some delay could have arrived soon enough to prevent the joint Representation of the two allied Courts to that of Petersburg being sent off from Berlin (this with other papers went by the preceding messenger a few days only sooner).

The Chancellor said he hoped not, and thought there had been a fortunate east wind which would prevent the second messenger arriving time enough for that purpose. The Duke seemed nettled at this answer, and replied, I suppose then you wish to read Homer, my Lord. What the Devil, retorted the Chancellor, has Homer to do with this business? Only, replied the Duke, I suppose y^r Lordship may want to have sufficient Leisure to read Homer in comfort, which, from your situation, you have not at present. After a little more snarling on one part, and a great deal of Grumbling on the other, the Dialogue concluded. The D. of Richmond then asked me if I recollected the day the second messenger went away. I told him he set out on Fryday, April 1st. Pitt could not help saying, Now do own, Duke, that you enjoy the date on this occasion. I told him I really answered the Duke tout bonnement, and was sure the date was accurate; however, since he mentioned it, I could not say I was particularly sorry at such a step being taken on such a day. Soon after this conversation Ld Grenville read the Dispatch to Jackson above mentioned, which, he said, in fact contained the substance of the others. Some trifling alterations were made it it, and Pitt asked me if I objected to sign it. (He had called upon me in Grosvenor Square on Thursday night to talk to me on the subject of my objecting to sign those Instructions I did not approve, stating it as if the signing was merely ministerial. I thought another Secretary of State would answer the same purpose, and told him if with a view to avoiding delay it was indispensably necessary for me to sign Dispatches I did not approve of I must accompany my signature with a protest, a circumstance, I believed, unprecedented, which would have a strange appearance in the records of the office, but which under such circumstances if obliged to sign my name I could not dispense with.) I told him I certainly could not but object to sign what I did not approve of, and could not see any difficulty in the papers in question being signed by the other Secretary of State, as was frequently done in cases of indisposition or absence. This difficulty was however in the course of 24 hours settled by application to the King for permission to L⁴ Grenville to sign the Dispatches of the Foreign Office.

I dined at Lord Stanhopes, a mixed company, Lord Chatham and L⁴ Grenville both dined there. The Duchess was much struck with L⁴ Grenville appearing extremely out of spirits and scarcely speaking the whole time. In the evening I went to Whites. The Speaker came there a few minutes after. We went to the upper end of the Room and had a long conversation. After having talked on common Parliamentary business for some little time we got upon the subject of the late Debates and of course to the present situation of the Government. He lamented Mr. Pitt not having opened the business more that he had even yet done when it first came to be discussed in Parliament, as he was sure it would have produced the best effects; that what he had said the preceding evening had been productive of good consequences, and that the House of Commons, he was convinced, were now impressed with a far more favourable opinion of the measures of Gov' than at the close of the preceding debate, and much more disposed to join in an active support of them. I told him my own opinion respecting the line Mr. Pitt might more successfully have taken perfectly coincided with his, and that I had more than once remarked to Mr. Pitt that from the silence observed by the King's Servants in both Houses it could not be said the question had had fair play. I told the Speaker I saw with real regret the situation in which the Gov¹ now stood, and added in confidence to him my intention to resign. He appeared greatly surprised, and expressed in the kindest manner the sincere concern he felt at this information. I told him I flattered myself he would agree with me in the motives on which my conduct was founded; that having the misfortune to disapprove of the measures now adopted I thought it neither consistent with what I owed to the King or to my own character to retain my official situation any longer. He expressed the highest approbation of my conduct and added great satisfaction at finding we agreed so perfectly in sentiment upon the present situation of affairs, stating his having at first imagined I had differ'd with my colleagues as thinking the modifications did not go far enough, whereas now he learnt with pleasure I was firm to the manly principles on which we had acted previous to the present system of caution bordering upon timidity. We both lamented the particular situation of Pitt, it was the first instance in which the present Gov' had shrunk from its plans, that at all times to shew one's teeth and then declare one dare not bite was obviously the worst of policy; in the present instance it would, he apprehended, prove particularly injurious both from its effects abroad and at home. I perfectly agreed with him in his observation, adding that besides the bad effects to be apprehended in the first instance from so apparent a want of stability in our councils, namely, the distrust of our allies, the Triumph of Russia, and the insulting clamour of opposition in general, I was, I confess, apprehensive of a new description of enemies starting up, who would, I am sure, appear to him above all men the last to be encouraged, I mean nothing less than a Russian Faction in the House of Commons. He owned my apprehension appeared but too well founded, and after again lamenting the situation of Ministers, and bestowing the strongest encomiums on my manly and consistent conduct (as he was pleased to term it), this interesting conversation was put a stop to by several people coming up to us.

Su. April 17th. The Cabinet was summoned for twelve. I did not attend it, but went to the Drawing Room, it being necessary for the Duchess and myself to go to St. James' that day on account of their Majesties having honoured Lady Holdernesse with their presence on Fryday night. I went from Court to the office and conversed with the Ministers, who stayed some time after the Cabinet was over.

M. April 18. I walked down to the office. I had a long conversation with Burges, who expressed an anxious wish to consult me in respect to the conduct he ought to hold under the present circumstances. He told me both Nepean and Smith (Mr. Pitt's Private Secretary) had severally hinted to him a wish that he might

remain in office, evidently with a view to sound him upon the
subject for the information of Mr. Pitt and Lord Grenville: he added
he would not give them or any other Person who might question
him upon the subject any answer till he had consulted me: he then
in the most affectionate terms expressed his sense of the obligations
he said he lay under to me, repeating his sincere and warm attachment even independent of these obligations, and declared he would
be determined only by my wishes as to the conduct he was to
observe. I answered by assuring him how gratefully sensible I
was of his friendship and regard for me; that supposing I had given
up from any quarrel with the K.'s servants or with a view to break
with them and even oppose the Gov^t I should still have thought it
unjust to him to have expected him to sacrifice his situation to my
ill humour whether well or ill founded, that on the contrary under
the present circumstances, where I resigned upon principle not
pique, it was a great consolation to me to think that there existed
no reason upon earth which in my mind could make his remaining
in office a matter of hesitation, and that therefore I seriously wished
him to encourage the opening made to him by Mr. Nepean and
Mr. Smith, the first opportunity that presented himself. He appeared extremely pleased with the manner in which I expressed
myself to him upon the subject, and we parted. In the evening I
received a summons to the Cabinet to be held the next day.

T. April 19th.

I had a message in the morning from Count Wedel, the Danish
Minister, desiring me to name a time when he might come to
me. I appointed three o'clock the same day at the office. I
went there a little before three, the business of the Cabinet was
over but the Members not gone. I chatted some time with them
till the Danish Minister came. I found his business was merely to
express a wish that some answer might be sent to the proposals[1]

---

[1] The proposals of Denmark were that England should not insist upon the strict *status quo* and the absolute cession of Oczakow and its district, but, 1, the demo-
lition of the fortress of Oczakow with an agreement not to restore it, or to build any

he had communicated by order of his court respecting a plan of pacification between Russia and Turkey. I told him the answer had been above a fortnight since, but going thro' Berlin had probably not reached Denmark when his letters left Copenhagen. With this he appeared perfectly satisfied, and we conversed upon general subjects till he withdrew. I went to Burges' room; as soon as we were alone he told me he had had in the course of the day two of the most interesting conversations he had ever known, the one with the Chancellor the other with Mr. Pitt.

The Chancellor being come some time before the rest of the Cabinet Burges took the opportunity of going to him to have some conversation with him; he appear'd very cross and sullen, confess'd I had acted like a man of honour in resigning, but did not appear much disposed to follow my example. Among many other curious parts of his conversation there is one that appears too curious not to be particularly noticed. Upon the bare mention of a future war he made use of the following very extraordinary words: "I do not believe that there can be any danger of a war while the present Ministers continue in place; what can they go to war for? We have given up everything for which a war could be commenced, and after swallowing *this Disgrace* what other disgrace can we scruple to swallow."

other fortress within the district ceded; 2, the agreeing not to establish any Russian colonies, or to build towns, or to introduce any inhabitants within the district; and, 3, that the cession should be made so as not to give to Russia the command of the navigation of the Dniester and the consequent influence which she might thereby acquire in Poland.—Lord Grenville's instructions to Mr. Ewart, April 22, 1791. Mr. Drake, our representative at Copenhagen, was ordered on April 20 to ask that immediate orders may be sent to the Danish minister at St. Petersburg to help in making peace with Russia on the terms proposed. Lord Grenville informs Lord Auckland in a private letter, dated April 16, 1791, " with respect to our present measures the great fear which I entertain is that the line of concession which what has happened here compels us to adopt will too evidently betray our weakness, and that the Empress will rise in her demands, instead of being disposed to modify them." This probably is what the Duke of Leeds was afraid of.

Such being his Lp's sentiments it seems we are much nearer agreeing in Theory than Practice.

The second conversation was of a very different sort. Mr. Pitt came into Burges' room, and talked to him in the most friendly manner, directly expressing his hopes that he would continue in his present official situation, accompanying his wishes on the subject with the strongest testimony of approbation of his conduct. Burges in reply express'd the deep sense he entertained of the honour Mr. Pitt had done him, not only by approving his past conduct, but by the very handsome manner in which he had expressed his wishes that he should continue in office; that in return for so flattering a mark of Mr. Pitt's approbation he thought it his duty to speak to him with equal confidence. He began by stating the Friendship that had subsisted between himself and me for many years, the obligations he should ever consider himself as laying under to me: that it was to me, and to me alone, he owed his present situation. adding his sincere attachment to me, and determined resolution to be guided by me in every part of his public conduct: that such being his sentiments, grateful as he was for Mr. Pitt's very obliging proposal, he could not, of course, under the present circumstances, accept of it. When Burges told me of this conversation I immediately asked him if he had mentioned nothing of what had passed between us on the subject the preceding day: he answered not a syllable. I owned I was much surprised and sorry he had not, as the substance of his conversation with Mr. Pitt appeared to me too like declining the very handsome offer made him, and which it was so much my wish he should accept. I therefore desired him to go immediately to Mr. Pitt and mention to him his having communicated their conversation to me, and that I had earnestly desired him to remain in office.

It seemed to me I own absolutely necessary to avoid the least delay in coming to an explanation on this subject, as it was difficult to know what applications might not be made for his office, and how far they might avail under the impression that he declined continuing in it. Coming out of Burges' room I met Mr. Ewart, who told me he was to set off for Berlin on Thursday morning, and wished to know when he might call upon me to take leave. I told him I should be very happy if he would come and dine with me, which accordingly he did; he and Burges came together. The latter told me in consequence of what I had said to him he had been to wait upon Mr. Pitt, who was not at home: that not being able to see him he had written to him upon the subject of his offer, and shewed me a copy of the letter. After dinner we had a great deal of conversation, not only on the immediate subject of my resignation, but on the present situation of affairs in respect to foreign politics; and Mr. Ewart when left alone with me asking if I had any particular commands for him, I earnestly desired he would explain to the King of Prussia the motives which had induced me to quit my official situation; that having stated them to my own Sovereign, and having had the good fortune to find them approved of by him, I thought it a mark of respect due to his Prussian Majesty as the King's Ally, and particularly interested as he was in the whole of the proceedings in question, to have my conduct likewise explain'd to that Prince. Ewart, with tears in his eyes, assured me he should be happy in such a commission, as he was sure it contributed highly to my honour in the opinion of the King of Prussia and of all others who were made acquainted with the circumstances of my conduct. He again lamented the situation in which he thought the late change of system would involve this country, and after repeating his assurances of regard and esteem for me in the most affectionate manner we parted.

W. April 20. I went to St. James' after the Levee and had a conference with the King. I mentioned to H.M. my not being able to find any copy of the minute of Cabinet[1] which I had the honour to deliver to him on the 25th of last month, and which I was extremely sorry not to have by me; as important as its con-

---

[1] This minute of Cabinet is not to be found in the Duke of Leeds' papers.

tents were in every sense they were particularly so to me. The King told me he perfectly recollected the Paper, and obligingly added he thought he knew exactly where to find it, and would take care to send it to me. During our conversation I told H.M. I wished to receive his commands when and where I should attend him with the seals. He again expressed his concern at my intended resignation, which he assured me was sincere, and not the effect of compliment, and desired me to consult my own convenience in delivering them up, since it must be. I went from Court to the office, where I stayed but a short time, and returned home to Dinner. Being informed there was to be a Drawing Room next day I wrote to Burges, desiring the seals might be sent up to my house that evening. They were sent accordingly, accompanied by two most kind and affectionate letters from Mr. Burgess and Mr. Aust.

Th. April 21.

In the morning I walked with Dr. Jackson down to the office where I pack'd up my private papers and returned the different Keys I had belonging to the office to Mr. Burgess. I came home to dress, and between three and four went to St. James'. The Drawing Room was not over; I did not however go to it, but waited in the King's Apartment. I was in the Bedchamber when their Majesties returned. The King stopp'd and spoke to me in the most Gracious manner. The Queen I daresay guessed the business I was come upon, as when she stopped to speak to me she gently shook her head accompanying that action with a kind smile, and then addressed herself to me in the most affable manner, as did the three Princesses.

The King beeing returned into his closet I was immediately admitted to an Audience and delivered up the Seals into His Majesty's Hands.

The King said he was very sorry to receive them from me, adding a great many flattering expressions of regard and approbation. I remained in Conversation with His Majesty about twenty minutes, and then withdrew and returned home.

Fr. April 22ᵈ (Good Fryday). In the morning I received a packet from the King containing the Minute of Cabinet I had mentioned on Wednesday with permission to take a copy of it, which I did, and returned the original immediately after to His Majesty.

S. April 23ᵈ. Baron Nagel, the Dutch Minister called upon me; he spoke of my resignation with tears in his eyes, and at the same time he warmly applauded my conduct and lamented not only the disgrace the change of system would probably bring upon the Allies, but the probability of the Alliance itself materially suffering from the consequences of it. He begged I would still continue my Friendship to him which he should endeavour to deserve; he appeared much affected when he took his leave of me.

I left London, and with the Duchess and my three Sons came down to Mims.

1792.

This part of the Memoranda refers to a supposed attempt at coalition between the followers of Pitt and Fox. The main object was to oppose a more united front to the internal disturbances resulting from the French Revolution, and to intervene with more effect in case England was forced to take part in the European war. Historians have generally taken their information with regard to these matters from Lord Malmesbury's Diary; but it will be found, on close examination, that most of Lord Malmesbury's statements rest solely on the authority of Lord Loughborough, who was himself very eager for office. His trustworthiness has not been borne out by the verdict of succeeding generations.

On Thursday, July 19th, in the afternoon, I received an Express at Mims from Sir Ralph Woodford with a letter from him inclosing one to me from the Duke of Portland[1] wishing to call upon me in Grosvenor Square if in town. I returned for answer I would come up the next morning and should be happy to see his Grace either at my own house or at Burlington House or anywhere else most convenient to him.

Fryday, 20. I arrived in town before eleven. Sr R. Woodford came to me and told me no person knew of the proposed meeting but Mr. St Andrew St John, Mr. Aust, and Mr. Rolleston. The Duke of Portland came a few minutes afterwards and was shewn

---

[1] We find in Lord Malmesbury's Diary, vol. ii. p. 470, under date July 25, 1792: "At Burlington House, in the evening, Duke of Portland told me that the Duke of Leeds had through Rolleston expressed a wish to see him. On the 26th they met at the Duke of Leeds in Grosvenor Square; and after strong expressions of his sincere wish for an arrangement the Duke of Leeds offered to speak to the King at Windsor.

upstairs, where I attended him. His Grace appeared much agitated and embarrassed, and after apologizing for the trouble he had given me of coming up to Town began by observing, It was pretty well known that the subject of an Administration upon a more extensive plan had been in contemplation, and that although no direct negotiation could be said to have taken place, yet communication had been held between some members of both parties; that he owned in the present situation not only of this country but of Europe in general, he thought it highly desirable that everything that could give weight to Gov^t by uniting Talents, Character, and Property in the Executive Administration of the Country should be exerted, and that whatever former differences might have subsisted between parties, a union not upon the narrow grounds of interested support, but upon principles of real public and general advantage to the Country, should be formed. I perfectly agreed with his Grace in the advantages to be derived from such an event if practicable, that I had no scruple in confessing that I had long and sincerely wished to see the Country possessing what it was merely entitled to, the joint exertion of the abilities of Mr. Pitt and Mr. Fox. That some years ago, in private conversation upon the subject of the P. of W.^{s} personal politeness to myself at a time when H. R. H was particularly cool to most if not all the rest of the K.^{s} Servants; being asked in case of any accident happening to His Majesty, and my being sent for or officially attending the Prince, what my first advice would be, I answered it certainly would be to send for Mr. Pitt and Mr. Fox both. This I mentioned merely as a proof of what my sentiments had long been respecting so desirable an event as their acting in concert together for the public service; that however I sincerely wished the accomplishment of such an arrangement I feared it would be difficult to bring about, the Best and Greatest men were often liable to be influenced by the same passions as the most insignificant and personal considerations of self-importance and perhaps pride (almost justified by Public opinion) might make the slightest sacrifice on either side, tho' evidently for the public good and strictly honourable, very hard to be submitted to. The D. agreed with me in the remark I had made, but flattered himself with hopes that in the present situation of things Mr. Pitt and Mr. Fox would be ready to forego every consideration of the nature I had alluded to.

I told his Grace I had understood there had been several meetings between Lord Loughborough and Mr. Secretary Dundas; he said there had, that Dundas seemed eager for the arrangement, and had not only assured Lord L. of Mr. Pitt's readiness to concur in it, as far as practicable, but had referred his Lordship to Mr. Pitt himself at Wimbledon, who appeared ready to consider it as a wise and necessary measure. I asked the Duke if any hint of it, or direct intimation upon the subject, had been submitted to the King; he answered not to his knowledge, but added he thought under the present circumstances neither *St. James'* or *Buckingham House* could object to it. Upon this I could not help remarking that by this last expression his Grace seemed to suppose the existence of a separate interest between the King and Queen, the existence of which I owned I did not believe, altho' I was sorry to say some of the Royal Family either did, or affected to believe, and of course induced others to believe, such different interest actually did exist. I then wished to know if any other of the K.'s Ministers except Mr. Pitt had been sounded on the subject, or had given any opinion with respect to it. His Grace told me the Duke of Richmond had gone from the Sussex meeting to Sheffield Place on an invitation from Lord Sheffield; that Mr. Pelham was there, and the subject had been much discussed. That the Duke thought it a measure highly adviseable. I observed the Duke of Richmond would scarcely have expressed himself so favourably to it had he not thought Mr. Pitt himself disposed to it. The Duke assured me that he was informed Mr. Pitt *himself* had no objection to act with Mr. Fox in the most cordial manner; that some of his friends he believed, however, might object to that gentleman's coming into office from personal dislike. The Duke could not, he told me, on my asking him guess who the persons alluded to were; he had not learnt that they were any of the Ministers. I said Mr. Pitt I knew had several people called his Friends, whom he listened to more than perhaps he ought to do, and that like many other great men, not excepting Mr. Fox himself, I thought he had more than once got into a scrape by following the advice of those whom he supposed were in truth what they professed to be—his friends. I told the Duke there was *one* person, a friend of Mr. Pitt's, of whom I had the highest opinion, with whom I had no claim to boast of intimacy, but of a character that demanded, and had indeed met with universal respect in his public situation, and I believed was entitled to unlimited confidence in his private capacity, I meant Mr. Addington, the Speaker. That in conversing upon General Politics he had always expressed himself in the most candid manner towards Mr. Fox, and with the most liberal sentiments upon any subject of a public nature where any predilection for a particular man or set of men could be supposed to have operated ; that I mentioned that not only in justice to the Speaker, but to prove to his Grace my opinion that Mr. Addington was not in the number of those *Friends* of Mr. Pitt, to whom I understood Mr. Pitt to have referred. The Duke did not understand Lord Grenville to have been at all alluded to, and of course no one of the Cabinet seems to have been comprehended in the description of those who might object to act with Mr. Fox.

The Duke stated a circumstance of difficulty in the arrangement supposing the plan to be adopted, which was Mr. Pitt remaining at the Head of the Treasury, which of course would give him in point of Etiquette a nominal superiority over Mr. Fox in the House; his Grace added he did not believe Mr. Pitt would make any difficulty upon this point, as the Idea was that He and Mr. Fox should be the two Secretarys of State, and therefore some person of character and unexceptionable to the country at large and in whom both parties at their outset (meaning hereafter to form one mass) could have confidence should be appointed First Lord of the Treasury, by which neither of those gentlemen could officially claim a superiority in the Cabinet. To this I made no particular answer, having heard from Sir R. W^d that the Friends of the D. of P. had thought of me for that situation. I said the whole matter was deserving of the most serious attention; that I wished to hear of a direct communication between Mr. Pitt and Mr. Fox upon the subject, and above all things that the King's sentiments might be known respecting it; that having had no private communication (since my resigning the Seals) with either His Majesty or His Ministers I could only judge of things from appearances; that to me it appeared the Dismission of the Chancellor was rather a measure of necessity than of choice on the part of the King; that had I been consulted by the Ministers I should have advised the measure now in contemplation. Ld Thurlow, whatever faults he may have, must make a pretty considerable blank in the Cabinet, and the Gov^t at all times, particularly in the present, ought to be efficient. Such were my sentiments. I perfectly agreed with his Grace in wishing for the arrangement he mentioned, and if I could be of any use in forwarding the communications necessary for that purpose, I mean with the King himself or Mr. Pitt, should my interference be thought expedient in that quarter, I was perfectly ready to be employed for that purpose, and, to use his own words, hold the scales between the two parties with a view to do an essential service to both King and Country by contributing to bring them in every sense of the word to a good understanding.

Wednesday, July 25th.

Sir R^h Woodford came to Mims while I was dressing, and sent me a sealed Paper, by way of Memorandum; the contents informed me the Duke of P. had communicated to Mr. Fox the substance of the conversation which had passed between us; that Mr. F. *had stated his sentiments to Mr. Rolleston for my information, the essential points of which seemed to turn upon the necessity of my communicating the same to the King.*

That in order to remove any delicacy on my part as to taking such a step without having it in my power to state to His Majesty that I did so at the desire of the Duke of Portland, Mr. Rolleston felt no difficulty in engaging to bring a note from the Duke of Portland if necessary, that in case I saw the propriety of making the wished-for communication to the King, Mr. R. was ready to set out for Cheltenham in order to bring me the note from the Duke of Portland already alluded to, and that he (Mr. R.) would meet me at any place which might be most convenient and agreeable to me.

After a long conversation with Sir Ralph he left Mims, and carried a message from me to Mr. Rolleston saying I should be very happy to see him at Mims on the Fryday following.

Fryday, July 27th.[1]

Mr. Rolleston came to Mims; he confirmed every part of the memorandum delivered to me by Sir Ralph Woodford, adding the Duke of Portland and Mr. Fox had expressed their wishes that I should be acquainted with the arrangement in contemplation as I could be trusted by both Parties, and might be of service by communicating directly with the King. Mr. R. told me an offer of one of the vacant blue Ribbands had been made to the Duke of Portland by His Majesty's command. That Mr. Fox was both ready and willing to enter into the most fair and ample explanations of any part of his conduct which he supposed to have given offence at St. James's, and that the principal difficulty seemed to be Mr. Pitt's remaining at the head of the Treasury rather than being Secretary of State with Mr. Fox: in mentioning the propriety of my having a letter from the Duke of Portland to authorise me to communicate the substance of what had passed between us to the King, Mr. R. thought it extremely proper such a letter should be written, though perhaps it might be liable to some objection as appearing to proceed from an eager desire of the Duke of Portland to precipitate the arrangement. I said I thought his remark was just, and that a method occurred to me which I thought would answer our purpose

[1] Lord Malmesbury's entry under this date is, "The Duke of Portland, although he placed no great faith in the intervention of the Duke of Leeds, in consequence of Fox's promoting it, acquiesced in the Duke of Leeds seeing the King."

and was unexceptionable, which was my writing to the Duke of Portland and informing his Grace that I should be in the neighbourhood of Windsor for some days about the time of the Prince's birthday, and therefore wished to know if I might be permitted by his Grace to communicate our conversation to the King. Mr. Rolleston charged himself with this letter, and return'd to London in the evening.

Lord Malmesbury came to Mims before dinner, and stayed with us till Sunday morning. We had several conversations upon the subject of the proposed arrangement: he confirm'd to me what Mr. Rolleston had mentioned concerning the offer of the Garter to the Duke of Portland, which the Duke himself had informed him of (after he had with the utmost gratitude and respect begg'd leave to decline it in the present moment for obvious reasons). Lord M. told me the most respectable people in the country wished most heartily for the success of the arrangement in question. The Duke of Devonshire, Lord Carlisle, Lord Fitzwilliam, Lord Egremont, thought it a measure likely to be of the utmost advantage to the Public, that the Duke of Bedford was the only person of consequence he knew of who seemed to object to it, that at first he had approved, but had since alter'd his mind. Lord M. thought perhaps Lady Melbourne might have influenced him, that Mrs. Bouverie was much against any arrangement with Mr. Pitt, and would probably use her weight with Mr. Fox, tho' he trusted ineffectually, to throw every possible difficulty in the way of this arrangement. Ld M. added the Duke of York was friendly to the measure. That the Prince of Wales had not been nor was it meant he should be consulted on the subject any more than Sheridan, who probably would endeavour to prevent its success; that the Duke of Portland had received the strongest assurances of approbation of the measure and support of it when completed from Sir George Cornwall, Mr. Mundy, and several other gentlemen of weight and influence in the House of Commons and in the country. That with regard to the difficulty of Pitt no longer remaining First Lord of the Treasury, neither Lord Carlisle nor Lord Loughborough thought it a point necessary to insist upon. That Fox thought the *Pride of the Party* must be humoured so far as to avoid the appearance of Pitt being at the Head of the proposed Administration, which would be the case should he retain that office.

Ld M. told me Ld Lauderdale was heartily sick of the Association he had joined with, but did not know how to get rid of it. I found neither Lord Thurlow nor Ld Rawdon were thought of as either proper to be consulted or employed. The Marquisate of Rockingham had been offered to Ld Fitzwilliam probably at the same time with the Garter to the Duke of Portland. Lord Auckland I was very happy to learn was no longer in confidence with Ld Loughborough. I gave Ld Malmesbury a Paper of Minutes to be communicated to Mr. Fox, in which I stated the substance of the conversation I had had with the Duke of Portland, to be communicated to the King, and wishing to know if it was thought advisable I should have any direct communication with Mr. Pitt on the subject, and how far I was at liberty to make use either of his or the Duke of Portland's name in any conversation I might have on the subject with Mr. Dundas. Ld M. left Mims[1] after Breakfast on Sunday Morning the 29th, and told me he would go to Mr. Fox at St. Anne's Hill the next day, and that I should hear from him in a day or two.

Monday, July 30th.

About nine in the evening I received an express from Mr. Rolleston with a letter from the D. of Portland at Cheltenham (in answer to mine of the 27th). The Duke expresses himself highly sensible of my delicacy in wishing to be directly authorised by him to state to the King the substance of what had passed between us on the 20th, a communication which he thinks very desirable, and

---

[1] Lord Malmesbury's account gives a very different impression of the interview (*Diaries*, vol. ii. p. 471). He concludes that "the Duke of Leeds was in earnest, but, as he always is, carried away more by his imagination and sanguine hopes, in which his string of toad-eaters encourage him, than by reason and reflection."

again states his general ideas of the subject with great good sense, and in the most respectful manner towards the King.

Fryday, August 3ᵈ.

I received a letter[1] from Lord Malmesbury in which he acquaints me that *Mr. Fox had great satisfaction from my idea of seeing the King, as he considered the success of the whole to depend on His Majesty's having an arrangement in his wishes; that he had no objection to my speaking fully and without reserve to Messrs. Pitt and Dundas, but thought it unadviseable for me to communicate with either of them till after I had seen the King.*

That Mr. Fox repeatedly dwelt on the indispensable necessity of an alteration in the Treasury, and that without that was admitted nothing could be done.

*L*ᵈ *M. expresses his fear that this will be an unsurmountable obstacle, altho' if an arrangement takes place with everybody belonging to it in the same mind and acting on the same principle, he still thinks it might be got over.*

Saturday, August 4ᵗʰ. Sir R. Woodford came to Mims. He told me that he understood from Mr. Rolleston that Mr. Fox had some doubts whether it might not be adviseable to have the business in question mentioned to Mr. Pitt even previous to its being communicated to the King. Mr. Aust mentioned the same thing when he came to Mims the Monday following. I told them both that till I heard directly from Mr. Fox upon the subject I should think myself in a manner bound to communicate first with the King, as agreed upon already.

Sunday, August 12ᵗʰ.

On my arrival at Ditton I found a letter from Mr. Rolleston informing me that the *Person* * who had written to me from the

---

* Duke of Portland.

[1] This is printed in the *Malmesbury Correspondence*, p. 473, and may with advantage be compared with the entry in the Diary of July 30, in p. 472. Evidently Fox was not sanguine about any arrangement being possible.

country was in Town and intended to remain there or in the neighbourhood of London till the latter end of the next week.

In the evening we went to the Terrace [1] at Windsor Castle; it was extremely crowded. The King was standing in a circle talking to Mr. Pitt and Mr. Dundas, the former appearing uncommonly grave. He afterwards however resumed his usual cheerfulness and talked and laughed with the Duchess and me in the old style. The King very gracious to us.

Monday, August 13th.

The Duchess, Miss Anguish, and myself accompanied Lord Beaulieu to Windsor; the ladies went to Mrs. Henly* and we to leave our compliments at the Prince of Wales' apartments. The Duke and Duchess of York arrived from Oatlands just as we were at the entrance of the Great Court, and the Duke on alighting from his curricle came and talked to us for some time with great affability and good humour. In the evening we went to the Queen's Ball. During the circle the Duke of Richmond expressed to me his concern at the present situation of Poland, and I thought meant to have entered into some interesting conversation; he was however interrupted I think by some of the Royal Family and did not resume it during the course of the evening.

When the Royal Family and the company removed to the Ball Room the Duke of York drew me into one of the windows of the Great Council Chamber, and having talked some time on the affairs of France and the movements of the Armies, his Royal Highness being (as I had understood from Lord Malmesbury) informed of the proposed arrangement I, by degrees, got upon the subject of the present situation of Europe in general. I found H. R. H. agreed with me in regard to the Russian business of last year, and thought we had now no connection with any power on the continent; I told him I was almost ashamed whenever I had the good fortune to

---

[1] The King and Royal Family always walked upon the Terrace on Sunday.

meet the Duchess, at thinking how little the King her father[1] could trust to any assurances from this present Government after what had passed last year. He smiled and seemed to admit the justice of my observation. I then stated the reports I had heard of some proposed arrangement for the purpose of obtaining a stronger and more efficient administration. He expressed his approbation of such a plan if practicable. I asked if there was any ground to suppose the King had been sounded on the subject or was likely to object to it. He answered he did not know, but suspected there must be something of the sort in his contemplation from certain things which had fallen in conversation from Lord Chesterfield, who was so much with his Majesty, and who would scarce drop a hint of anything of a public nature without speaking in compliance with the King's ideas on the subject. H.R.H. added that he had been surprized at the Duke of Richmond (between whom and himself there was so little communication) having talked to him about Poland, and expressed the necessity of this country's interference in its affairs. That H.R.H. had answered he had no doubt that his Grace would give his opinion upon the subject in the proper place. He stated how eligible he thought it would be to have a new arrangement which would unite abilities and property. That the country must ever look up to those whose situation gave them an additional interest in its welfare and whose possessions of course added weight to their situation. That Mr. Pitt must ever be considered as a great Trump in the hands of any administration; that he thought the principal persons in opposition had behaved most honourably and wished they could be brought to act together, that this he told me in confidence was his opinion. I assured H.R.H. I perfectly agreed with him, and told him in confidence I wished much to have the honour of a private conference with His Majesty, wishing to know from His Royal Highness the proper method of

[1] The Duchess of York was the daughter of the King of Prussia. The Duke refers to the English desertion of Prussia on the question of the Russian armament.

procuring that honour. The Duke told me he was sure the King would be very glad to see me and that I need only express a wish upon the subject this evening and His Majesty would appoint a time for me to wait upon him.

The Duke went to the Ball Room. In going thither I met Mr. A. St. Leger, who told me he had a letter for me from Ld Malmesbury, and wished to have an answer by eleven the next morning if convenient to me. I put the letter in my pocket and afterwards took an opportunity of looking at it when I thought I was unperceived, having seen many of the attendants peeping round the doors during my conference with the Duke of York. The letter was merely expressive of his wish to be informed of the result of my conference at Windsor.

In the course of the evening I met Ld Chesterfield. We had some conversation, tho' for a few minutes only. He expressed himself as sorry for the Cinque Ports being given to Pitt and not to the Duke of Dorset, that office being his object. Upon laughing with him for having called me a Brother the preceding evening on the Terrace (meaning a Brother Director of the Concert of Antient Music) I put my hand to my Riband and said I hoped we should soon be Brothers in another capacity. He answered that it would be telling a direct lye to say he should not be glad to have the Garter, but that he had no pretensions to it, and did not mean to ask for it. He inquired if I had heard anything of a coalition of Parties, for such a thing was talked of. I answered I had seen something of the sort mentioned in the Papers. He said no more on the subject. I observed the Duke of Richmond and Mr. Pitt were in close conversation for a considerable time in a corner of the Cartoon Room when the King's card party broke up. H.M. stopped in one of the rooms to speak to me, and I took the opportunity of mentioning a wish to trouble him for a few minutes the next day at any time most convenient to H.M. He said any time I pleased in the afternoon, as it would he thought be more convenient to us both than the morning.

Tuesday, August 14.

In the afternoon we went to the Terrace. The King, the Duke of York, and all the Princesses, except the Princess Royal, were there, and but little company besides. The Royal Party extremely gracious. The Duke of York talked a considerable time to Ld Beaulieu[1] and myself. His Majesty took me afterwards aside, and I had the honour to walk with him the whole time he remained on the Terrace. Our conversation was general, as I did not think the Terrace by any means a proper place for what I wished to communicate. Upon the K. withdrawing I mentioned my wish for a few moments' conference. H.M. ordered me to come with him, and carried me through the Castle to his Library in the Queen's Lodge, where, I believe, we remained in conversation half an-hour.

I mentioned to His Majesty the interview I had had with the Duke of Portland at His Grace's desire on the 20th of last month, and stated the general substance of the conversation that had passed between us. I told the King I thought it expedient to have something more than verbal authority from the Duke to make the communication to His Majesty, for which purpose I had written to the Duke. I then shewed the K. my letter and the Duke's answer to it from Cheltenham. The answer was so proper in every point of view and so respectful to the King that I flattered myself it might create a favourable impression on his mind towards the Duke of Portland.

I told His Majesty that tho' I had not seen Mr. Fox I was fully authorized to declare his concurrence in every thing the Duke of Portland had stated to me. I likewise mentioned the queries I had sent to Mr. Fox by Lord Malmesbury, with Mr. F.'s opinion that it would be improper to communicate the business to Mr. Pitt or Mr. Dundas until His Majesty himself had been acquainted with it. This I endeavoured to turn to Mr. Fox's advantage as a mark of proper respect towards His Majesty. Whether it had any effect I

[1] Edward Hussey, created Lord Beaulieu, 1762; Earl Beaulieu, 1784; died 1802, when his honours became extinct.

am ignorant, for H.M. did not, I believe, mention Mr. Fox's name more than once if even that during the whole conversation!

I mentioned the several interviews which had passed between Ld Loughborough and Mr. Dundas, at one at least of which Mr. Pitt had been present (and which had been mentioned in the newspapers), as affording sufficient reason to suppose His Majesty's Servants not indisposed to an arrangement, and that I took for granted His Majesty was informed of everything that had passed down to the present time. To my great surprize the K. answered that he had not heard anything upon the subject for a long time. That Mr. Pitt had indeed some months ago mentioned something like an opening on the part of the Duke of Portland and his friends, to which H.M had answered, *Anything Complimentary to them, but no Power!!!* (The first part of this brief but pretty copious answer explains the circumstance of the offer of the Garter to the Duke of Portland, and of the Marquisate of Rockingham to Lord Fitzwilliam, and the latter proves but too clearly the great difficulty, if not impossibility, of succeeding in the proposed arrangement.)

His Majesty informed me he had been talked to on the subject of the Duke of Portland by Lord Bute (probably in the audience he had to deliver up his Father's Ribband), who is connected with his Grace and who was full of expressions of the Duke's good intentions and dutiful attachment to His Majesty. The King very truly observed that it frequently happened that people from eagerly wishing an object to succeed deceived themselves by thinking it much nearer its accomplishment than in truth it was. That in the year 1780 during the Riots the Administration had made some approaches towards Lord Rockingham and the Duke of Portland which seemed calculated to effectuate a union of parties. That this was done not only without any authority from H.M. but even without his knowledge, nor was he informed of it till a long time afterwards.

With regard to the change in the Treasury mentioned in the Duke of Portland's Letter, H.M. thought it impossible either Mr.

Pitt or his Friends could consent to it. I observed that some of the Duke of Portland's Friends, viz. Ld Carlisle and Ld Loughborough, did not think it necessary, and that I believed it was not meant by any that Mr. Pitt should not still remain Minister of the Finances, that this might be managed by his continuing Chancellor of the Exchequer altho' appointed Secretary of State. The King asked me who was proposed to be First Lord of the Treasury. I answered that I could not tell, but that it was meant that some one should be in that situation who was upon terms of Friendship and Confidence with both. Parties. H.M. replied it would be very awkward for Mr. Pitt after having been so long at the head of that Board to descend to an inferior situation at it, and that whoever was the First Lord must either be a Cypher or Mr. Pitt appear as a *commis*.

I observed there certainly must be some difficulty in any arrangement of the sort. That both Mr. Pitt and Mr. Fox had People they called Friends who frequently had led them into scrapes, and who upon this, as upon other occasions, might be troublesome. That sometimes the most important objects were sacrificed to mere circumstances of Etiquette or mistaken notions of honour. That whatever could contribute to strengthen His Majesty's Government, and distinctly prove who were really attached to the constitution and to His Person and Government, must be most desirable.

In the course of the conversation the K. told me that Ld Loughborough[1] had expressed his happiness at the Great Seal not having been offered him, as he could not quit his Friends. (Qu. If Ld Guilford's death[2] will make any alteration in his sentiments?)

His Majesty did me the Honour to say He should always consider himself as obliged to me for the communication I had made to him, and immediately returned to the Queen and Royal Family at the Castle.

[1] Lord Loughborough, as a matter of fact, became Lord Chancellor a few months later.

[2] This had taken place, August 5, 1792, nine days previously. Lord Guilford was better known as Lord North; he was an intimate friend and a connection of Lord Loughborough.

I ought to have mentioned the King having said he could only thank the *Duke of Portland for his good intentions,*—as likewise H.M.ˢ supposing L.ᵈ Grenville would probably object to anything like the arrangement in question. To which I answered I thought it most likely he would, as I thought with all his merit and abilities he was a very ambitious man, and one whom Mr. Pitt ought to be very *attentive* to.

Remarks.

It appears to me that altho' no expression directly pointed at Mr. Fox dropped from the King during this conference, that His Majesty's dislike to that gentleman remains in full force, and is perhaps the sole ground of objection to anything like a union of Parties. His Majesty certainly did not commit himself so far as to say he never would hear of an arrangement like that in question, but the answer formerly given to Mr. Pitt and the thanks now expressed to the Duke of Portland for his *Good Intentions* do not afford much expectation of His Majesty (to use Mr. Fox's words) *having an arrangement in his wishes.*

It would be very desirable to ascertain how far Mr. Pitt is really disposed towards the arrangement, either as a measure of expediency or necessity; and in case he sincerely wishes it to succeed, to what degree he might be able, or judge it adviseable, to induce the King to think more favourably of the measure, should His Majesty continue in his former sentiments, considering the recent mark of His Majestys Goodness to him in giving him unasked the Cinque Ports.

Wednesday, August 15. I returned across the country to Mims, where I found Sir Ralph Woodford, who stayed till the next morning. I sent by him a letter to the Duke of Portland, informing His Grace of my interview with the King. *That I wished I could make a more favourable report of the Conference. That I was however certain it had done no harm, and if any good should arise* from it it would be the result of reflection on what had passed during a tête-a-tête, which had been conducted with great good humour and attention. I proposed seeing the Duke on the following Sunday, if convenient to him.

Saturday, August 18.

Lord Malmesbury came to Mims; I told him the general substance of what had passed at Windsor ; he thought with me no harm could arise from the communication, particularly after the manner in which the King had received it; he informed me that on the King's return to the Castle after our conference he had addressed the Duke of York and told him he had *seen me* in private; that he found, like a man of business, I was determined not to open what I had to say during our remaining on the Terrace. The Duke observed he thought the King seemed desirous of drawing from him whether he was apprized or not of the subject of my conference. That H.R.H. however took no notice of such conference having taken place, but observed the King appeared more pleased than otherwise with what had passed. Ld M. told me Ld Loughborough and Mr. Dundas had had a meeting the day before (Fryday); he did not know the result of it as yet. He brought me a letter from the D. of Portland, and one from Sir R. Woodford. The Duke being engaged at Bulstrode on Sunday, offered to come to Mims or meet me in Town on Monday ; I desired Ld M. who was going to Bulstrode to settle our meeting on Monday at his Lp^s House in Spring Gardens. Sr Ralph in his letter mentioned Mr. Aust[1] having told him there was a rumour among the Foreign Ministers of some change being in contemplation in which I was to be employed, and therefore suggesting (from Mr. A.) the expediency of communicating to Mr. Pitt without delay the business in question.

Monday, Aug 20.—I went to town and met the D. of Portland at half-past one at Ld Malmesbury's; we went over a great deal of

[1] Mr. Aust was Under-Secretary in the Foreign Office, and one of his Grace's "toad-eaters."

what passed in our former conversation; I informed him of course of the general substance of my conversation with the King. He mentioned the circumstance of the K.'s telling the Duke of York I had been with him as above stated. In addition to many other reasons for strengthening the Government, the Duke dwelt much on the situation of Ireland, and the proceedings of the Catholics in that Kingdom, who are convening meetings in different parts for the purpose of appointing Delegates to form a Committee at Dublin.

The D. asked me if I thought the K. read the newspapers. I told him I thought very likely he did, as there were many both at Windsor and St. James's. He said he had heard from very good authority that H.M. had been very anxious to see my speech on the Russian business last Session, and was desirous to have the paper where it was most accurately taken.

We agreed the sooner I could talk over the matter in question with Mr. Pitt the better. I had seen him come to town thro' the park just before I came to Ld M.; as it rained I sent for a Hackney Coach and drove to his house; he was gone to Ld Grenville's. I returned to Ld M. directly. The Duke of Portland went to the Duke of York, as did Ld M. after walking with me. He was anxious to meet Ld Loughborough (at Sir Ralph Payne's, where they were to dine) to know what had passed between his Lordship and Mr. Dundas in their interview of Fryday, the latter having been with the King subsequent to my interview with His Majesty at Windsor on Tuesday last. That he wished me to point out a safe method by which he could convey to me such information as he might be able to collect on the subject. I told him if he would send a letter to me by Rolleston it would come safe; it was agreed I should desire Mr. R. to come to him the next morning at ten. He went to York House and came to me afterwards in Gro^s Square; he said the Duke of York had mentioned to him his having frequently seen the King since my interview, and that His Majesty had appeared uncommonly cheerful and pleased, and that H.R.H.

augured very favourably of the impression my conversation had left upon the King's mind. I wrote to Mr. Pitt stating a wish to wait upon him; I had a very curt note from him, and the next morning received a second at Mims by a messenger, and we settled I should come to him on the next day (Wednesday) between twelve and one.

I dined at Sir R. Woodford's; Mess. Aust and Rolleston were there; Mr. R. told me Mr. Fox had heard from the Duke of York of my conference with the King, and H.R.H." hopes that it had by no means been disagreeable. Mr. R. clearly of opinion that the whole principally if not entirely now depends on Mr. Pitt being sincere in wishing to promote anything like a fair union of Parties, for the public advantage. I was surprized to hear from Ld Malmesbury in the course of to-day that tho' he could not say how the case stood at present, it was certain that some time ago Lord Grenville himself had wished for an union of Parties, and had expressed himself to be so to his brother, Mr. Thomas Grenville.

In the evening I returned to Mims.

Tuesday, Augt 21.

About two o'clock I received by express a letter from Mr. Rolleston (enclosing one from Lord Malmesbury), in which Mr. R. mentions Ld M. *being in high spirits at the last report made to him by Lord Loughborough,** *that he himself was going at Ld M.'s desire to St. Ann's Hill to make it a point with Mr. Fox to be in town tomorrow, that on his return to night he was to call at Burlington House, or should otherwise have delivered to me the enclosed in Person.*

Ld M. in his letter states *Ld Loughborough to have been perfectly satisfied with what passed between the King and me, and thought*

---

* Probably alluding to an idea Mr. R. had entertained that Lord L. had thought the negotiation taken out of his hands by my being sent to the King. Ld Malmesbury on my asking yesterday did not think Ld L. had taken it at all amiss.

nothing but good could come from it. That he could not collect from his Lp. that when he saw Pitt and Dundas together last Friday that from anything they said they had taken any alarm from my conference; that they indeed expressed a wish that I had spoken to one or both of them about it, and an expectation that I still would. He then observed how proper my visit and subsequent note to Mr. Pitt yesterday were, and adds that the whole business is in as good a train as possible, concludes that, hoping to see me to-morrow, it was unnecessary to go into further detail in this letter of what L.ᵈ Loughborough had said.

I wrote him word I was to be in Downing St. to-morrow between twelve and one, and would call in Spring Gardens about two.

Wednesday, August 22.

I went to Town, and, according to appointment, waited upon Mr. Pitt between twelve and one. He received me very civilly, but I thought did not appear quite at his ease. I told him I wished to communicate to him the substance of the conversation I had had with the Duke of Portland the 20ᵗʰ of July, which I should have done much sooner but for circumstances which I would now mention to him. Having stated the Duke's sentiments, I told him I had been authorized, both verbally and by letter from His Grace, to communicate them directly to the King. That Mr. Fox had sent me word he fully concurred in what the Duke of Portland had expressed to me in our conference. I told Mr. Pitt of the Queries I had sent to Mr. Fox by Lord Malmesbury, and that in consequence of Mr. F.'s answer it appeared to me totally impossible to communicate the subject consistently either with good faith or delicacy to any person, till I had made it known (agreeably to my instructions) directly to the King.

Mr. Pitt listened attentively to all I said, and answered that *there had been no thoughts of any alteration in the Government, that circumstances did not call for it, nor did the people wish it, and that no new arrangement, either by a change or coalition, had ever been in contemplation!!!*

I told him I understood there had been several interviews between Mr. Dundas and Lord Loughborough, at some of which it was reported he himself had been present; he said it was true, but that such meetings had not in view any change of Administration.

I observed the object of the Duke of Portland was not so much a change of Administration as an accession of strength to the Government in general; that to me it seemed an event highly advantageous to the country, tho' the arrangement might be attended with many difficulties; that perhaps the name of Mr. Fox might not at first be very agreeable to the Royal Ear. He answered *if anything could be devised to make an union with Mr. Fox more difficult than it had been for many years it was precisely the conduct he had held towards the close of the last session.*

I told him I disapproved that conduct of Mr. Fox as much as he could do, and expressed my surprize at Mr. Fox' condescending to act so trimming a part, which must prejudice his character even among his own Friends, and merely for the purpose of not offending a few rash hot-headed persons belonging to his party.

Mr. Pitt told me the King had mentioned to him the conversation I had had with His Majesty at Windsor the following day at St. James'. He stated accurately the civil expression His Majesty had made use of with respect to the Duke of Portland. I likewise quoted the strong answer the King told me had given to him, Mr. Pitt, on a former occasion; he said I stated it correctly, he remembered it well. Qu: How is this consistent with no change having ever been in contemplation? ! ! ! !

He turned the conversation for some time to the affairs of France. I brought him back, however, to the subject of our conference, by stating that the Duke of Portland knew I was to see him, and indeed had wished me to do so on Monday last; he again reverted generally to my conference with the King, and owned he could have wished a business in which he himself was so materially and immediately concerned had been mentioned to him first, altho' he was convinced the mode in which it had been conducted was founded in motives of the purest and most honourable delicacy.

I again repeated the grounds on which I had proceeded, which I still thought the only one on which I could have acted with propriety, that the commission I had been charged with was by no means of my own seeking: he asked me if the Duke of P.'s note desiring to call upon me was the first intimation I had received upon the subject. I told him it was the first direct communication of it, having before only heard some vague rumours of anything of the sort, being in contemplation. He said reports of that sort were generally exaggerated, if not totally without foundation; that the least cessation of hostilities between contending parties, or anything like common attentions passing between them, frequently gave rise to reports of coalitions and arrrangements which were never thought of.

I stated to him my opinion that in a business of so much importance and delicacy I could wish Principals to meet, adding that tho' I did not consider myself as directly authorized to mention anything of the sort, I could not avoid asking him (for my own satisfaction) whether he would have any objection to see the Duke of Portland. He answered he could certainly have no objection to see His Grace, but he thought it could answer no purpose whatever, as he had in truth nothing to say upon anything approaching to the idea of an alteration of the present Government.

I took my leave and withdrew.

I went to Lord Malmesbury's and communicated to him the general substance of Mr. Pitt's conversation. We agreed it would be right to soften it to the Duke of Portland and particularly to Mr. Fox, for as he had all along doubted Mr. Pitts being sincerely disposed towards the arrangement in question, what had now passed would be a matter of triumph to his discernment, and he might perhaps not have discretion enough to be silent, and the whole getting wind might be productive of many bad consequences.

I told Lord Malmesbury I thought it would be right to observe whether all communication between Dundas and Lord Loughborough would now be at end. That it seemed strange Lord L. should have expressed himself so sanguine in his hopes of things being *en train*, the day only before my conference with Mr. Pitt, unless it could be supposed that Mr. Pitt chose to put an end to my being any more employed in the negotiation, either out of resentment for the former, or apprehension of any future direct communication from me to His Majesty, and at the same time wished Dundas still to continue his conferences with Ld Loughborough. In that case Mr. Pitt's language to me was throughout contrary to truth, or else the conferences were for some separate purpose, in which case Ld L. would appear to have misled his Friends by encouraging the idea of the arrangement itself being in any degree likely to succeed.

I added there must have been some strange *mistake*[1] somewhere which perhaps time would clear up.

Upon the whole Lord Malmesbury thought it of use to know Mr. Pitt's sentiments were so decidedly hostile to the arrangement in question, as by trusting to the contrary opinion however *well* or *ill* founded we were only deceiving ourselves and every other person who were sincere in their endeavours to promote the success of a measure which seemed to promise the greatest advantage to the country.

ADDITIONAL NOTES AND OBSERVATIONS.

The language of Ld Chesterfield referred to by the Duke of York I understood from the Duke of Portland afterwards at Ld Malmesbury's to have passed during the encampment. That his

[1] The mistake appears to have been that Lord Malmesbury and others put too much confidence in Lord Loughborough's reports of interviews at which he was present with one or two others. Lord Loughborough was probably extremely desirous of office for himself, and objected to no steps which were likely to secure that end.

Lordship observed to the Duke of Richmond (in His Grace's Tent) how necessary some arrangement was with a view to render Gov' efficient, as every body knew there was nobody in the Cabinet who had any power but Mr. Pitt and L' Grenville; that Mr. Dundas was only Secretary of State *pro tempore* till some other person could be fixed upon for the office. N.B. The Duke of Richmond being himself in the Cabinet, the remark appears more likely to have proceeded from *sincerity* than *politeness*.

By comparing my conference with the Duke of Portland on the 20th of July with my conference with Mr. Pitt on the 22d of August following it is clear that either the Duke's *Information*, or Mr. Pitt's *Memory*, must have been uncommonly defective. Perhaps Ld Loughborough and Mr. Dundas could fix one's judgment upon this material point.

It is not a little remarkable that as late as Monday, the 20th August, Lord Loughborough should have given such information as had induced Ld Malmesbury not only to declare his opinion that *the whole business was in as good a train as possible*, which he does in his letter to me of the 21, but to make a point with Mr. Fox that he should be in town the next day, the 22^d, on which identical day I had the memorable conference with Mr. Pitt. N.B. Lord Loughborough had seen Mr. Pitt and Mr. Dundas together on the preceding Fryday, August the 17th.

This again requires explanation. It is scarcely probable Lord Loughborough's report should have been directly contrary to what had really passed at his interview with the two Ministers, or that had any new and hitherto unforeseen difficulty occurred, so as to suspend any further meeting, or put an end to the discussion of the subject in future, his Lp. might possibly from common attention have been informed of it from Mr. Dundas at least, if not from Mr. Pitt, in the course of four days which elapsed between his interview on the 17th and mine on the 22^d, and this probably must have been known, as he dined at Burlington House on Tuesday the 21st. This I own appears to me as affording sufficient ground for my observation to Ld Malmesbury respecting Mr. Pitts wishing me to be excluded from any concern in the negotiation.

Wednesday, August 29. The Duchess, Miss Anguish, my two eldest sons, and myself, went by appointment to Hatfield to meet their Royal Highnesses the Duke and Duchess of York; as soon as the Duke returned home before dinner he honoured me with a conversation which lasted a considerable time, in which he expressed himself in the most flattering manner on the subject of my conference with the King, adding he was sure His Majesty himself was pleased with it. H.R.H. seemed convinced of the necessity of a strong Government; that at present a weak Administration and a weak Opposition must furnish occasion for the Factions to promote their schemes, and perhaps become formidable. He thought great attention ought to be paid to the numbers of French daily coming into England; that although many of them were in the strictest sense of the word objects of compassion, several might conceal the most mischievous designs under the pretence of being driven from their country by the intestine commotions of France. H.R.H. told me that one day during the encampment Ld Chesterfield remarked that he hoped the present Ministers might be entitled to places in Heaven as he was sure their Kingdom was not of this world, adding we cannot go on well unless we have some acres added to our abilities, and that an accession of Property to the Gov^t was absolutely necessary.

In the evening the Duke tooke me into the Gallery, where we had a very long conversation, both on the subject of the present situation of the country, and of many past events, particularly respecting the King's illness, and the transactions which occurred at that time with regard to the formation of a Regency. The D. said his opinion always has been, and ever would be, that the Executive power ought to have been vested in the Regent pure and entire, and told me he was convinced that had the Regency taken place the K. himself was determined (and has declared so much long since his Recovery) never to have resumed the Government. I mentioned to H.R.H. the cruel reports which had been circulated with so much injustice respecting the Queen's eagerness to have the care of the K.'s person, and in fact to interfere in Gov^t, which I knew to be false, as it was with very great difficulty she could be prevailed on to take any part in the melancholy business entrusted to her. I likewise lamented Mr. Fox having been absent at the beginning of the K.'s illness, as much worse advice had been given in a *certain quarter* than that Gentleman would have given. The D. perfectly agreed with me, and expressed his bad opinion and confirmed detestation of Sheridan in the strongest terms.

H.R.H. told me he was going to Weymouth for a week, and that perhaps something might fall from the K. upon the subject of the proposed arrangement, that he perfectly agreed with me to let things remain quiet for the present, that the foundation was laid for the K. to form a deliberate opinion upon the subject, and that he thought the public very materially obliged to me for the communication I had made to the K. by which the whole was now upon fair and honourable grounds.

In speaking of the establishment of a strong and effective Government the Duke mentioned two points to which he thought Ministers ought in the strictest manner to engage themselves and on no consideration depart from, viz. the Resisting any Parliamentary Reform and the Repeal of the Test Act, whether partial or total, that at all times (particularly in the present) it was dangerous to make any alteration (however apparently trivial) in the Constitution, and no one could answer for the consequences of either of those measures should they unfortunately be submitted to.

1792.

[These Memoranda refer to negotiations which were taking place between Pitt, Grenville, and the Whigs for a coalition in view of the dangers of the French Revolution. Windham notes in his diary, under Nov. 12, 1792: "My day too has been for the greater part spent in promoting the measures necessary at this time to be pursued. Conversations at Burlington House (the Duke of Portland's) with Fox. Grenville, and the Duke of Devonshire." Also under date November 25: "Called in the morning in consequence of a note from Lord Loughborough. Adair had called before, and walked with me the greater portion of the way. Heard the result of his communication with P[itt], being a refusal of the seals, his letter very good. It was the day before that I had been with Mr. Pitt." Lord Grenville writes to the Marquis of Buckingham the same day, November 25: "Our hopes of anything really useful from opposition are, I am sorry to say, nearly vanished. In the meantime the storm thickens. Lord Loughborough has declined, and Fox seems to govern the rest just in the old way." Lord Campbell, vi. 220, says of the negotiation generally: "A negotiation was now opened—one of the most important in our party annals; for upon the result of it depended, not merely the disposal of the Great Seal, but whether Fox or Pitt was to be Minister and whether there was to be peace or war between this country and the new Republic of France." This last statement is hardly correct. The issue of peace or war depended on other circumstances.]

Bath.

W. Nov. 21st. I received a letter from Moore, informing me that in consequence of a letter from Mr. Pitt Lᵈ Loughborough had had a conference in Downing Street on the preceding Sunday, which had lasted above an hour; that a Letter, marked secret and confidential, had been immediately after dispatched to Lᵈ Grenville at Dropmore, who, after being shut up by himself for three hours, had redispatched the messenger with a letter marked in the same manner, and with orders to follow Mr. Pitt in case he should have left town, before the messenger's return. That Mr. Pitt lived very retired at Hollwood, having ordered his servants to admit nobody, not even his most intimate friends.

F. Nov. 23. I received by the Coach a letter from Sr R. Woodford, packed up in cotton, inclosed in a small box like a watch, and one from Mr. Rolleston lapped up in Brown Paper, tied with tape and sealed. The former informed me the Flirtations were seriously renewed between Mr. Pitt and Ld Loughborough. That Rolleston had been sent down to St. Anne' Hill; that Mr. Fox was for no deviation whatever from the First Plan; but that Pitt threatened *them* with the consequences in case they did not afford him a spontaneous support in the present critical situation of affairs; that Lord Malmesbury, who had seen the Duke of Portland and Ld Loughborough subsequent to the latter's interview with Mr. Pitt, had told him (Sir R.) they were of opinion nothing was to be done at present for fear of exposing the weakness of Government, but to give their support *spontaneously*, all change to be deferred for the present. That he (M.) spoke out as to Fox, *laying a stress on its being as difficult to do without him as to arrange anything with him!* Sr R. adds that in his own mind he begins to think Ld Loughborough and Ld Malmesbury are joining to get the D. of Portland to separate from Fox; he likewise mentions Ld M.^{s} desiring him for the present to communicate to me that the measure was to assist Government without any further idea for the moment, and concludes with informing me he was just come from the Drawing room where Lord Carlisle had been very much distinguished. Mr. Rolleston begins with stating his surprise and concern at the report of several strong symptoms of the renewal on the part of Mr. Pitt, thro' Lord Loughborough, of the late negociations at Burlington House, while I remained unconsulted upon the subject, but that reflecting on the sentiments uniformly and very recently expressed both by the D. of Portland and Mr. Fox towards me, and knowing that the latter was not consulted either directly or indirectly upon the occasion, he is convinced that no negotiation of the kind can be seriously on foot in Piccadilly under such circumstances. That he is confirm'd in this belief by a conversation of three hours with the Duke of Portland the preceding evening, in which the Duke assured him that Mr. Pitt had not hitherto made the most distant overture of the kind alluded to since his interview with me; that the Duke still remained convinc'd that the plan of a Person to hold the scales between Fox and Pitt, as suggested last summer, was the wisest and best arrangement that could be devised to encounter with effect the existing difficulties.

R. observes that from some flippant conversation which was said to have lately taken place at Whitehall on the part of one or two very worthy and well meaning men attached to the D. of Portland, he had reason to think that it was from thence concluded that his Grace meant to separate from Fox, and give his full support to Pitt. That the Duke was very animated upon this point, and declared to him in the strongest terms possible that *whatever shades of difference there might be between their way of thinking with respect to one or two particular subjects* (*which may be pushed and dwelt upon by Mr. Pitt in Parliament for Party purposes*) *that he never could be satisfied till Mr. Fox was seated in the Cabinet, and that he* (*the D. of P.*) *would never enter it while he lived unless accompanied by Mr. Fox.*

S. Nov. 24. Lord St. Helens dined with me. After the Ladies were gone upstairs we conversed for some time on Foreign affairs; he mentioned the King of Prussia as a very weak man, who by his absurd conduct had exhausted his finances, spoilt his army, and

---

* Messrs. Burke and Windham. Aust had informed me by a letter of the 19th that a conference between these gentlemen and Mr. Pitt had been arranged by the Home Department, and that Mr. Windham had expressed much alarm at the progress of *Painism* in this country; this conference was on the 13th.

given to the House of Austria a decided superiority over him. Speaking of the Russian business of last year he reprobated in the strongest terms the conduct of Fox in sending an Agent (Mr. Adair) to Petersburg to counteract the negociations of this Court at that of Russia. He told me he knew for certain that Mr. Adair had shewn to some English merchants at Petersburg the Empress Picture set in diamonds which had been given to him. That it was not one of the sort usually given, but of much greater value, being set round with large Brilliants, and the whole Picture covered with a Table Diamond instead of Chrystal. That this was a present seldom made but on some very particular occasion or to some great favorite (I remember to have seen such a one in the possession of P. Orlow). Ld St H. thought it must have been worth six or seven thousand pounds, and of too much value probably to have been meant for Mr. Adair. The conclusion we both very naturally drew from this circumstance was not very favorable to Mr. Fox!

Su. Nov. 25. I wrote to Sir R. W. and Mr. R. To the first I merely acknowledged having receeived *the watch* safe by the coach, which did not appear to have been at all injured by the journey. Vide, p. 1.

I sent Mr. Rolleston my answer likewise by the post, but under cover to Mr. Aust, and both were sealed and directed by Miss Anguish.

I told Mr. R. I should have been happy to have heard the negociation had been resumed in a manner likely to ensure the success of the great object in question. That I was much flattered by the concern he had expressed at the supposition of its having been renewed without my being consulted, tho' had that been the case I had no reason to complain, as I considered my commission as terminated the moment I had made the communication at Windsor. I mentioned not having seen Ld Loughborough for many months but at Guild Hall, when I had no conversation with him but on general subjects and even that across Ld Grenville. That I had been assured Ld L. was steady (I did not mention my authority, but Ld Malmesbury, who supped with me the night before I set off for this Place, assured me he was so in the strongest terms). That perhaps Ld Guildford's death might make no alteration in L^d L^s conduct tho' I had once thought it might. That the conference with Pitt might have been upon some legal point, and that it was pretty well known the Great Seal (upon certain conditions) was at his service. I stated how much I was flatterd by the D. of P. and Mr. F.'s attentions, recommended *Firmness* tempered with *Discretion* as likely to ensure success, told him I heard a report of a considerable difference of opinion,[1] tho' on what subject I knew not, existing between Mr. Pitt and Ld Grenville, which had been mentioned by a Relation of them both,* and concluded with a wish to be informed from time to time what was going on, and an offer of my services with any of the parties concerned whenever they could be thought useful.

I received no further intelligence during my stay at Bath. On my return to town Sr Ralph Woodford dined with me.

T. Dec. 11. Sr R. brought me a letter from Mr. Rolleston, in which that gentleman acknowledges the receipt of my very *Liberal* and *interesting* Letter from Bath, mentions his having been in daily hope that something new might have occurred on the subject in question, but that to the best of his knowledge nothing hitherto had arisen in respect to it. He continued his Letter in these words, *I really looked forward with a kind of dread to the approaching collision of Parties, in both Houses of Parliament. Although I have never heard Mr. F. intimate anything of the kind yet, I am not without my apprehensions that after the very fair, moderate, and*

---

* Genl Grenville.

[1] This was most probably on the question of going to war with France. Pitt was ready to make any reasonable sacrifice in favour of peace.

conciliatory Disposition which he manifested last summer, he may feel the conduct of P. towards him upon the occasions to which I allude as amounting to a DECLARATION OF WAR against him.— What a very different situation this country and perhaps the rest of Europe would be in at this alarming crisis, had your Grace' late Patriotic exertions been crowned with success!

[Here follow six blank pages.]

1794.

On Tuesday, October the 7th, Mr. Rolleston came with Dr. Jackson to Mims, and stayed there till the next morning. We had a great deal of conversation respecting the times, the situation of Parties, and the general state of the country. I told him that, considering the bad success[1] of our arms on the continent during the last campaign, the Administration could not meet Parliament with much satisfaction; that, however desirable Peace must be, I flatterd myself Mr. Fox would act with moderation and discretion in bringing forward any motion with a view of obtaining it; that I thought his plan should be to lament the present circumstances of the country, rather than boast his having foretold them; and by recommending rather than dictating a different line of conduct he might conciliate many respectable persons both in and out of Parliament, who were already weary of a war so little likely to prove successful. Mr. R. having very obligingly stated in his visit a probability of Mr. Lindsay (lately appointed Governor of Tobago) being able to do something for Mr. Cha⁸ Anguish, I made an application to Mr. L. which that gentleman regretted not being able to comply with on account of prior engagements. This I stated in a Letter to Mr. R. at the same time renewing the subject of our late conversation at Mims. In the answer to this Letter, Oct. 17, he mentioned Mr. Fox being extremely grateful for the

---

[1] The Duke of York's expedition to the Netherlands had been a complete failure. Other great disasters were the failure at Dunkirk and the evacuation of Toulon.

very good and sound advice I had sent him, and which he had said
he would act up to in every respect as far as laid in his power. He
added that Mr. F. was going to a distant part of the country, but
meant to return about the 10th of Nov. after which period he meant
to visit Lord Thurlow, and would not fail to make me acquainted
with the result.

Oct. 26. Mr. R. wrote me word that Mr. Fox had intimated a
wish to wait upon me before the meeting of Parliament in order to
communicate to me candidly his opinions, and how far he felt himself committed with other individuals upon certain points; that his
opinion seemed to be that a motion for a cessation of Hostilities
would have the better chance of success if it was brought forward
by a person not connected with either party; he talked of L^d
Thurlow, Lord Moira, and myself, but that he could not form any
certain judgment whether L^d Th. in particular could be induced to
believe that the *proper moment* had arrived for taking a step calculated to produce the effects which he knew L^d Th. so anxiously
wished. That he had not lately seen Ld Moira, but would take an
early opportunity of seeing him. That in case I should feel an
inclination to bring forward any motion of the kind above alluded
to Mr. Fox would previously arrange with me confidentially that
the full support which he and his Friends would give me upon the
occasion should carry the appearance as it would in reality be of a
concurrence on their part to a measure originating with me and not
a support given to a proposition suggested by them. Mr. Fox
desired R. not to omit to express his concern that he had already
committed himself to move an amendment to the Address which he
said he should not have done had he received a previous intimation
of my sentiments upon that point. N.B. This refers to my having
mentioned to Rolleston when at Mims that I thought Fox might as
well lye by the first day and rather keep back his arguments till a
specific motion could be brought forward.

In my answer to the above (Oct. 27) I desired Mr. R. to make
my best acknowledgments to Mr. Fox for his polite proposal of

seeing me previous to the meeting of Parliament his offer of support and concern for having committed himself on the subject of the amendment, observing that the amendment might come perhaps better from him than his Friends, and, taking for granted one would be made in the House of Lords, recommending Ld Guildford as most likely to give it weight and effect. I mentioned reports I had heard of Ld Hawkesbury and Windham being rather inclined to Peace, and expressed a desire to know Ld Thurlow's sentiments and also those of his old friends the Marquises of Stafford and Bath. I took for granted nothing was to be expected at present from Carlton House.

Nov. 5. Sir Ralph Woodford sent me an account of the Differences occasioned by the state of Parties in Ireland, and in his Letter inclosed a Paper marked separate and private in which he mentioned a person having come to him the preceding night after he was in Bed, who said he had dined in company with the Westmoreland Party, when some conversation of a secret nature had passed with regard to their proposing to Mr. Pitt a negociation with me, to whose terms the Irish Administration would submit and most likely the other party. To this I wrote an answer expressive of my gratitude for the good opinion entertained of me by the persons in question, but at the same time declaring my dislike to the office alluded to. Sr Ralph came soon after to Mims and quoted what had passed between him and Mr Burton Conyngham on the subject, still endeavouring to convince me of the use I might be of by accepting the mediation between the two parties and going over as Ld Lieutenant. This however produced no alteration whatever in my sentiments with respect to Ireland.

Mr. Rolleston in a letter of Nov. 8 informed me of a particular circumstance that had happened at Brooks two nights before, and which had been related to him by a Friend (and of Mr. F^s) who was present, viz. Mr. Sheridan and one or two of his Friends entered upon the subject of a Parliamentary Reform in the hearing of L^d

Fitzwilliam, and after Sh. had declared it to be the present intention of the Friends of the People to abandon all thoughts of Parliamentary Reform unless called for by two-thirds of the People, Lord Fitzw^m took General Tarlton by the arm and told him that if the Opposition would really give up the question of Reform that he should have no objection to act with his old Friends again.

Nov. 10th. I went to Town to dine at Guildhall. Mr. Pitt and Mr. Fox were both there. I had no convenient opportunity for any conversation with the latter. The next day Mr. Rolleston came to me before I left town, said he had been at Mr. F.'s who was not yet up, having sat up all night in endeavouring to prevent his Friends from adopting the violent measure of expelling the D. of Portland from the Whig Club, which was to meet the following evening. In a letter of that day's date, written after I left Town, R. mentions Grattan^s having been with Fox the last time he was in Town, and mentioned the Discordant state of parties in Ireland.

Nov. 12. Mr. R. wrote me word at the desire of Mr. F. that he, Mr. F. had seen Lord Thurlow, that he candidly own'd he could not venture to say Lord Th. would have resolution enough to hazard his opinion in Parliament, but that it was not impossible his Lp. might say something. That Ld Bath's opinions were also right, but he did not chuse to publish them, and that this appeared to be the case with many persons of weight. That Mr. F. hearing that I should be in Town the 24th (Parliament being expected to meet the next day) said he should be happy to meet me anywhere I would appoint, that he approved of the Elector of Mentz^s declaration as much as I did (this I had mentioned to R.), and if I was inclined to make any motion on the grounds of it, would make a similar one in the House of Commons, or give his full support to any person I wished should move it there. Mr. R. observed that Mr. F. had certainly been very uniform in declaring that in making the various motions he had brought forward on the subject of Peace that he had had two grand objects in view, viz.:

1st. To prove to all parties in France, as well as to the Emigrants here, and elsewhere, that we were not (as they imagin'd) fighting for conquest or extermination:

2ndly. To unmask the Designs of the Convention if they should *refuse* to us a secure and honourable Peace, and thereby convince all classes of People in this Country of the indispensable necessity of uniting Heart and Hand in the War, for the Preservation of everything dear to them as individuals and as a nation.

It was afterwards settled that Mr. Fox and myself should meet at Mr. R.'s house on the 24th. This Interview, however, did not take place on that day, Parliament having again been prorogued to the 30th of December.

Nov. 29th. Mr. R. wrote me word that the French had offered to make peace with the Dutch on the terms of the *Status quo ante Bellum*, and that the conduct of the Stadtholder and the Dutch Ministers in respect to this, pending negotiation, had been exceedingly unwarrantable and offensive towards this Court, and that in consequence very strong Remonstrances or threats had been made on the part of this Gov^t. He added that Lord Wm Bentinck had no more confidence in any of the King's allies abroad than he had in those of his *Father* at home, and that Windham had told Ld William that *they* (meaning the D. of P^{ds} Friends in the Cabinet) had had no reason to alter the opinion which they had long entertain'd of Pitt; that Ld William had examined with great apparent anxiety the grounds of Difference between his Father and Mr. Fox, and after expressing an earnest wish that they could be reunited, ask'd his (R^s.) opinion whether or not he thought Mr. F. would come to his Father if he sent for him, to which R. of course answered in the affirmative.

In my answer to the above letter, Nov. 30th, I stated my opinion that it would be madness in the Dutch not to accept the terms offered by the French, and next door to it in our Ministers wishing to prevent them: that surely it would be of no trifling advantage to us, if we *must* carry on the war, neither to have the wealth or the Fleet of Holland in the hands of France, nor to be obliged to defend those who seemed unwilling to accept our assistance, even supposing it could be successful.

With respect to the differences between the D. of P. and Fox, I had always understood they had arisen from their different views of the French Revolution, and subsequent war, and that if the latter could be put an end to, their reasoning on the former need no more interrupt a renewal of their former Friendship than any other past transaction respecting which a difference of opinion might have prevailed between them.

Monday, Dec. 29. I came to town for the winter (the Parliament was to meet next day), and met Mr. Fox by appointment at Mr. Rollestons, in Eaton Street. We talked over the present state of the country so far as related to the grand subject of Peace, and tho' we perfectly agreed upon the expediency of endeavouring to promote so desirable an object, I could not but observe how little sanguine he was in hoping for any considerable accession of strength in either House towards carrying any amendment of a pacific nature which might be proposed to the Address in answer to the Speech, which was understood to recommend an unqualified Prosecution of the War. He said Ld Thurlow in private conversation was decidedly for peace, but did not know whether he would declare himself in Parliament. Three of the new Peers, viz. L^{ds} Yarborough, Bradford, and Dundas, he thought wished for Peace; that Ld Carlisle had been represented likewise as thinking the war had been long enough persisted in to wish for its speedy termination as soon as with propriety it could be obtained. Mr. Burdon (member for Durham) and Mr. Brandling (member for Newcastle) had likewise been mentioned as wishing for Peace, and if they declared their sentiments to that effect in Parliament would doubtless from their very respectable character create a great impression. He showed me the proposed amendment, which appeared moderate and proper, assuring the K. of support in maintaining his Rights and the constitution of the Country, but recommending a negotiation for Peace. It was nearly the same as that propos'd last year. In mentioning reports of a different nature he had heard respecting the sentiments of the lower order of people, he made use of this (for him very) remarkable expression, that the husbandmen and labourers thought so little of public matters that he should as soon think of consulting the sheep on the propriety or impropriety of Peace as the people who had the care of them, or in general the lower order Peasantry. That in towns, from their ale-houses, clubs, &c., they turned their thoughts more to political subjects

I brought him away in my Hackney Coach and set him down in St. James' Street, at the end of St. James' Place, as he was going to Lord Moira*; I then went and called at Lord Thurlow*, who was not come to town though expected in the course of the day.

Tuesday, Dec. 30th, Parliament met. I objected to a paragraph in the Speech and Address which I thought intimated a resolution not to treat with France as a Republic, altho' qualified by the expression "under the present circumstances," and in consequence of this objection declared I could not vote for the Address. In the House of Commons Mr. Wilberforce moved an amendment expressive of a negotiation for Peace being desirable; he was seconded by Mr. Duncombe and supported by Messrs. Banks, Burden, Brandling, Mainwaring, Sr Richard Hill, Alderman Anderson, and several other Friends of Government, which occasioned some surprize. The Minority were 72.

1795.

Tuesday, Jan. 6th. Ld Stanhope brought forward a motion stating this country having no right to interfere in the internal Govt of France, and that it was expedient to declare so now. This motion was not directly negatived, but on a Division on the question of adjournment, moved by Ld Carlisle, Ld Stanhope divided singly, though the opposition Lords attended, the numbers being—for adjourning 60, against it 1.

I stayed but a very short time in the House, and should not have attended that day but under the idea that Ld Stanhope might have called upon me in consequence of what had passed on the 1st day of the Session, when amongst other topics I repeated what I had formerly said, that in case France was satisfied with her Gov^t I cared not of what nature it was as long as the safety of this country was provided for.

Soon after the House met Ld Abercorn expressed a wish to speak to me, and taking me to the Archbishop's seat told me from what had fallen from me the day of the meeting he was happy to find our sentiments in general agreed, although he did not quite feel the force of my objection to the paragraph in the Address before mentioned; that however he wished to inform me that the D. of Bedford intended to make a motion relative to France, and that it had been represented to him of so moderate a nature that both he and myself might concur in supporting it. I told him I was very glad to hear it; that the situation of the D. of Bedford in this country was such that I certainly should feel more satisfaction in supporting any motion I approved of coming from him than from any other of the Opposition Peers. I met him again at the opera, and we appointed an hour the next day to meet at my house to talk the matter over more at large.

Wed. Jan. 7. Ld Abercorn called upon me and shewed me a paper he had drawn containing two propositions he had prepared, and on which he wished the D. of Bedford to ground his motion. The purport of them, that no Establishment of any particular Gov^t in France should impede the entering upon a negotiation for the concluding a Peace with that country upon terms safe and honourable to this—to these I gave my free and unreserved consent; he talked over the situation of the country with great good sense, and mentioned his former intimacy with Mr. Pitt, for whom he still preserved the greatest personal regard, though totally unconnected, and could not but lament Mr. Pitt's junction with the D. of Portland, and which he thought, instead of strengthening Government, had most essentially weaken'd it, and had only increased the number of Jobbs without adding to the weight or satisfaction of either party.

Th. Jan. 8. Late at night I received a letter from Lord A. inclosing one he had received from the Duke of Bedford, Ld A. mentioning his apprehension that the D. and his *Friends* (whom his Gr. stated he must consult) would be satisfied with nothing short of a Party Question. It was, however, agreed the D. of Bedford and Lord Guildford should meet Ld Abercorn and myself.

F. Jan. 9. Ld Abercorn came to me and repeated his apprehensions already stated in his Letter of the preceding night, lamenting the D. of Bedford whom he so much respected being tied down by a party that we, being both independent men, must after our conference with the D. and Ld Guildford wait for their determination till they had seen their Friends, but proposing in case his proposals did not meet their concurrence to move them himself, to which I promised my support. We go to Bedford House to-morrow.

Sat. Jan. 10. Lord Abercorn called upon me and we walk'd to Bedford House (according to appointment), we found Lord Guildford there. The Duke was dressing, but came to us in a few minutes; we immediately enterd upon the subject of our interview, namely, the motion his Grace was to make in the House of Lords, and no difference of opinion respecting the expediency of the motion seemd to exist. Lord Abercorn objected to a particular word or two as put down by the Duke of Bedford, the force of which objection I confess I did not comprehend, but the Duke politely giving way, and Lord Guildford and myself wishing it to be drawn in as unexceptionable a way as possible, the following words were unanimously agreed to : *That any particular form of Government which may prevail in France should not prevent negociation or preclude Peace consistent with the Interest, the Honour, and the security of this Country.*

After settling the words of the motion (the business on which we had met) we continued in conversation I believe at least half an hour, and, in talking over the manner in which the war had hitherto been conducted, Lord Abercorn expressed himself in stronger terms of disapprobation than fell from either the Duke of Bedford or Lord Guildford. On leaving Bedford House L.ᵈ Abercorn expressed himself as much pleased with our conference, and expressed great satisfaction at finding the Duke and Lord Guildford so ready to adopt the alterations proposed by him, without being obliged previously to consult their Friends; he told me he hoped several independent Peers would support the motion, and particularly named Lord Hardwicke as likely to vote with us in support of it.

Tuesday, Jan. 13. I went to the House of Lords (nothing but common business). Mr. Fox came there and took me aside to tell me it was in contemplation to bring forward Sir Gilbert Elliot' appointment as Viceroy of Corsica¹ in the House of Commons, and, as probably a writ might be moved for, he wished me to be informed of it, that I might take the necessary steps at Helston.

Fryday, Jan. 16. Mr. Rolleston called upon me, and, after conversing some time upon general topics, told me that as I had ever shown myself attentive to his interests he should be ungrateful indeed if he was ever to prove inattentive to mine; that in a conversation that lately passed at Mr. Fox' house, where the possibility of Mr. Fox' being applied to for the purpose of negotiating Peace was mentioned, he (Rolleston) had expressed his wish that I might be of the new Cabinet, that Mr. Fox immediately answered he himself wished exteremely that I should be. Rolleston mentioned the office of Privy Seal; Mr. Fox replied there were many people Friends of his who had particularly applied for that place who were fit for nothing else. (Rolleston understood the Duke of Norfolk would probably have it should the arrangement in contemplation take place, notwithstanding the many applications above stated.) That his (Mr. Fox's) wish was that I should be Lord

¹ George III. had lately accepted the crown of Corsica.

Chamberlain (which he thought would be agreeable to the King), and likewise of the Cabinet. I do not believe there is much chance of these very polite professions being very speedily put to the proof, and when they are I shall endeavour to say something in favour of my Friend L.d Salisbury. Soon after Rolleston left me I went down to the House of Lords where I met L.d Hardwick; we stayed there some time after the House adjourned; he began upon the subject of the Duke of Bedford's motion, and a similar one to be made by Mr. Grey in the House of Commons, and declared his opinion to be that if Ministers gave way to them he should think they acted wisely, and that no harm could possibly result from their being carried, but that if on the contrary they either resisted them directly or endeavoured to get rid of them by the Previous question or a motion for adjournment, he thought the minority in the House of Commons would be so strong (he thought probably 150) that perhaps the Ministry might throw up, a measure neither he nor myself he was sure could wish for, and of course the worst consequences might ensue; to this I only replied that I did not see any real occasion for such a step in the event of either or both these motions being carried, particularly when the nature of them was fairly and dispassionately considered.

Tuesday, Jan. 20. Mr. Sheridan called at my house and did not stay a minute; he wished to inform me he was going down to the House of Commons previous to the call, to take notice of S.r Gilbert Elliott' appointment, and knowing my connection with Helston wished me to be apprized of his intention. I thank'd him for his politeness. He only moved I believe or at least expressed a wish for the Instrument of Sir Gilbert's appointment to be laid before the House, but no motion was made for a new writ.

Tuesday, Jan. 27. The Duke of Bedford[1] brought forward his

[1] His motion ran thus: "That any particular form of government which may prevail in France should not preclude negociation or prevent peace consistent with the interest, the honour, and the security of this country." Lord Grenville moved an amendment to support the King in the war, relying "on the desire uniformly

motion, to which Lord Grenville prepared an amendment, which was carried by a great majority, 88 to 15, present, besides proxies. The Debate lasted from Five in the afternoon till Four the next morning. Ld Abercorn and myself spoke in favour of the original motion, which was supported by the Bishop of Landaff[1] in one of the finest speeches I ever heard. Neither his Lordship or Lord Lansdown stayed the Division. Ld Abercorn, Lord Clarendon, and myself were the only Peers except the Opposition who divided in the minority on a similar Discussion in the House of Commons the preceding night (on a motion of Mr. Greys to which an amendment was proposed by Mr. Pitt and carried, and afterwards another by Mr. Wilberforce[2] which was negatived); there were two Divisions, in one of which the minority was 86, and in the other 90.

Wed. Jan. 28. In the evening at Carr^s I met Sr Wm Young, who asked me if the Marquis of Buckingham had been in the House of Lords during the late Debates. I told him he had not. He said he had been with the Marquis a day or two before, who had desired him to stay and sup with him; that his Lp. was much dissatisfied with Govern^t and particularly offended at their new system with regard to Ireland.

The Duke of Richmond was a few days ago *removed* from the office of Master General of the Ordnance.

Sunday, Feb. 8th. I went with Lady Holdernesse to Kew to wait upon the Prince and Princesse of Orange. The Prince informed me he had just received a letter from Zealand mentioning the French having made a Requisition to an enormous amount on

manifested by his Majesty to effect a pacification on just and honourable grounds with any government in France, under whatever form, which should appear capable of maintaining the accustomed relations of peace and amity with other countries."

[1] Dr. Watson. The speech is remarkably eloquent.

[2] His motion was thus worded: " That the existence of any particular government in France ought not to preclude such a peace between the two countries as both in itself and in the manner of effecting it should be otherwise consistent with the safety, honour, and interest of Great Britain." This was the first beginning of an estrangement between Pitt and Wilberforce.

the Province of Holland, and that it had been made in the name of the States. His Serene Highness agreed with me in thinking that their adopting violent measures would probably prove much less injurious to the Common Cause than had they by a different conduct endeavoured to conciliate the minds of the Dutch and thereby rendered their own Government popular instead of oppressive.

Tuesday, Feb. 10th. I dined at Lord Guildfords. There were present his Lordship, his brother Col. North, the Duke of Bedford, Lord Lauderdale, Lord Robt. Spencer, Mr. Fox, Gen¹ Fitzpatrick, Mr. H. Andrew St. John, and myself. No mention was made of any other motion than that of the Duke of Bedford, which had for some time been settled to come on the following Thursday being intended for the present in either House. Ireland was much talked of, and it seemed expected that the very strong measures now pursuing there must create some dissension in the Cabinet. Mr. Fox thought they would probably produce the recall of Lord Fitzwilliam, but could not agree to the idea that they might eventually produce the retreat of Mr. Pitt from office. In conversing on Foreign Politics I took an opportunity of privately speaking to Mr. Fox who sat next me on the subject of the very violent language which had on different occasions been held in Parliament, conveying the most violent personal reflections on the K. of Prussia, which appeared to me I confessd not only highly improper but even unjust, as I had some suspicion the Ministers here had perhaps not strictly observed the conditions of the Treaty with that Prince by not paying the sums stipulated in advance. Mr. Fox seem'd to agree with me. I mentioned this in consequence of a conversation I had had by appointment the day before with Baron Jacobi, the Prussian Minister, who came to cousult me respecting a misrepresentation in a newspaper of what L.ᵈ Grenville had said some days before in the House of Lords respecting the King his master. The Baron afterwards stated to me the conduct of both Courts with regard to the late Treaty, and I must confess removed some suspicions I had hitherto entertained of a direct and voluntary infraction of the Treaty on the part of the Court of Berlin.

Feb. Towards the end of this month Lord Fitzwilliam was recalled from the Lieutenancy of Ireland.

[Here follow some blank pages.]

On Wednesday, April the 8th, 1795, the Marriage[1] of His Royal Highness the Prince of Wales with Her Serene Highness the Princess Caroline of Brunswick was solemnized at St. James' Palace. It being usual at the Marriage of a Prince of Wales for the Bridegroom to be attended by two Bachelor Dukes to the Chapel, and by two married Dukes on his return from thence, the Dukes of Bedford and Roxburgh were appointed to attend His Royal Highness to the Chapel, and the Duke of Beaufort and myself on his return. In consequence of this honour I walked immediately before the Prince, who handed the Princess from the Chapel, and I could not help remarking how little conversation passed between them during the Procession, and the coolness and indifference apparent in the manner of the Prince towards his amiable Bride. I was afterwards informed by those who were in attendance on different branches of the Royal Family and stood upon the Haut pas during the ceremony that the Prince appeared much agitated on entering the Chapel, and that during the ceremony (which was performed by the Archbishop of Canterbury in the most solemn and impressive manner) H.R.H. was perpetually looking at his favorite Lady Jersey. A circumstance happened at the time which was thought to confirm the unfortunate suspicion of his ill-fated attachment to that Person. The Earl of Harcourt, Master of the Horse to the Queen, whose wife was also Lady of the Bedchamber to Her Majesty, and the most

[1] The marriage took place at night.

intimate female friend of Lady Jersey, was desired by the Prince to hold his hat during the ceremony, which over when His Lordship returned the Hat H.R.H. insisted upon his keeping it. The Hat was ornamented with a most beautiful and costly Button and Loop of Diamonds.

Sat. May 28, 1796.

I was in my box at the opera when the Princess of Wales arrived. The Pitt and some of the Boxes began to applaud, and the whole House almost instantly rose and joined the Applause. The Duchess said, Good God, how fine! they are applauding the Princess. I looked down at her box and seeing her appear agitated immediately went down to her. Her R.H. had nobody with her but Lady Carnarvon, Mrs. Fitzroy, and Col. Thomas. The applause and Huzzas continued several minutes. She appeared much struck, and said to me, Mon Dieu! qu'est ce que tout ca veut dire? I answered, Je n'ose guere dire ce que j'en pense, Madame. Mais scavez, dit elle, que cela fera une *cruelle Histoire*. After repeated curtseying to the audience she sat down; the audience called for God save the King, which the orchestra immediately played; the Princess rose instantly, as did the whole House, and the acclamations were universal of God save the King; one Person with great emphasis calling out, God save the *Princess* too, say I.

The Princess during the performance recovered her spirits, which were much agitated at first. She told me she had been surprized at having received a letter from the Margravine of Anspach offering her R.H. the use of her House in the country in case the Princess thought proper to remove from Carlton House. She said the Prince was to return to town on Monday, and then she supposed she should be guillotined that day for what had passed this evening.

Tuesday, May 31, 1796.

The Princess this evening came in during the first Ballet, which was instantly stopped, and the acclamations began, God save the King, &c. &c. She lamented the situation and the effect which might be produced by the public applause she met with as perhaps offending still more the P. She did not attribute his cruel treatment of her to himself but to Lady Jersey. On my expressing a wonder that Lady J. had not common sense enough to resign on pretext of ill-health, rather than venture actual danger from the mob, she said it was otherwise ordered, and the P. would not hear of her resignation. She added that *Lady J.* had left her house in Pall Mall and was gone to her Daughters in Berkeley Square. The Princess understood she went on Saturday night; and, on my asking whether in consequence of what passed that night at the opera, she said she believed it was.

She wondered how the Public could be informed of what was but too true, that the Prince had not *seen* her for three months except in public or the Queen's House. That the Correspondence which had passed between them was of a most extraordinary nature, and which if her Grandchildren were to see they would scarcely believe possible. The Letters were dated from the Green or Yellow room according to the parties who wrote them, and some of his Letters in such a style as she scarcely conceived any *man would have written to any woman.*

That she knew he had represented her as the most infamous character, had imputed to her among other crimes that of immoderate ambition, and intending to create a party against him. God knows, she continued, I had no other ambition than to make him and of course myself happy; what was I independent of him had I been ambitious? nobody; my only consequence was derived from being his wife, and which I wished to profit of to render him every comfort and to shew my affectionate Duty to the King and Queen and the Royal Family; at the same time I wished not to cultivate popularity any further than to be well thought of by the Nation as at least an innocent character. The first thing that surprized me was dining with the P. at Carlton House and observing that the Company spoke English only, and after sitting a long while at Table; the same thing happened after supper, in short she was treated as if *elle n'avoit pas y port.*

That the great apparent change was after the birth of the Princess.[1] The King and Queen frequently came to her. The K. once knocked at the Door without being announced; she said naturally come in and *Voila le Roi!* The Prince was then out of Town, and on his return seemed offended at such a Circumstance having taken place in his absence.

Wednesday, June 1, 1796.

I had been to St. James' to present Carmarthen on his return from his travels. Coming home I passed Ld Thurlow near my own house, and getting out of my carriage asked him to walk in. He stayed with me near half an hour, during which time the conversation turned entirely on the unhappy business of Carlton House. He thought with me the Prince' strange conduct could alone be imputed to madness, and expressed himself as much struck by the good sense and discretion which the Princess had manifested under so cruel a tryal. He declared the Letter to the King, for which he very undeservedly had the credit, was written by the Princess of her own accord, and tho' in his presence, without any assistance from him; that nothing could be more judicious than her conversation, and that in many instances he preferred her mode of arguing the subject to his own.

---

[1] This took place on **January 7, 1796.**

Thursday, June 16, 1796.

I went to the Drawing Room; the Princess of Wales came there. She told me her jewels felt very heavy, but she was determined to wear them now, as she could not at the Birthday. I told her I was glad to see them *de retour*. (N.B. I believe the circumstance of the Prince taking the Key of the Jewels with him was really accidental.)

The Duchess and myself were invited to the Pss. party in the evening. Ld Cholmondley told me at Court the Pss. wished to have some conversation with me either before or after the card party, and on my return from Court the D_{ss}. said it was wished we might come a quarter of an hour sooner than the time appointed—9 o'clock. Accordingly we went there a quarter before 9, and found the Princess with her Lady of the Bedchamber (Lady Carnarvon) and Bedchamber woman in waiting (Mrs. Vernon). After some conversation Her R.H. observed to her Ladies she wished to speak to the Duchess, and they retired from the Dressing Room into the Tapestry Room (where the card table was placed). I offered to withdraw, but the Princess desired I would stay, and immediately addressed herself to me. She expressed great concern at the unfortunate circumstances which obliged her to inform me that perhaps it might be necessary (here I expected being forbid coming any more to Carlton House) for her to employ me in a message to the King or Prince. I assured her Royal Highness in whatever mode I could be of service she might command me. She said she considered me as a Friend of the Prince; that those of her former acquaintance, whom she had always looked upon in that light, namely Lords Thurlow and Malmesbury, were forbid all communication with her; that Ld Cholmondley, whose behaviour throughout the whole of this unfortunate business she spoke of with the highest commendation, was the Servant of them both, being Chamberlain to the Prince as well as to herself; and therefore as an independent man, and one who could be trusted by all parties, she wished to employ me when circumstances made it necessary for further communication on her part, either with his Majesty or the Prince. That Lord Moira, she believed, meant well, but certainly had rather embroiled than reconciled matters, and to her great surprize she heard had been with Lady Jersey and communicated to her all that had passed between Her R.H. and him previous to his returning to the Prince in Hampshire. It appeared as if his Lp^s visit to Lady Jersey was in consequence of the Princess having stated her Ladyship as having advanced certain positions which Ld Moira chose to enquire into the truth of.

The Princess shewed us a Letter from the Prince[1] dated April 30th, 1796, in which he lamented *our affections not being at our own disposal,* and giving Her Royal Highness to understand that should the young Princess die, *which Heaven in its goodness avert,* it was his resolution never to cultivate any connection beyond the common usage of ordinary civility. The letter was couched in cold formal language! Tho' the subject went beyond any degree of ordinary coolness or formality, I ever met with, she talked to me of the proposal of the Prince contained in the Paper communicated to me by H.H.R. command on Sunday last, adding that the latter part was added by Lord Moira, and shewed me the substance of the part alluded to in his Lp^s handwriting. She owned she thought it bore an intimation somewhat severe on the Queen, but was advised to consent to it, and was rejoiced to find the whole paper met with my approbation. She mentioned with visible emotion the Prince's behaviour to her soon after their marriage, what among other circumstances she observed would scarce obtain credit, his having obliged her after dinner to smoke a pipe; his having likewise carried her to the Inn at Staines to dine with the officers without any other Lady, and to sleep at a common Inn tho' so near Windsor. As to his abuse of me she added, I know not upon what grounds it is founded, for he has been so little with me that it is impossible he can judge

---

[1] This letter is printed in Fitzgerald's *Life of George IV.* vol. i. p. 308.

1796.

whether I am wise or foolish, good or ill tempered, in short he can know no more of my character from intimacy than I do that of Mr. Pitt from seeing him half a dozen times at Court. The cruel stroke of all she said was what she never could be perfectly happy if her Honour were not completely satisfyed by his positively denying before the King, what he had wickedly asserted, namely, that *the young Princess was not His child.* During this dreadfully interesting conversation Lady Carnarvon came to inform Her R.H. that the company were come. She continued however with us a considerable time after this notice, and then we attended her into the Tapestry Room. The company consisted of H.R.H. Lady Carnarvon and Mrs. Vernon (both in waiting), my wife The Duchess, Lord and Lady Cardigan, Mrs. Howe, Lord Sudley and myself. Near the end of the pool Lord Cholmondley came, and when the card table broke up, the Princess desired I would stay, as she wished to speak to me and Lord Cholmondley. I attended H.R.H. again into her dressing room, and she soon after beginning her conversation called Lord Cholmondley; we remained with H.R.H. I believe at least half an hour.

Lord Cholmondley was to wait upon the Prince at Richmond (H.R.H. being at the Duke of Clarence's Villa) the next morning in hopes of obtaining an answer to the Princesses proposal of Sunday last sent to the Prince by Lord Moira, but of which no notice had hitherto been taken. The conversation naturally began on the subject of that proposal, and of course on the material condition of Reconciliation, namely, *The Retreat* of Lady Jersey. Ld Cholm. who in common with myself and I believe almost every one else who were at all informed on the subject, thought that step absolutely necessary, but with respect to the mode of its taking place wished it might be left to the Prince. To this the Princess did not object, but remarked how little time remained for determination, as on the ninth of July Lady Jersey[s] waiting would commence, and that Her Royal Highness wished to have a successor appointed in the place of Lady Jersey by that time, as she ought

not and would not insist upon her other Ladies being slaves to the
caprice of any one, and certainly had no intention of being left
without a Lady to wait upon her. I told Her R.H. I flattered myself
the determination would not require much time, that although I
conceived that H.R.H. was clearly entitled by right to appoint or
dismiss her own servants, I certainly wished the Prince might be
apprized of her wishes on the present occasion, and thought the
precise mode of obtaining the object scarce worth consideration.
That all things considered perhaps Resignation might be preferable
to Dismission, certainly not with a view to spare Lady Jersey, but
to prevent as far as possible any disagreeable eclat, which might
produce consequences extremely unpleasant in the present unfortunate situation of things both with respect to the Royal Family and
the Public in general; that however I must observe that supposing
the dismission of Lady Jersey to be absolutely necessary, the
Prince himself appeared to me (however unintentionally) to have
furnished Her Royal Highness with a very strong argument in
case that measure should be thought proper to be adopted. I referd
to the Prince^s Letter of the 30th of April, and to other similar professions of H.R.H. respecting all intimate connection being for
ever at an end. That if such was unfortunately to be the case, an
interference in the Princesses establishment of her own servants
could neither appear consistent with reason or equity, and I earnestly
entreated Her R.H. not to lose sight of that consideration. I added
how much I had flattered myself that the King would have effectually interfered to have brought about a reconciliation so desirable
upon every account. The Princess answered with emotion that
the King, whom she was convinced meant well, was ignorant of
many circumstances, and had been deceived with respect to others.
I sincerely lamented such being the case as I could have wished as
many others of Her R.H.'s well wishers did, that the King should
be apprized of every circumstance (however unpleasant) of the
case, and that Her Royal Highness should take every step under

the advice as well as Protection of His Majesty. The Princess observed that she had some formidable enemies at the Queens' House, but spoke in the highest terms of her cousin Sophia (Pss. Sophia of Gloucester) as being sincerely attachd to her. I could not help mentioning Princess Sophia of England (the King's Daughter), whom I highly respected for the regard I understood she entertaind for H.R.H. The Pss. answered, she was always good to her. The Pss. in the course of this conversation referred frequently to Lord Cholmondley respecting circumstances that had pass'd at different times which gave her too much reason to foresee what would happen; that L^d Ch. had formerly differed with her respecting some of them, but was now convinced that Her R.H. was right, to which he repeated his full assent, lamenting the Princess had shown more talents for prophecy than himself.

In the course of these two conversations I could not help remarking that in case a separation should unfortunately take place, I thought it highly probable that in the space of a few months the Prince himself might sue for a reconciliation and be miserable at the idea of a separation. The Pss. said that was quite impossible; I answered it might appear so, but from what I knew of His R.H. I thought it extremely probable. She lamented, amongst other cruel circumstances attending her, the being taken away from her Friends and connections at home where she lived in comfort, and then, under the prospect of increased happiness, be brought over to England to be plunged into the unceasing misery she had experienced ever since her Marriage. She said the Prince had told her how much he respected her Father, the Duke of Brunswick, to which she could not help expressing her surprize that if such was the case he did not transfer a little of that respect, or at least entertain some esteem, for his Daughter. After quitting the Pss. dressing room L^d Ch. and myself remained some time together in the Tapestry Room. He lamented with great feeling the cruel situation of the unfortunate Princess, and the strange infatuation of the Prince, who seem'd equally insensible both to his reputation in the world and his own comfort, as to the situation in which his conduct might place him eventually whether as Heir apparent or actually entitled to the Crown.

Fryday, June 17, 1796.

I went to Lady Cholmondley's Assembly. As soon as I had made my bow the Duke of Gloucester, who was talking to Her Ladyship, took me aside and told me L^d Ch. was returned, and that things were as bad as ever. H.R.H. said he had heard I had had a long conversation at Carlton House the preceding evening, of which he was extremely glad, as he wished me to be apprized of the whole of this unfortunate business.

Lord Cholmondley came late and on seeing me took me with him into Lady Ch^s Cabinet. He told me he had been with the Prince at Richmond, that he found him more violent than ever, his chief wish seemed to be a total separation from the Princess, that he declared in the strongest terms his antipathy towards her, adding he had rather see toads and vipers crawling over his victuals than sit at the same table with her ! ! ! That as to appearing with her at the Theatres it was out of the question, as it could not be very pleasant to him to know the whole applause was directed to her and not to him (this seems to be pretty nearly the only mark of sense H.R.H. has manifested throughout the whole of this unpleasant business). With respect to Lady Jersey's quitting the Princess' service it did not appear the Prince made any very strong objection, but would not be dictated to, and was determined to see what Company he pleased at any time at Carlton House. He mentioned having heard Mrs Pelham was wished to retire, to this he objected, and said if she is to go others must go to, who I understand have been pretty free in their conversation about me. I did not collect from L^d Ch. that he named any body, but his l.p.

thought the Prince alluded to Lady Carnarvon and Mrs Fitzroy, knowing how much they were attach'd to the Princess and esteemed by Her Royal Highness; L^d Ch. said the poor Princess was ill and gone to bed before he reached Carlton House on his return from Richmond; that Doctor Warner had been sent to, but being confined to his house by illness could not come, but had ordered Her R.H. a dose of Laudanum. L^d Ch. said if the Princess was not better in the morning he should send for some other Physician, as he thought it his Duty so to do.

Saturday, June 25, 1796.

The Duke of Gloucester called at my house before I was up; from the stupidity of my servants I knew nothing of H.R.H.'s visit till the Duchess informed me of it between twelve and one, and said he would call again. He came about one o'clock, and after laughing at me for not being an early riser (in his good humour'd way) said he came from Carlton House at the desire of the Princess of Wales to shew me the letter (in answer to H.R.H.'s of Wednesday last) from the King. The Duke, I should here mention, the moment the door was shut, told me he brought good news, and such as he was sure would give me pleasure; he gave the letter into my hand, which I read several times. It was couched in the kindest terms, beginning, Ma chere Fille, and ending, Ma chere Belle Fille. This difference (immaterial in itself) struck me as convincing proof of its being written from the Heart, and that the Letter itself conveyed the K.'s own sentiments, and then and not till the end was H.M. aware of the exact relationship in which the Pr. and himself were placed. The K. stated in his Letter in the kindest terms the disagreeable reports that had taken root, and thought no way so likely to obviate the mischief they might produce as in consideration of the Prince of Wales having consented to Lady Jersey' quitting the Princesses service and her private Society (N.B. the Princesses own words), Her Royal Highness should express a wish for his return to Carlton House. The letter was throughout of the most affectionate nature to the Prince of Wales. The Duke of York had been consulted, and indeed, I believed, carried a message from the P. to the K. some days past. He, I have no doubt, has acted in this, as I firmly believe he does in every other occurrence, a most honourable part. And the Duke of Gloucester was perfectly satisfied with the letter, as I own, under the present circumstances, I was. The great point of Lady Jersey's removal being carried, and the K. in a dignified as well as affectionate manner appearing the Princesses Protector, at the same time shewing a degree of *menagement* for his unfortunate Son and Heir.

Tuesday, July 12.

Being in the Princess of Wales' Box during the Ballet of L'heureux Naufrage ou Les Sorcieres Ecossaisses, I thought it right to prepare Her R.H. for the Firing of the Robber; she answer'd *Quand la Fille d'un Heros epouse un Zero, elle ne craindra pas des coups de Fusil.*

Thursday, July 14, 1796.

After the Drawing Room we dined at Lady Holdernesse's, and when the Ladies had withdrawn Mrs. Nugent told the Duchess that she had reason to know that Lady Cholmondely, conversing with the Queen on the subject of the Prince of Wales' return to Carlton House, had observed to Her Majesty that *she was surprised the Prince should ever have returned there after the usage he had met with from the Princess!!!* Mrs. N. added she knew *some* of the Royal Family particularly wished the Duchess and myself to be apprized of this extraordinary anecdote. Mrs. Nugent, not being disposed to mention the names of the persons who had informed her of this anecdote, the Duchess and myself, when she acquainted me with it, could only hazard a guess upon the subject; we both agreed, however, in thinking it came either from Prince Ernest or Princess Sophia.

Some days afterwards I communicated this circumstance to Mr. Lee (Groom of the Bedchamber to the D. of Gloucester), in order that thro' the Duke his master the Princess might be upon her guard before Lady Ch. Mr. Lee told me he was not surprized; that Lady Ch., tho' he acquitted her of any bad intention, might do mischief if not attended to; that she was very weak and extremely open to flattery, and that the Prince of Wales, by paying great court to Her, had completely got her over to him: that Lᵈ Ch. was sensible of the true character of his wife, but could only endeavour by his own discretion to prevent as far as possible her Ladyship doing any serious mischief by her want of so requisite a quality.

Sat. July 30, 1796.

The last opera of the season. I went into the Princess' Box. Her R.H. was extremely glad to see me, thinking I was gone with the Duchess to Weymouth. She told me her journey to Brighton would not take place, that she understood the Prince meant she should have a country House taken for her, but where was not yet settled. She informed me the Parliament was ordered by Proclamation to meet in September for the dispatch of business, and in the course of the conversation expressed a suspicion that it was meant she should not be in town whenever it did meet. Upon her asking how long the Duchess stayed at Weymouth, and my answering it depended upon the Bathing agreeing with her, and her liking the place, she observed, *vous n'êtes Tyran!* She mentioned that amidst all the unpleasant circumstances which had occurred, one had taken place which gave her real pleasure, namely, Mrs. Goldsworthy being appointed to attend upon Princess Charlotte during the necessary absence of Lady Dashwood, whose extreme bad health rendered it necessary for her to go into the country. I congratulated her R.H. most sincerely on the choice, as Mrs. G. is an excellent woman, and respected by everybody. The Pss. informed me she understood Lady Jersey was to have the house formerly Marshal Conways lately inhabited by Jack Payne, and which the Prince bought a few years since, adjoining to Carlton House Gardens, that a wall was to be built as a sort of screen on the side of Carlton House, and that this and other works necessary would probably be done during her absence! She took leave of me very kindly and said, God knows what may happen before the next opera. She appeared to me this evening less gay than usual. I took the liberty of again recommending Patience and to remain perfectly quiet.

Thursday, Sept. 22.

At the Drawing Room I saw both the Prince and Princess of Wales. The Prince did not speak to me tho' near me several time; he made me a cold formal Bow in the outward Room when going away.

The Princess very gracious as usual, told me she was to have her new neighbor Lady Jersey very soon, that the situation of the House was well calculated for a spy, as the windows looked directly into those of Her Royal Highness's apartment. She added how strange it seemed for Lady Jersey to take possession of her new house just before the meeting of Parliament, as if to remind the Public of all that had passed. Her R.H. desired the Duchess and myself to dine at Carlton House the next day to meet the Prince and Princess of Orange.

Fr. Sept. 23.

We dined at Carlton House with the Princess of Wales; the rest of the company were the P. and Princess of Orange, Lady

Holdernesse, my daughter, Lady Mary de Reede, Lady Carnarvon, Mrs. Fitzroy, and Lord St. Helens; there was music in the evening. The little Princess (a charming child) was brought into the Room before Dinner; she is extremely like the Prince. During the evening Lady Carnarvon took me into the inner room, and told me her fear lest the Dinner might disoblige the Prince. I told her I took for granted he knew of it, or at least allowed the Princess to invite her own company. She wished me to discourage the Princess from giving dinners. I told her it was a subject on which I wished not to interfere, but took for granted she would do nothing she could suppose was improper. I told both Lady Carnarvon and Mrs. Fitzroy I flattered myself things were taking a more favourable turn for the Princess at the Queen's House, having reason to know P'ss. Elizabeth wished much for things to remain quiet in the family, that the Queen had spoken twice (in apparent good humour) to the Princess at the Drawing Room the preceding day, and that Her R.H. had nothing to do but to observe the same prudent line of conduct, and that matters I hoped would soon come round so as to make her situation far more comfortable than of lately it had been. I had scarce any private conversation with the Princess. The P'ss. of Orange agreed with me that things looked better than some months past, and strongly recommended prudence and patience.

APPENDIX.

I have printed in the Appendix the most authoritative account that exists of the Revolution in Denmark which recalled the younger Bernstorff to power. I have taken it from the original despatches of Hugh Elliot, preserved in the Record Office. These despatches were considered so secret by their writer that they were delayed some months until they could be conveyed to England by a safe hand. Although alluded to in Lady Minto's life of Hugh Elliot, they have never been published, nor, I believe, consulted by historians.

A.

Denmark. No. 149 (6).

Copenhagen, Sept' 1st, 1784.

MY LORD,

I have no other apology, for having so long delay'd transmitting to your Lordship a full account of the late total Revolution in the Government of this Country, than a chain of circumstances which, unavoidably, obliged me to postpone Mr. Johnstone's journey to England.

Your Lordship has, in the meantime, been made acquainted with the principal events which attended the Prince of Denmark's confirmation and entrance into the Council. I, consequently, flatter myself that no inconvenience hath arisen from my not having given a more minute detail of the origin, progres, and conclusion of a transaction equally important to the interior politicks of this Court and to those foreign Nations who are interested in its publick concerns.

Since the Revolution which was effected in 1772, the only hope of overturning a system of Government, no less detrimental to the most distinguished Families than destructive to the Country, rested entirely on the preservation of the Prince and His arrival at the legal age of majority. He was not entitled to a seat in the Council before confirmation ; and, though the Law enacts that a Prince of the Blood may be admitted to that Ceremony at thirteen, yet the Party in power succeeded in protracting the time till His Royal Highness had attained his sixteenth year.

It is not requisite to trace through so long an interval the numberless instances of incapacity, profusion, and extortion by which this Kingdom has been impoverished and nearly ruined. It is sufficient to observe that, after a peace of above sixty years, its finances are in great confusion, its specie annihilated, the necessaries of life at an exorbitant price, the principal merchants on the brink of insolvency, and both the naval and military force reduced to a state of weakness and langour unknown in any former Reign.

The Queen Dowager and her son, from the year 1772, continued to direct the wheels of Government through the same means by which they got into power. They flattered themselves with the hopes of over-powering even the Prince Royal, by being able to command the signature of an unfortunate Monarch, whose pen was guided by those in possession of his person.

It is evident that the King of Denmark is deprived of the use of reason; and his insanity is of that species which leaves no lucid intervals. In any private rank of life he would have been withdrawn from the publick eye. Upon the throne it has been judged expedient to oblige him to go through the pageantry of so elevated a station; and by long habit his subjects have become less sensible to the striking improprieties of his demeanour than Foreigners, who are not accustomed to so melancholy an exhibition of diseas'd understanding.

The constitution of Denmark is purely despotic, and the will of the sovereign, expressed either by word or writing, supersedes law. In the Council, the King's uttering "Le Roi le veut" puts a close to discussion. A royal mandate, with the sign manual affixed, is absolute, and this, particularly distinguished by the appellation of an order of Cabinet, is the instrument by which Denmark has been governed for many years.

As soon as the Queen Dowager had, in 1772, gained the uncontrouled disposal of her Stepson, she consigned him over to the management of M. de Schach, late Great Marshal of the Court. That gentleman never quitted his Sovereign night nor day, and, by the treatment usual in similar cases, established an authority so arbitrary, that he cou'd make him apply his remaining powers of action to any purpose for which they were still competent. It is well known that even compulsion was sometimes exercised to get the King to copy a letter, or to teach him a phraze which he was to repeat. M. de Schach, while in this office, shewed himself devoted to the views of the Queen Dowager, and received every reward of rank or fortune which she could bestow. In return, he was assiduous in preventing all access to his Danish Majesty, and in procuring his subscription to any papers which required the Royal sanction.

The Queen Dowager is not possessed of talents for business, tho' she is intriguing, and has a great share of artifice and cunning. Her son, Prince Frederick, who appeared as the ostensible agent in publick affairs, was still less able to conduct them. M. de Guldberg was, in fact, sovereign in Denmark. From having been private preceptor to Prince Frederick, he acquired, not only the confidence, but also the entire direction, both of the Queen and of her son. He was thus raised from the humblest situation to be Secretary to the Cabinet, and the supreme Minister of his country.

M. de Guldberg did not trust solely to his own credit, but was supported and seconded by all the weight of the King of Prussia, who rivetted His influence over the Queen by peculiar attentions to Her Favourite. He frequently corresponded with him, and was not sparing of every species of adulation that was adapted to dazzle an aspiring mind. He was also more liberal in the presents He made on different occasions than was consistent with His usual parsimony. By these means the King of Prussia acquired the compleat direction of the Cabinet of Copenhagen. In all matters of consequence he was consulted, and His advice implicitly followed. Every secret communication entrusted to the Danish Ministry was conveyed to Potzdam; and whatever opinion or proposition came from thence was adopted. He was, at the same time, very cautious in not interfering with any views of Russia, being too well apprized of the weak and defenceless state of this Country not to know that its existence, as a separate Power, depends upon the protection of the Court of Petersburg. Concealing, therefore, as much as possible, his intimate correspondence with the Queen and her Favourite, he directed all his intrigues at Copenhagen to the attainment of commercial advantages and other more private and secondary objects.

This system prevailed from the time the Queen Dowager seized the reigns of Government till the Prince Royal asserted his own Rights and entered himself upon the management of publick affairs, an event which, tho' long preparing, through many secret causes, was little expected by those who were not immediately in the confidence of His Royal Highness.

From the instant that M. de Guldberg began to grasp at the uncontrouled power which he nearly reached, he took measures for gradually removing from Court and publick office those of the Nobility whose Opulence or abilities he had reason to dread; and in pursuing this end exhibited great exertions of deceit and low cunning.

Count Bernstorff was the most formidable object of his jealousy, and stood principally in his way. That Nobleman's distinguished fortune, reputation, and talents enabled him, for some time, to support the interests of the Nobility and the Nation against a system which the Queen Dowager was endeavouring to establish upon the ruin of both.

The person in high office who, next to Count Bernstorff, enjoy'd the most general estimation in point of capacity, was M. de Schach Rathlow. In order to gain his assistance in the removal of that Minister, M. de Guldberg amply provided for the numerous class of M. de Schach's relations and dependents, who either needed or were ambitious of employment in the State.

Your Lordship is well acquainted with the real origin of the Neutral League, and the manly resistance made by Count Bernstorff to a combination subversive of justice and the faith of Treaties. Your Lordship also knows that, tho' the Empress of Russia at last adopted that system as her own, yet it was first started at Berlin, and the principal emoluments arising from it accrued to His Prussian Majesty. Naturally, therefore, Count Bernstorff's opposition drew upon him the resentment of that Monarch; and Duke Ferdinand of Brunswick, after having been at Potzdam, was sent to Copenhagen with no other errand than to effectuate the dismission of a Minister who had dared to withstand a measure no less beneficial to His Prussian Majesty than injurious to the interests of Denmark. The Count has since informed me that Duke Ferdinand, upon his arrival at Copenhagen, assured him that if he would meet the wishes of the King of Prussia he would have the full countenance and support of that Monarch. This proffer M. de Bernstorff rejected, and accordingly he soon after received his dismission from all his places.

After this event M. de Guldberg appeared to have established his ascendancy in the Danish Counsels upon a foundation not to be shaken; and it was soon manifest to M. de Schach Rathlow that he was marked out as the next victim. His Genius, therefore, naturally versatile, easily led him to follow the biass of his interest, and to connect himself with the Friends of Count Bernstorff, in order to overthrow a favourite whose ambition knew no bounds.

At the time of my arrival in Denmark in 1782 Count Bernstorff was settled upon his estate in Mecklenburg, M. de Schach Rathlow hardly retained a shadow of his former importance, and M. de Guldberg as Ministre d'Etat, and Secretary of the Cabinet, acted with exclusive ministerial power.

M. de Rosencrone, formerly my Colleague at Berlin, had been appointed Secretary of State for the Foreign Department. The principal reason for this choice was because that Gentleman and his Lady had formed very intimate connexions with the Queen of Prussia and the Ladies immediately attached to the Prince of

Prussia's eldest daughter, whom the Queen Dowager already looked upon as the future Consort of the Prince of Denmark. Upon this Marriage she intended to lay the foundation of her influence when the Prince Royal should have attained the age of Majority. So early as the year 1779 the King of Denmark's hand had been used to ask the Princess of Prussia for his Son; and, at the age of thirteen, the Prince himself was prevail'd upon to send a letter of his own writing for the same purpose.

Notwithstanding the pains which had been taken to protract the Prince's childhood and to cramp his Genius His Royal Highness possessed, almost from infancy, an uncommon share of penetration, firmness, and self-command; he sensibly felt the treatment he met with, but concealed those feelings till the opportunity of emancipation occurred. Here may I beg leave to insert an anecdote which shews how soon the Prince was determined to assert that pre-eminence and dignity so justly due to his Birth.

He had been taught to kiss the hand of Prince Frederick. The Queen Dowager, either from vanity or from a desire of impressing the Nation with a sense not only of her own superiority but also that of her Son, insisted upon the Prince's continuing that mark of respect much longer than is usual here even among private Families. She carried this so far that the heir of the Danish Throne was compelled to submit to this etiquette openly, at the play, in the presence of his Father, and before his own future subjects. The publick could not abstain from discovering symptoms of dissatisfaction at a ceremony which they consider'd as degrading and improper. The Prince soon perceived the general impression, and resolved at once to rid himself of a piece of homage to which, tho' with reluctance, he had long complied. Prince Frederick one evening presenting his hand his nephew threw it from him with such violence as nearly overturned his Uncle, who is both feeble and deformed. These and similar demonstrations of resolution encouraged the discontented to turn their views towards His Royal Highness.

I entered upon my Mission at the Court of Denmark under

APPENDIX. 241

circumstances so little favorable to myself, on account of my sudden and unexpected recall from Berlin, that I was not consider'd as enjoying the particular confidence or approbation of my superiors. I had therefore little reason to expect that men embarked in measures big with danger to themselves wou'd venture to make me their confidant. Neither was there at that time to the publick eye any symptoms of those changes which have since taken place, nor had the least intimation been given to me that designs existed which escaped the observation of even those whose interests were most deeply concerned.

During the Spring in 1783 I began to entertain suspicions of the good intelligence that subsisted among the remaining members of Count Bernstorff's Party, and consequently exerted myself to obtain a farther insight into their views. Count Schimmelman was the first who with great caution surmised the hopes they rested upon the Prince Royal's secret support, and I collected from him that there was a regular intercourse kept up between Count Bernstorff and certain individuals of great note at Copenhagen. He also repeatedly expressed a wish that I had been personally known to that Minister. The very perilous situation in which from this moment I saw the Prince of Denmark and his adherents placed determin'd me not to neglect a suggestion of such consequence.

Having soon after been obliged to go to Berlin upon business of a private nature which had attracted the general attention of the publick, I profited of the opportunity to effectuate an interview with Count Bernstorff. I had no reason to repent the trouble I had taken in returning round through Mecklenburg, where I passed some days with the Count on pretence of hiring his Villa near Copenhagen. He gave me as explicit an account of the Prince Royal's plan and of the state of their Party as was consistent with his duty. He was also pleased to mark out the line of conduct most advisable for me to pursue, in order to forward the success of measures he represented as not indifferent to the interests of Great Britain. These communications were however made to me conditionally and upon a supposition that they were to serve merely as a rule for my conduct, but not to be disclosed to any person whatever.

I must acknowledge that, on reflecting how much the chance of success depended upon the discretion and resolution of a young Prince in his fifteenth year, I could not help distrusting the issue. I learned, besides, that some of those in whom Count Bernstorff was obliged to repose the greatest confidence were persons who had contributed to his own dismission—who were in full credit with the Queen Dowager, and who had taken an active part in the most odious transaction of her government. I even understood it was principally to them I was to address myself; and, by entering into intimate habits of society with them, to quiet their apprehensions of any remains of resentment that might still be entertained in England. On my return to Copenhagen, therefore, I connected myself as much as possible with the Queen's party, and succeeded so far as to have been useful in preventing any suspicions of the plan going forward, or that I was co-operating in its execution. I am happy to say that my conduct in this respect has since met the warmest thanks of Count Bernstorff, and of some of his Friends, as having been of essential service.

My next object was to shew great attentions to M. de Schach Rathlow, a most necessary and important instrument for the execution of His Royal Highnesses designs. This gentleman, naturally suspicious and distrustful, had borne too open and too unjustifiable a share in the fatal transaction from which the misfortunes of this country are to be dated not to be alarmed at the thoughts of overturning a system he had so much contributed to establish. I perceived that nothing would encourage him so much to go through with the intended revolution as a certainty that it would be agreeable to Great Britain; and that the part he might act in it would entirely obliterate the remembrance of what was past. I believe, my Lord, I may with truth arrogate to myself a degree of merit in having strengthened the resolutions and fixt the purposes of a wavering mind, without his being able to discover that I had any knowledge of the plan in agitation farther than what I could infer from his own communications.

Although I was apprized that other individuals were privy to the Prince's designs, I studiously avoided any conversation concerning them. I thought myself the more obliged to maintain this reserve, by Mr. Fox's answer of August 26th, 1783, to my Dispatch No. 23 of Augt 5th. I considered that letter of Mr. Fox's as an instruction not to intermeddle in the interior politicks of this Court, and, therefore, confined myself merely to observe the secret directions I had received from Count Bernstorff, without seeking to obtain information from other quarters.

For some months previous to the Revolution the Prince Royal seemed to grow more and more attach'd to those very people whom he had determined to overthrow; and in proportion as he approached that period of life which would entitle him to a share in the administration, M. de Guldberg grew more impatient to get quit of all those who were not thoroughly of his own party. I was every day witness to the dismission of persons upon whose presence at Copenhagen I had reason to think everything depended. M. de Numsen, a near relation of M. de Schach Rathlow, was abruptly, and to the general surprise, displaced from office. Knowing this gentleman to have been one upon whom C^t Bernstorff had a principal reliance, I attributed his disgrace to M. de Guldberg's having discovered their connexion. Every subsequent change was adapted to support the interests of the party in power; and the Prince, even after his confirmation, affected the appearance of so much unanimity with his uncle that it was generally supposed his unexperienced mind had been gain'd over by the art and cunning of the Queen Dowager. M. de Rosencrone having also about this time informed me that a clandestine correspondence between Count Bernstorff and some people in Copenhagen had been detected, I considered the attempt as now in a great measure defeated, and, accordingly, expressed to your Lordship my doubts of its success.

The Queen Dowager and M. de Guldberg thought themselves so sure of commanding the Prince's concurrence that they had not scrupuled to new-model the Council, and to fill it entirely with their own creatures. When they came, however, to take their seats on the 14th of April, the very hour they looked for as the hour of Triumph, put a termination to their power, and covered them with ridicule and disgrace.

Notwithstanding the specious appearances, which had imposed upon the publick, the event demonstrated that the young Prince remained faithful to the plan which Count Bernstorff had made me acquainted with. His Royal Highness, tho' only in his thirteenth year at the dismission of the Count, had given that nobleman a promise that he might rely upon his future countenance and protection; and such trust had Count Bernstorff in the steadiness of the Prince that he, some time after, began a private correspondence with him upon the most important subjects.

Although Count Bernstorff pays too great respect for the secrets of others to add to his own reputation by detailing the share he had in the whole of so important a Transaction, yet I think myself authorised to affirm that for two years he contrived to furnish daily directions for His Royal Highness, and which he implicitly follow'd. There were but two methods of communication, the one by writing, the other through the medium of those who had an opportunity of appearing in the Prince's presence. I am informed that the packets were delivered by * * * *, a *valet de chambre* to the Prince; and that His Royal Highness, after perusal, immediately committed them to the flames, trusting to his own memory for the contents. When it is recollected that General Eichstedt, his Governor, and M. de Sporon, his private preceptor, both equally creatures of the Queen, were constantly about the Prince's person, it is astonishing that he should have succeeded in concealing, through so long an interval, not only the correspondence with Count Bernstorff, but also with others whom the Prince, by that nobleman's advice, had gradually attached to his cause. There is sufficient reason to sup-

APPENDIX. 245

pose that Count Schimmelman, with the Brothers Count Christian and Count Louis Reventlow, were the chief agents who were, from the beginning, entrusted with Count Bernstorff's verbal communications.

I am not exactly apprized at what time the Prince had been induced to turn his eye towards M. de Schach Rathlow, but that Minister has since acquainted me the first letter he received from His Royal Highness was dated a year and a half before the accomplishment of the Revolution; and that during this period not a week had past, while he was at Copenhagen, in which he had not private conferences with the Prince. Some months before the Revolution the persons who, to my knowledge, had embarked in it were Count Bernstorff, M. de Schach Rathlow, M. de Stampe, and General Huth, members of the new Council, together with Count Schimmelman, the two Count Reventlow's, General Haxthausen, M. de Numsen, M. de Bulow, one of the Prince's Chamberlains, besides other inferior Agents. Among those I consider General Huth, Count Schimmelman, and the two Count Reventlow's as particularly attached to Count Bernstorff. The Prince of Hesse was indeed acquainted with what was going forward, but, being at a distance, he had no immediate concern in the execution.

In the present unhappy situation of the King of Denmark there could be no doubt of the legal right the Prince Royal had to assume the reins of Government as soon as he had been confirmed. But, as the Queen Dowager and M. de Guldberg were sensible that not only their importance but even their safety depended upon their continuation in power, so it was to be imagined they would exert every means to uphold the Fabrick they had so artfully erected. Many acts of their administration, particularly in regard to finance and expenditure of the publick money, were highly criminal, and, if rigidly enquired into, might have exposed several to capital punishment. No motive, therefore, but the conviction that the Prince Royal wou'd, by compliance, add strength to her Party, could have induced the Queen to consent to his taking a seat in the

Council. She trusted to the infirmity of the King and the youth of the Prince for preserving the unlimited influence she had hitherto enjoyed.

The Queen Dowager and M. de Guldberg had now reigned with unquestioned sway for fourteen years. During this interval they had founded an authority so absolute that the property, liberty, and lives of the principal Malcontents might have been forfeited had their designs been disclosed before they had brought over a sufficient military force to secure the palace and the Capital. General Huth, seconded by M. de Schach Rathlow's brother-in-law, General Haxthausen, who commanded the Norwegian life guards, were entrusted with this commission, and succeeded in it beyond expectation.

As violence is usually employed to overturn a legal constitution, so power is necessary to preserve a Government founded upon injustice. It is seldom that those in possession of usurped authority rely on mere habits of obedience. The Queen Dowager and her party did not seem attentive to this maxim, and, consequently, neglected the proper precautions. They did not apprehend that their designs could possibly meet with any check which they cou'd not immediately suppress by the supreme command of the King. They were, therefore, so little watchful of the Prince Royal's secret motions that his party had secured the assistance of the Norwegian Guards, of the Artillery, and of the Garrison in the Citadel some time before their help was actually requisite. It must be owned that the situation of people so deeply engaged in this transaction was exceedingly hazardous, because an order of the King might either have put the Prince Royal in arrest or sent him to travel till his marriage with the Princess of Prussia had been concluded—and, indeed, this last was an expedient often in agitation. A similar mandate would have been sufficient to have sent all his Partizans to confinement. I am assured by Count Reventlow and General Huth that they are now certain, had they been discovered, imprisonment at least would have been their fate.

About a week before every thing was ripe for execution the

discontented had finally settled upon the best measures for bringing their purposes to a happy termination. During this short space they were, however, much alarmed by several accidents. I had, as mentioned before, been acquainted by Count Rosencrone that the Queen Dowager certainly suspected the correspondence with Count Bernstorff, and had even put some very home questions to the young Prince on the subject. His Royal Highness did not lose his presence of mind, but answered with so much unconcern and adroitness that he dispelled every suspicion. Another incident occured a few days afterwards that disconcerted his Party not a little. The Prince Royal's adherents were assembled at Count Schimmelmans to agree upon the decisive exertion, when an unexpected message arrived from the Queen desiring Count Louis Reventlow to come forthwith to the Palace, which was the more striking as he had never before been sent for in that way, nor cou'd they conjecture any plausible reason for such a summons. It happily turned out in the sequel that the message originated from some trivial incident, and occasioned no farther apprehension. I was myself witness to a more trying case the very evening before the Revolution. M. de Schach Rathlow, who was still acting in the most unsuspected confidence with the Queen Dowager's Party, was conversing with the Minister of the Finances, M. de Stemman, one of M. de Guldberg's confidants, when a number of papers were brought in and delivered by a Servant to M. de Schach Rathlow. M. de Stemman expressing some surprise, M. de Schach Rathlow, with great composure, drew off his attention by some sudden break in the conversation, and, disposing of the papers in different pockets, contrived to leave the room without allowing the other time to ask any farther questions. He told me, a few days afterwards, that these were the very papers which were to be sign'd the next evening by the King in Council, and which, by mistake, instead of having been conveyed privately, were delivered openly at an assembly.

On the 14th of April M. de Guldberg and his Friends took their places in the Council. There were present the King, the Prince

Royal, Prince Frederick, Count Gotsche Moltke, M. de Guldberg, M. de Schach Rathlow, and M. de Stemman. This last Gentleman held some writings in his hand, which he was preparing to lay before the Council, when the Prince Royal, rising from His Chair, desired to read a memorial he drew from his bosom where it had been concealed.

This instrument contained in general the reasons he was pleased to alledge in order to prove the necessity of a total change in the measures of Government, as also the names of those His Royal Highness entreated his Father to call into the Council.

When the Prince had finished he stretched out the paper to the King begging that it might have his royal sanction. Prince Frederick endeavoured to make some opposition, but the Prince insisting with warmth the King took the Paper from the hand of his son and sign'd it.

His Royal Highness then produced a second Memorial, which was drawn up with a view to regulate the use of the Orders of Cabinet, and which provided that no Order of the King should in future be valid which was not both signed by His Danish Majesty and countersigned by the Prince Royal. The King having also subscribed this, orders were drawn up to acquaint the heads of the principal Departments with its purport, and these papers were all delivered by the Prince Royal to M. de Schach Rathlow, the only Minister of the Council in his confidence. M. de Schach Rathlow carried them to the outer Chamber, where they were put into the hands of M. de Bulow to be forwarded to the different Chanceries.

The Prince's manner in this trying moment was full of dignity and firmness. M. de Schach Rathlow assured me that it struck all present with astonishment, and did not a little contribute to prevent them from making any immediate attempts to withstand this decided measure.

His Royal Highness next waited upon the Queen and acquainted her himself with what had passed. As Her Majesty's passions are naturally strong, she could not refrain from tears and invective, and indeed for several hours after there was a good deal of confusion in the Palace.

I was that evening, with many of the Danish nobility, at Count Moltke's Assembly, when the news was brought of the unexpected Revolution. At first it was not credited, but Count Moltke receiving certain intelligence of its having taken place, and that his son was dismissed from the Council, he appeared to be much agitated, and said to me, with visible emotion, that the King's signature might again be made use of to reverse any innovations. Reports were soon propagated of there being much tumult in the Palace. It was not till near midnight that my apprehensions were quieted by the following note from one of my intimate friends most deeply concerned.

A 11 heure et demi.

Je ne rentre chez moi que dans ce moment, et Je ne puis m'arrêter que quelques minutes. Tout est heureusement achevé— le Comte Bernstorff est rapellé, le courier est deja parti—le General Huth, Stampe, et Rosencrantz sont nommé Ministres de Conseil— M. de Guldberg, Stemann, et le Comte Moltke ont leur congé— aucune mesure violente n'a eu lieu—personne n'est ni exilé ni arreté—la Providence voudra achever son ouvrage, et faire en sorte que ce qui doit fonder le bonheur futur du Dannemarc ne fasse le malheur d' aucun individu.

The Prince Royal, after having seen the Queen, insisted that a ball, which had been announced at Court for that evening, should not be interrupted, and assisted at it with so much coolness and composure as greatly animated his partizans. For greater security Count Schimmelman and Count Reventlow passed the first, and some of the ensuing nights, in the Prince's apartments; and for several mornings his Royal Highness walked through the town, attended by Baron Bulow and a single running footman. He was followed by a great concourse of people, who expressed the highest satisfaction at the publick appearance of their Prince, tho' the more brilliant demonstrations of joy had been strictly forbidden, in order to prevent all disturbance.

M. de Schach, Marshal of the Court, was removed from the King's presence, and his place filled by M. de Numsen, who, with four Chamberlains, was charged with the delicate commission of attending the King.

An express had been sent to Count Bernstorff on the evening of the 14th to call him to Copenhagen, and the department of Foreign Affairs; but it unfortunately happened that that minister was confined by a fit of the gout, and seventeen days elapsed before his arrival. In that interval, serious apprehensions were entertained by some of the Prince Royal's nearest adherents that the Queen Dowager might recover her power by getting possession of the King, and I did not look upon the Revolution as compleat till M. de Bernstorff had entered into office. He immediately remov'd Mr. Guldberg, Count Gotsche Moltke, and M. de Stemman from Copenhagen. With great address he next prevailed upon the Queen Dowager to separate her summer residence from that of the Prince Royal, and employed every proper means for giving stability to the new Government.

Before I conclude may I beg leave to call your Lordship's attention, once more, to the singular feature in the Prince Royal's character, which enabl'd him, at the age of sixteen, to liberate himself from the fetters into which he had been so artfully entangled. He not only kept his own secret for two years, but carried on private communications and secret correspondences through that period with various individuals, till the hour came when he was to display as much vigour as he had formerly done pliancy and discretion. If his Royal Highness is so fortunate as to escape the danger he is exposed to, from being not only his own master at so early a period of life, but also in possession of uncontroulable dominion, it may well be expected that his reign will be equally glorious to himself and to his kingdoms. Denmark is at present low in the scale of Europe, but it may soon rise again to be an object worthy of the political attention of the greatest Powers.

I have the honor to be with
the greatest truth and respect,
Your Lordship's
Most obedient
Humble Servant,
H. ELLIOT.

Endorsed:

Copenhagen. Sept" 1st, 1784.
Mr. Elliot.
R. 28th
by Mr. Johnstone,
(A.)
The Right Honorable the Marquess of Carmarthen.

(B.)

Denmark. No. 149. (6).

Private. Copenhagen, 1 September, 1784.

MY LORD,

I have, in a former letter, had the honor of laying before your Lordship an account of the late Revolution in the Danish Government. I shall now proceed to state, more particularly, some circumstances I think worthy of attention, and beg leave to explain, at the same time, the Part I have acted in so important a transaction.

Your Lordship will have perceived that M. de Schach Rathelow was a decisive Agent in the accomplishment of the Prince Royal's measures, and indeed they could hardly have succeeded without his concurrence and co-operation. The necessity of securing him to the Prince's Interests made it indispensably requisite for His

Royal Highnesses other adherents to be very careful not to alarm the timidity natural to this Gentleman, and which at this conjuncture he might rationally be allowed to entertain. I am here obliged to recur to that fatal incident of His Danish Majesty's Reign, which involved this Court in a continued scene of Intrigue, Confusion, and Distrust.

M. de Schach Rathelow embarked with warmth into the Views of the Queen Dowager when first she seized the Reins of Government by getting Possession of the King. His Name, from that Period, has ever been quoted by the Publick, as one whose Conduct, in several instances, had been conspicuously reprehensible. A singular Anecdote may have reached your Lordship's knowledge, and which, if true, would have been sufficient to render all connections between him and the Prince highly improper. It is, however, no more than a duty I owe to truth when I assure your Lordship of my having the greatest reason to believe, that what has been alledged upon that point was not only exaggerated, but even fabricated long after the date at which it was supposed to have taken place. Count Bernstorff Himself, aware of the bad impression that the general belief of this Story might have made in England, once more took the liberty of mentioning a transaction to me, which, by Mutual Stipulation between the two Courts, was never more to have been made the subject of future discussion. The Count, in whose veracity and integrity I cannot but have the most perfect reliance, expressed a desire that I would do justice to M. de Schach Rathelow, whom He now considers as thoroughly attached to the good Cause, and that I would endeavour to prevent any false surmises that might be carried to England tending to excite Prejudices in the Bosom of my Royal Master. Without entering more circumstantially into this Matter, I beg leave to assure your Lordship that I consider the Imputations particularly alledged against M. de Schach-Rathelow as groundless; and that I look upon Him as a Person who should, by every means, be convinced that no resentment is harboured against Him in England.

APPENDIX. 253

I know this Gentleman was long persuaded that all future Connection between the Courts of Great Britain and Denmark was impracticable, and that many Individuals here could never be forgiven. Hence it is not surprising that He continued to espouse the Queen Dowager's System as long as it suited His Personal safety and the convenience of His family. Had not the Plenitude of Power, which the Queen and Her Favourite attained, infatuated their Judgement, they never would have ventured to disgust the only Man of rank and ability who remained steadfast to their Party. M. de Schach Rathelow had not only approved but even furthered Count Bernstorff's dismission; and it was the discovery that He Himself was destined to be the Next Victim, which at length forced Him to take refuge under that very Minister to whose disgrace He had contributed. I must repeat that it was Pique against M. de Guldberg, joined to a fear of falling Himself a Sacrifice to the Arrogant Ambition of the Favourite, which prompted M. de Schach Rathelow to close in with His present Connections. I have thought it the more necessary to state this circumstance fully, as the recollection of it will evidence to your Lordship with what great delicacy it was necessary to proceed, that neither M. de Schach Rathelow's feelings should be hurt nor His Apprehensions awakened. It seemed also essential to explain fully the grounds upon which He acted, as this, added to the knowledge of His private Character, will account for the anxiety of the Prince's Adherents, during the interval which elapsed between the Revolution and the Arrival of Count Bernstorff.

In my first letter I have had the honour of acquainting your Lordship that I had, Agreeably to the Wish of Count Bernstorff expressed to me while in Mechlenbourg, been very assiduous in my attentions to M. de Shach Rathelow. I have often taken upon me to insinuate, indirectly, that degree of encouragement which circumstances permitted, in order to abate the uneasiness He evidently felt with respect to England. But the only one of Count Bernstorff's Partizans with whom I maintained a real and uninterrupted Intercourse, at Copenhagen, was Count Schimmelman. To Him I made no Secret of the Progress I made upon M. de Schach Rathelow, or of any other information I thought of Importance. He, in return, shew'd me the utmost Confidence. It was from Him I received the Note transcribed in my former letter; and I also, without losing a moment, communicated to Him my Conversation with Count Moltke on the 14 of April, and the very remarkable observation of that Nobleman: That a new order from the King might reverse what His Majesty had then just signed.

The Situation of the Prince Royal was from that instant most critical. The whole Court then resided in the same Palace; all the officers and servants had been placed by the Queen Dowager. Had she therefore attempted any violence there was in my opinion within the Walls of the Palace a force fully sufficient to have put Her again in possession of the King's Person and to have obtained His Signature to an Order for annulling what had been done.

As a proof what little dependence was to be put upon the military in case the Queen Dowager had made any sudden Exertion, I had it in my power to inform Count Schimmelman of a circumstance which showed the Necessity the Adherents of the Prince were under of trusting solely to themselves for His Royal Highness's Preservation.

The very Officer who was to have been upon Guard in the Prince's Anti-chamber, the night of the Revolution, had endeavoured to excuse Himself on pretext of Sickness. As I thought it of material Importance to be exactly informed of the Disposition of the Norwegian Guards, I learnt from a Person whom I employed to frequent a House where their Officers generally resorted that the Gentleman above mentioned had acquainted some of His Brother Officers that He was much averse to the whole Business, since He believed all those engaged in it would be totally ruined. As His family Connections were themselves interested in the success of the Revolution, I was the more alarmed at His Conduct. I must say that on this, as well as every other occasion, Count Schimmelman neglected no Hint nor Information which could be of Use, but without delay took proper measures for remedying unforeseen Accidents.

In this Crisis I also spared no means of acquiring hourly Intelligence of every thing transacting in the Palace. I did not even scruple to concert measures for securing a reinforcement, which, coming from an unexpected though hearty quarter, might have added considerable strength to the Prince's Party, had that violence been attempted to which the Queen was instigated by some of Her Dependants.

Count Schimmelman communicated to me the following instance of the Prince's Intrepidity. When His Royal Highness was going to bed His attendants, among whom was the Count, were desirous of securing the Door, but were not a little disconcerted at finding the Bolts had been removed. They proposed to have them instantly replaced, when the Prince said that he should be ashamed to betray any symptoms of Fear, as He trusted sufficiently to the Justice of His Cause and the Precautions His friends had taken; adding that, although the Emperor had often exposed Himself for the good of His Subjects, yet that He had escaped any Harm.

Next forenoon, while His Royal Highness was proceeding through the Streets, in order to show Himself to the Publick, I went to the Russian Chargé des Affaires and took Him with me to the great Place through which the Prince was to pass. I walked arm in arm with this Gentleman till the Prince arrived, when We saluted Him conjointly in the presence of the concourse of People assembled there.

The general Impression produced by this Step was on the following day much increased by the distinguished Notice His Royal Highness was pleased to take of me, when again, attended by many followers, He stopt to address me, and graciously accepted a Compliment which I made Him suitable to the occasion. The Idea which from thence universally prevailed that the Courts of London and Petersburg were privy to the Revolution strongly contributed to damp the Spirits of the opposite Party, and to encourage those who favoured the Prince. With a view to confirm these Sentiments in the Danish Nation, the first time His Royal Highness went to the Play I appeared in the most conspicuous Box to pay my respects to Him in the face of the Publick. This attention was the more remarked, as none of the other Foreign Ministers were there, and especially as the Prussian Envoy declared He did not think it decent for Him to show that mark of respect so soon after the treatment the Queen Dowager had met with. Prince Frederick, who indeed from the beginning of my Mission was jealous of my frequent conversations with the Prince, could not abstain from saying harsh things to me in consequence of this unequivocal support of His Nephew's Cause; but, as I knew it was the intention of Count Bernstorff to gain over that Prince for future Purposes, I avoided betraying the least resentment.

I have in another place acquainted your Lordship that M. de Numsen, one of M. de Shach Rathelow's nearest Relations, had been appointed Great Marshal immediately upon the Revolution, and that the custody of the King's Person had been principally committed to him. M. de Numsen, therefore, was obliged to give up a large Hotel he occupied upon the great Square. I did not hesitate to hire it, and bought all His furniture at His own Price, notwithstanding I already possessed a smaller House in a more retired situation of the town, and which was more suitable to my private circumstances. I did this, not merely for reasons which I thought essential in other respects, but also that I might add additional strength to the sentiments now prevalent among the Publick, by receiving in my House with due distinction and without loss of time, the Prince's adherents, and by adopting every method of keeping up that Harmony and Good Humour among themselves so very necessary for the final success of their undertakings. I likewise relinquished my intentions of spending the Summer in the Country, where I had already procured a House by the advice of my Physicians for the recovery of my Health.

The Prince Royal, having eluded the danger of the violent measures which for some days were dreaded, was exposed to new and unforeseen difficulties. Count Bernstorff was, unfortunately, laid up with a fit of the Gout when the express arrived at His Seat in the Country with an account of the Revolution. As this prevented His coming to Copenhagen, the management of every thing in the Interim devolved upon M. de Schach Rathelow. The Queen Dowager ably profited of this circumstance, and began to operate upon His timid and suspicious mind. I was very early apprized of Her Intrigues, and did not fail to impart them to Count Schimmelman.

The Moltke family, of great weight and influence in this country, was the only one which had remained attached to M. de Guldberg's Administration. Count Gotsche Moltke, son to the celebrated Minister of that name, had been, as mentioned before, dismissed from the Council. He was the Agent employed to address Himself to M. de Shach Rathelow; and had made considerable progress upon M. de Rosencrantz, a Member of the New Council. Count Schimmelman took the alarm, and thought it not improbable that M. de Schach Rathelow might give way, or be awed into compliance. One Evening in particular He was so much agitated that He expressed to me the strongest regret He had not placed a large sum of money out of the country, and asked whether, in case of misfortune, He might rely upon the Protection of my most gracious Sovereign. He remained firm, however, and gave me assurances that if any attempt was made against the Prince He, and some others, were determined rather to perish than to surrender Him into the Hands of those whose vengeance He was persuaded would not even spare the life of His Royal Highness.

I again in this emergency desired Count Schimmelman to let the Prince know that I should certainly be ready to second His Royal Highness with all the force I could command; and I am happy to say that, although this force would not have been inconsiderable, yet the Publick have never gained any knowledge of the resources

I had secretly prepared. I hope, therefore, my Lord, that I shall not be subjected to the imputation of imprudence in the arrangement of so delicate a Business.

In the mean time I exerted myself more assiduously than ever to counteract the effect of the Queen Dowager's Intrigues with M. de Schach Rathelow, and to keep Him true to the cause he had espoused. I pressed upon Him the little hope that those engaged so deeply in the Revolution could have of the Queen's forgiveness, and demonstrated in the most feeling manner that His own safety depended upon the continuation of His present connections.

Thus, although by various means every essential change was prevented, during the seventeen days that elapsed before Count Bernstorff's arrival, yet I am convinced nothing but that Minister's presence could have given stability to the new system of Government.

I have the honour to be, with the greatest truth and respect,

My Lord,
Your Lordship's
most obedient
humble servant,
H. ELLIOT.

Endorsed:
   Copenhagen, Septr. 1st, 1784.
      Mr. Elliot,
   R. 28th,
      by Mr. Johnstone.
         (B.) Private.
The Marquess of Carmarthen.

(E.)

Denmark. 149. (6.)

Copenhagen, 1 Sepr, 1784.

MY LORD,

The Prince Royal of Denmark is now in his seventeenth year. He is, for that time of life, of a proper stature, rather slender, very active, and to all appearance of a healthy constitution. His hair and eye-brows are light-coloured, his complexion fair and florid, and his eyes blue. It is to be regretted that, from the great want of attention to the Prince's education, his address in publick is not easy, on the contrary, has a degree of awkwardness, but I am happy to observe that this daily diminishes. There is also a peculiar desultory motion in His Royal Highnesses eye, which, I apprehend, is rather the consequence of embarrassment than of any natural defect. The Prince has little turn for reading; his chief passion is evidently for the military art, and he already displays great activity and genius in this pursuit. He rides better and more boldly than any of his attendants, but is very deficient in all the other accomplishments, upon which indeed he bestows little attention and sets no value. His Royal Highness, besides his native language, speaks French and German, but neither with any great degree of accuracy or elegance.

The Princess Louisa Augusta is more brilliant in her personal appearance and accomplishments than Her Brother. She is lively, engaging, and singularly advanced for her years. The Prince shews great affection towards His Sister, and it is indeed a pleasing and most interesting scene to see them together.

I have the honor to be
 with the greatest truth and respect,
  My Lord,
   Your Lordship's
    Most obedient
     humble servant,
      H. ELLIOT.

Endorsed:
 Copenhagen, Septr 1st, 1784.
  Mr. Elliot,
 R. 28th by Mr Johnstone.
  (E.)
The Right Hon'ble the Marquess of Carmarthen.

INDEX.

Abercorn, Lord, 214, 215, 216, 218
Abergavenny, Lord, 47 n
Abingdon, Lord, 47 n, 54, 55, 57
Adair, Mr. 201, 204
Addington, Dr. 122
Addington, Mr. afterwards Lord Sidmouth, 178
Amherst, Lord, 15, 44
Anderson, Alderman, 213
Anguish, Mr. Charles, 207
Anguish, Miss, 163, 183, 199, 204
Anspach, Margravine of, 221
Arden, Pepper, afterwards Lord Alvanley, 94, 124
Argyll, Duke of, 100
Armisted, Mrs. 138
Arnold, Mr. 9
Ashburnham, Lord, 21
Ashburton, Lord; *see* Dunning
Aust, Mr. 173, 175, 183, 191, 193, 203, 204
Aylesbury, Lord; *see* Bruce, Lord

Baker, Sir G. 122
Balfour, Col. 51
Bankes, Mr. 95, 213
Barré, Col. M.P. 3 n, 30 n, 39, 48, 64, 73
Barrington, Lord, 65
Barthélemy, Mr. 118
Bath, Lord, 209, 210
Bathurst, Lord, 43, 133
Beaufort, Duke of, 220
Beaulieu, Lord, 183, 187
Bedford, Duke of, 181, 214, 215, 216, 217, 219, 220
Bentham, Jeremy, quoted, 36
Bentinck, Lord E. 71
Bentinck, Lord W. 211
Bernstorff, Connt, 102 n, 103, 107, 235, 238, 239, 241, 242, 243, 244, 245, 247, 249, 250, 252, 253, 255, 257
Bessborough, Lord, 41 n

Bolton, Duke of, 26 and n, 33, 44 n
Bouverie, Mr. 117
Bouverie, Mrs. 181
Bradford, Lord, 212
Brandling, Mr. M.P. 212
Bridgewater, Duke of, 90
Bridgewater, Earl of, 36 n
Brooks, Mr. 60
Brownlow, Lord, 31, 35
Bruce, Lord, afterwards Lord Aylesbury, 6, 7, 9, 24
Brunswick, Duke Ferdinand of, 23 and n, 58, 118, 119 n, 228, 239
Buckingham, Marquis of, 24, 120 n, 201, 218
Buckinghamshire, Earl of, 12 and n
Bude, Mr. 7 n
Bulkeley, Lord, 55, 67
Bulkner, Capt. 46
Bulow, M. de, 245, 248, 249
Burden, Mr. M.P. 212, 213
Burges, Mr. 74, 148, 150, 162, 165, 168, 171, 172, 173, 178
Burgoyne, Genl. 51
Burke, Right Honble. Edmund, 3 n, 4 n, 17 n, 27, 30, 36 n, 39, 41, 42, 48, 43, 61, 203
Bute, Lord, 26, 188
Byng, Mr. 61
Byron, Admiral, 12 *.
Byron, Captain John, 12 n

Caldwell, Captain, 46
Camden, Lord, Lord President, 28, 38 n, 55, 63 n, 64, 104, 105, 106, 121, 128, 129, 132, 134, 139, 140, 146, 155, 156, 160, 165
Canterbury, Archbishop of (Cornwallis), 45
Cardigan, Lord, 226
Cardigan, Lady, 226

INDEX. 261

Carlisle, Lord, 19 and *n*, 25, 77, 78, 86 *n*, 88, 133, 181, 189, 202, 212
Carmarthen, Lord, 223
Carnarvon, Lady, 221, 224, 225, 226, 230, 234
Caroline, Queen, 23 ; *see* Wales, Princess of
Caroline Matilda, of Denmark, 102 *n*
Catherine II., Empress of Russia, 111 *n*, 151, 161
Cavendish, Lord John, 63, 64, 71. 79, 86 *n*
Chandos, Duke of, 54, 61, 93
Charles I., King, 26 *n*
Charlotte, Queen, 7, 9, 11, 20, 22, 77 *n*, 120, 124, 125, 126, 127, 128, 130, 137, 138, 225
Chatelet, Comte de, 25
Chatham, Lord, 50, 55, 57, 91, 123, 124, 125, 127, 138, 146, 151, 153, 155, 156, 157, 164, 167
Chesterfield, 4th Earl of, 7
Chesterfield, 5th Earl of, 23 *n*, 65, 93, 185, 186, 197
Chevrense, Madame de, 10 and *n*
Choisenl, Duke of, 25
Cholmondley, Lord, 224, 226, 228, 229, 232
Cholmondley, Lady, 229, 231
Clarendon, Lord, 216
Clinton, Lord Thomas, 3 *n*, 5
Cobham. Lord, 26 and *n*
Coke, Mr. 85, 98 *n*, 99 *n*
Constable. Mr. 15
Conyers, Baroness, Duchess of Leeds, 8 *n*, 12 *n*, 14 *n*
Conyngham, Mr. Burton, 209
Conway, General, 58, 64, 72, 75, 233
Cordon, M. de, or Cardon, 31 and *n*
Cornwall, Mr. Speaker, 4 *n*, 34, 137
Cornwall, Sir George, 181
Cornwallis, 34, 47, 49
Cornwallis, Captain, 2
Cottrell, Mr. 98
Coventry, Lord, 38 *n*, 41, 52, 57, 60
Cowper, Mr. 149
Cranborne, Lord, 20 ; *see* Salisbury, Lord
Cranley, Baron and Viscount; *see* Onslow
Craven, Lord, 57
Crillon, Duc de, 76
Crofts, Mr. 12
Cumberland, Duke of, 135
Cumberland, Duchess of, 37
Cust, Sir John, 4 *n*
Cust, Mr. Fr. 3 *n*, 4

Darby, Admiral, 46
Dartmouth, Lord, 19 and *n*, 134
Dashwood, Lady, 233
Dean, Jocelyn, 49 *n*
de Ferrars, Lord, 47 *n*
Delaware, Lord, 7 and *n*, 8
Denmark, Christian V. of, 102 *n*
Denmark, Frederick V. of, 102 *n*
Denmark, Prince Royal of, 102, and Appendix *passim*
Derby, Lord, 54, 57
D'Estaing, Admiral, 11 *n*
Devonshire, Duke of, 38 *n*, 57, 66, 181, 201
Dickson, Dean of Downe, 72
Digby, Col. 141
Dorset, Duke of, 55, 74, 90, 91, 93, 186
Drake, Mr. 170 *n*
Draper, Sir Wm. 76
Drummond, Dr. 9
Duncombe, Mr. 213
Dundas, Lord, 212
Dundas, W. afterwards Lord Melville, 94, 137, 140, 148, 149, 177, 182, 183, 184, 187, 188, 191, 192, 193, 195, 197, 198
Dunning, Mr. afterwards Lord Ashburton, 3 *n*, 4 *n*, 28, 39, 48, 64 *n*, 69, 76

Eden, Mr. afterwards Lord Auckland, 88, 119, 120, 140, 148, 182
Effingham, Lord, 54
Egerton, Bishop of Durham, 66
Egerton, Major, 66
Egremont, Lord, 57, 71, 181
Eichstedt, General, 244
Elizabeth, Princess, 234
Elliot, Sir G. afterwards Lord Minto, 123, 216, 217
Ellis, Mr. Wellbore, 4 and *n*, 5, 49 *n*, 138
Elphinstone, Lord, 100
Ernest, Prince, 232
Eustace, Lord, 138, 154
Evelyn, Mr. 40 *n*
Ewart, Mr. 172
Eyre, Chief Justice In, 1 *n*

Falconberg, Lord, 10 and *n*, 11, 19 and *n*
Faurès, M. 25
Fawkener, Mr. 78, 80, 162, 164, 165
Ferrers, Earl, 38 *n*
Finch, Lady Charlotte, 5 *n*, 9
Fitzherbert, Mr. afterwards Lord St. Helens, 81, 104, 203, 204, 234
Fitzpatrick, General, 71, 72, 219

Fitzroy, Lord Charles, 154
Fitzroy, Mr. 224, 230, 234
Fitzwilliam, Lord, 12 and n, 13, 27, 38 n, 47 n, 58, 71, 72, 77, 131, 135, 158, 181, 182, 210, 219, 220
Fitzwilliam, General, 142
Fox, Mr. afterwards Lord Holland, 25
Fox, Right Hon. C. J. 3 n, 31, 36 n, 55, 57, 63 n, 64, 65, 66, 67, 69, 70, 71, 72, 73, 79, 81, 83, 85, 86, 93, 94, 97, 98, 99, 124, 129, 130 n, 133, 134, 135, 138, 140, 141, 176, 177, 178, 180, 181, 182, 183, 187, 189, 190, 193, 194, 195, 200, 201, 202, 203, 205, 207, 208, 209, 210, 211, 212, 216, 219, 243
Franklin, Benjamin, 71
Frazer, Mr. 98
Frederick, Prince, see York, Duke of
Frederick the Great, King of Prussia, 166 n
Frederick William II. of Prussia, 111 n, 151, 157, 172, 203, 219
Fullerton, Colonel, 27 and n

Galloway, Lord, 33
Gates, General, 34
George III. King, 1, 6 n ; interview with Dr. Markham, 9, 11, 21, 22, 23, 48, 50; on Shelburne's ministry, 74; presses Pitt to form a ministry, 84 ; audience with Lord Carmarthen, 84 ; interview with Lord North, 87; question of the regency on his illness, 119; his removal to Kew, 121 foll.; his recovery, 141 foll.; receives the Duke of Leeds' resignation, 162
George IV. King, 23 n
Germaine, Lord George, afterwards Lord Sackville, 21 and n, 19, 53, 54, 55, 57, 58, 60, 70
Gloucester, Duke of, 135, 229, 230, 231, 232
Gloucester, Princess Sophia of, 228
Glover, Mr. 20, 70
Godolphin, Francis, 3 n
Godolphin, Lord, 40, 58
Godolphin, Sidney, 3 n
Goldsworthy, Mrs. 232
Goodrich, Sir J. 19
Gordon, Lord George, 30 and n; his riots, 31 foll.
Gordon, General, 30 n
Gotsche-Moltke, Count, 248, 250
Gower, Earl, afterwards Marquis of Stafford, 16 and n, 17 and n, 36, 63 n, 67, 83, 90, 92, 95, 99, 105

Grafton, Duke of, 30, 36, 37, 47, 48, 51, 55, 57, 63 n, 64, 81, 154
Grant, General, 30 n.
Grantham, Lord, 17 and n, 73, 76, 77, 78, 79, 80, 82
Grantley, Lord; see Norton, Sir Fletcher
Granville, Lord, 36 n
Granville, Mr., 33
Gratton, Mr., 210
Grenville, General, 205
Grenville, Mr. W., afterwards Lord, 71, 80, 120, 136, 137, 138, 146, 148, 149, 150, 151, 153, 155, 156, 157, 158, 159, 166, 167, 169, 178, 190, 192, 193, 198, 201, 204, 218, 219
Grenville, Mr. 7, 293
Grey, Mr., 218
Grosvenor, Mr. Thomas, 98
Guernsey, Lord, afterwards Lord Aylesford, 4
Guildford, Lord ; see North, Lord
Guildford, second Lord, 209, 215, 216, 219
Guldberg, M. de, 102 n, 237, 238, 243, 244, 245, 246, 247, 248, 250, 253, 257
Gwyn, Colonel, 121

Hampden, Lord, 60 and n
Harcourt, Earl, 38, 93, 220
Hardy, Sir C., 13 and n
Hardwick, Lord, 217
Harley, Mr., 29
Harris, Sir James, afterwards Lord Malmesbury, 110 n, 113, 117, 136, 142, 175, 181, 183, 184, 186, 187, 191, 192, 193, 194, 196, 197, 198, 199, 202, 205, 224
Harvey, Col., 15
Haslang, Count, 31 and n
Hawke, Lord, 77
Hawkesbury, Lord, 72, 125, 126, 127, 137, 138, 140, 209
Haxthausen, General, 245, 246
Haynes, Col., 51 and n, 52
Henley, Mrs., 184
Herbert, Lord, 77
Hertford, Lord, 5 n, 6 n, 90
Hertford, Lady, 6 n
Hertzberg, M., 114
Hesse, Prince of, 245
Hill, Sir R., 213
Hillsborough, 19 and n, 22, 45
Hilyard, Sir R., 15
Holdernesse, Lord, 5 and n, 6, 7 and n, 8, 10, 11, 12 n
Holdernesse, Lady, 14 n, 163, 164, 165, 218, 231, 234

INDEX. 263

Hope, Colonel, 46
Hotham, Colonel, 9
Howe, Lord. 92, 93, 95
Howe, Mr., 226
Hurd, Dr., afterwards Bishop of Lichfield, 6, 7 n, and 9
Huth, General, 245, 246, 249
Hyde, Lord, 40 n
Hyde, Sir Nicholas, 33

Irving, Lord, 12 and n
Irwin, Sir John, 55

Jackson, Dr. Cyril, afterwards Dean of Christchurch, 5 n, 6 n, 7 and n
Jackson, Mr. Prebend of Westminster, 11, 60, 65, 66, 69, 71, 72, 75, 173, 207
Jackson, Mr. Charles, 78, 152, 158, 164
Jacobi, Mr. 219
Jenkinson, Mr.; *see* Hawkesbury, Lord
Jersey, Lady, 220, 222, 225, 226, 227, 229, 230, 231, 233
Jervis, Capt. 46
Johnston, Lieut.-General, 50
Johnstone, Mr. 235
Jones, Paul, 14
Joseph II. of Austria, 106 n, 110 n, 145, 146, 147
Julia Maria, Queen of Denmark, 102 n and Appendix

Kaunitz, Prince, 101 n, 107 and n
Kazeneck, M. de, 113
Kenyon, Lord, 125, 126, 127, 133, 137, 138, 140, 150
Keppel, Admiral, 11 and n, 12, 13, 23, 33, 36 n, 42, 62, 64
Kereton, Lord, 36 n
King, Lord, 47 n

Lafayette, M. de, 145 n
Landaff, Bishop of, 218
Langstaff, 36 n
Lansdowne, Lord, 218
Lauderdale, Lord, 219
Lee, Mr. 232
Leeds, fourth Duke of, 1 n, 142
Leeds, fifth Duke of : born, 1 ; comes into Parliament, 2 ; created Lord Osborne, 5 n ; appointed Lord of the Bedchamber, 6 ; Lord Chamberlain to the Queen, 7 ; married, 8 n ; Privy Councillor, 10 ; Lord Lieutenant of East Riding, 12 ; divorced, 12 n ; resigns Gold Key, 23 ; dismissed from

Lord Lieutenancy, 22 ; asked to move address, 75 ; offered embassy to France, 77 ; offered foreign secretaryship, 91 ; succeeds his father, 145 ; account of his resignation, 148 foll. ; conversation with Duke of York, 185; conversation with George III. 187 ; interview with Duke of Portland, 191; interview with Pitt, 194
Leigh, Honble. Mrs. 12
Leighton, Sir Charlton, 86
Lewisham, Lord, 19 and n
Ligonier, Lord, 55
Lindsay, Mr. 207
Lloyd, Mr. 33
Long, Mr. Dudley, 50, 73
Lothian, Lord, 10 and n, 50, 136, 142
Loughborough, Lord, 13 and n, 50, 83. 86 n, 130, 133, 134, 150, 160, 175, 177, 182, 188, 189, 191, 193, 194, 195, 197, 198, 201, 202, 204, 205
Lowther, Sir James, 49, 68, 70

Macartney, Mr. 38
MacBride, Captain, 44
Mackay, 12
Mainwaring, Mr. 213
Malden, Lord, 3 n
Malmesbury, Lord: *see* Harris, Sir James
Manchester, Duke of, 49, 61, 93
Mansfield, Lord, 5 n, 7 n, 9, 25, 29
Marchmont, Lord, 100
Markham, Dr. Archbishop of York, 3 n, 7, 127
Marlborough, Duke of, 11, 83
Melbourne, Lady, 81
Mellish, Mr. C. 19 and n
Mentz, Electors of, 100
Meredith, Sir William, 1 and n, 2
Middlesex, Earl, 36 n
Milbourne, Lady, 24
Moira, Lord, 208, 213, 225
Moltke, Count, 249, 254
Montagu, Duke of, 6, 7 n, 9, 83
Montagu, Mr. F. 138
Montmorris, M. de, 119 n, 145 n
Montrose, Duke of, 148, 149, 150
Moore, Mr. F. 78, 201
Morpeth, Lord, 26 n
Mountstuart, Lord, 79, 93
Mulgrave, Lord, 19
Mundy, Mr. 181
Murray, Genl. 76 and n
Muskerry, Lord, 40 n

Nagel, Baron, 174
Nepean, Mr. 98, 148, 150, 168, 169
Neutrality, armed, 29 n, 38
Newcastle, Duke of, 83
Norfolk, Duke of, 216
North, Lord, afterwards Earl of Guildford, 1, 5 n, 11, 13, 17, 18, 20, 21, 36 n, 40, 49 n, 58 n, 61; his resignation, 63 n, 64, 79, 83, 81, 85, 86, 87, 135, 140, 189, 205
North, Colonel, 219
North, Mr. 28
Northington, Lord, 88, 98
Northumberland, Duke of, 3 and n, 18, 19, 24, 50, 82
Norton, Sir Fletcher, afterwards Lord Grantley, 4, 34, 90, 136
Nova Scotia, 101
Nugent, Lord, 24 and n
Nugent, Mr. 231
Numsen, M. de, 243, 250, 256

O'Birne, Mr. 87
Onslow, Mr. afterwards Lord, 1
Orange, Prince of, 117, 218, 233
Orange, Princess of, 117, 119 n, 218, 233, 234
Orleans, Duke of, 145, 146
Orlow, Prince of, 201
Osbaldeston, Mr. 15
Osnaburgh, Bishop of; see York, Duke of
Oswald, Mr. 71
Owen, W. 3 n, and 4

Palliser, Sir H. 11 and n, 12 and n
Payne, Sir R. 192
Payne, Mr. 126, 133
Pearson, Captain, 14
Peircy, Captain, 14
Pelham, Lord, afterwards Earl of Chichester, 2 and n, 24
Pelham, Mr. 177
Pelham, Mrs. 229
Pembroke, Lord, 23, 24, 25, 27, 38 n, 47, 50, 51 57, 62, 65, 76
Pepys, Sir Lucas, 122
Percy, Lord, 3 and n, 5
Percy, Lord Algernon, 15
Petersham, Lord, 3 n
Pitt, Right Hon. W. 36 n; his first speech, 39, 49, 50, 55, 58 n, 64 n, 68, 73, 74, 76, 79, 84, 85, 90, 91, 92, 93, 94, 95, 96, 97, 98, 99, 101, 102, 104, 105, 119, 121, 122, 123, 124, 125, 128, 129, 130, 131, 132, 133, 134, 135, 136,
137, 138, 139, 141, 146, 149, 153, 154, 155, 156, 157, 158, 160, 161, 162, 164, 165, 166, 169, 170, 171, 172, 176, 177, 178, 183, 184, 185, 186, 187, 188, 189, 190, 192, 193, 194, 198, 199, 201, 202, 203, 205, 206, 207, 210, 214, 215, 225
Pitt, Thomas, 67
Pomfret, Lord, 36
Porchester, Lord, 160
Portland, Duke of, 38 n, 61, 69, 70, 85, 86, 133, 175, 179, 180, 183, 187, 188, 190, 194, 195, 197, 201, 202, 203, 205, 210, 211, 212, 215
Portland, Duchess of, 88, 98
Potemkin, Prince, 153
Powys, Mr. 99 n
Pratt, Mr. 76
Pulteney, Mr. 138
Purling, Mr. 57

Queensberry, Duke of, 136, 141, 142

Rawdon, Lord, 51, 136, 182
Rayneval, M. de, 77
Reede, Lady Mary de, 234
Reventlow, Count Christian, 245, 246, 249
Reventlow, Count Louis, 245
Reynolds, Mr., 122
Richmond, Duke of, 17 and n, 21, 28, 30, 32, 34, 35, 38, 41, 42, 47, 51, 52, 54, 57, 61, 64, 66, 67, 70, 71, 72, 90, 92, 94, 95, 99, 100, 102, 122, 123, 124, 125, 127, 130, 132, 137, 138, 140, 141, 151, 152, 155, 156, 157, 165, 166, 177, 184, 185, 186, 198, 218
Rigby, Mr., 49, 83
Robinson, W., 11
Rochford, Lord, 25, 34, 48
Rockingham, Lord, 12, 15, 17 and n, 23 n, 27, 28, 30, 32, 35; on reform of parliament, 35 n, 36 n, 39, 40, 41, 42, 46, 47, 49, 51, 52, 54, 57, 58, 59, 61, 62, 63, 64, 65, 67; death of, 69
Roger, Mr., 33
Rokeby, Lord, 37
Rolleston, Mr., 175, 179, 180, 181, 182, 192, 193, 202, 203, 204, 205, 207, 209, 210, 211, 212, 216
Romanzov, Count, 115
Romney, Lord, 142
Rose, Mr. 94
Rosebery, Lord, 100
Rosencrantz, M. de, 249, 257
Rosencrone, M. de, 239, 243, 247

Ronse, Sir John, 62, 63
Roxburgh, Duke of, 220
Rutland, Duke of, 50, 57, 78, 82, 92, 93, 94, 95, 98, 105

Sackville, Lord ; *see* Germaine, Lord G.
St. Alban's Tavern, meeting at, 68, 98
St. Asaph, Bishop of, 41 *n*
St. David's, Bishop of, 43
St. John, Mr., 175, 219
St. Leger, Mr., 186
Salisbury, Lord, 93, 95, 217
Salgas. M. de, 7, 8
Sandwich, Earl of, 11 and *n*, 21 and *n*, 23, 32, 36 *n*, 43, 44
Savile, Sir George, 32, 63, 73
Schach, M. de, 237, 250
Schach-Rathlow, M. de, 238, 242, 243, 245, 246, 247, 248, 251, 252, 253, 257, 258
Schimmelman, Count, 241, 245, 247, 249, 253, 254, 255
Scott, Sir John, afterwards Lord Eldon, 132
Scott, Mr., 88
Sheffield, Lord, 177
Shelburne, Lord, 17, 22, 24, 25, 27, 28, 29, 31, 32, 35, 38 *n*, 41, 42, 48, 49, 50, 51, 52, 54, 55, 57, 58, 59; conversation with on independence of America, 60, 62 ; his acceptance of office, 63 *n*, 64, 65, 66, 68, 69, 70, 71, 72, 73, 74, 75, 76, 77, 78, 79, 82, 84, 85, 88

Shelburne, Lady, 57
Sheridan, Right Hon. B. 181, 200, 209, 217
Simolin, M. 104
Smith, Mr. 5 *n*, 7 *n*, 9
Smith, Mr. 148, 168, 169
Southampton, Lord, 58, 77
Sophia, Princess, 232
Spencer, Lord, 71, 76
Spencer, Lord Robert, 37, 138, 219
Sporon, M. de, 244
Stafford, Marquis of, 123, 124, 125, 127, 131, 133, 137, 138, 139, 140, 141, 153, 155, 156, 157, 209
Stampe, M. de, 245, 249
Stanhope, Lord, 167, 213, 214
Stanley, Lord, afterwards Lord Derby, 4
Stare, 71
Stormont, Lord, 34, 38, 57, 86 *n*, 100 and *n*, 133, 134
Struensee, Count, 102 *n*

CAMD. SOC.

Sudley, Lord, 226
Suffolk, Lord of, 10 and *n*
Surry, Lord, 63, 86 *n*
Sydney, Lord, 92, 93, 95, 98, 99, 102, 121, 124, 125, 126, 127, 128, 130, 131, 133, 141

Tarlton, General, 210
Temple, Earl, 54, 65, 66, 68, 71, 73, 75, 86 *n*, 87, 88, 90, 91
Thomas, Colonel, 221
Thompson, Sir Charles, 19, 55
Thurlow, Lord Chancellor, 21, 36, 43, 57, 61 *n*, 67, 70, 76, 83, 90, 92, 95, 99, 120, 121, 123, 124, 125, 126, 127, 128, 130, 132, 133, 135, 137, 139, 146, 148, 149, 153, 155, 156, 159, 163, 166, 170, 179, 182, 209, 210, 212, 213, 223, 224
Townshend, Lord, 43
Townshend, Thomas, M.P. 3 *n*, 62, 64, 72, 73, 74, 75

Vergennes, Comte de, 71, 76, 80
Vergennes, Vicomte de, 77
Vernon, Mrs. 224, 226
Vivi, Count, 26

Wales, Prince of, afterwards King George IV. account of his education. 5 *n*, 6, 8, 50, 58, 66, 102, 120, 121, 122, 124, 127, 130, 132, 133, 134, 135, 137, 138, 139, 140, 141, 176, 181, 220, 222, 223, 224, 226, 227, 229, 231, 232, 233
Wales, Princess of, 220, 221, 224, 230, 232, 233,
Wales, Princess Augusta of, 23 *n*
Walsingham, Lord, 57
Warner, Dr. 230
Warren, Dr. 120, 122, 123, 126, 129, 137
Wedel, Count, 169
Westmoreland, Lord, 34, 150
Weymouth, Lord, afterwards Marquis of Bath, 16, 17, 63 *n*, 83, 94, 125, 126, 133, 140
Wilberforce, Mr. 213, 218
William, Prince, afterwards King William IV. 66
Willis, Dr. 129
Winchelsea, Lord, 131
Windham, Mr. 88, 201, 203, 209, 211
Woodford, Sir R. 175, 179, 180, 183, 190, 191, 193, 202, 204, 205
Worcester, Marquis of, 135
Woronzow, Count, 116

2 M

INDEX.

Yarborough, Lord 212
Yelverton, Mr. 88
Yonge, Sir George, 73
York, Duke of, Prince Frederick, and Bishop of Osnaburgh, 6, 8, 121, 124, 125, 135, 136, 181, 184, 186, 187, 191, 192, 197, 199, 207, 231

York, Duchess of, 181, 199
Yorke, Sir Joseph, 30, 66
Yorke, Mr. 3 n, 4 n, 40 n
Young, Sir W. 218

Zouch, Mr 72

ERRATA.

Page 3, note 3, line 1, *for* " Smithers," *read* " Smithson
Page 4, note 1, line 4, *for* " Burning," *read* " Dunning."
Page 71, note 1. lines 7 and 12, *for* " Greville," *read* " Grenville
Page 119, note 1. line 7, *for* " Montmorris," *read* " Montmorin.
Page 124, note 1, line 1, *for* " Betham's," *read* " Botham's "
Page 223, line 6, *for* " port," *read* " part."

www.ingramcontent.com/pod-product-compliance
Lightning Source LLC
Chambersburg PA
CBHW032112230426
43672CB00009B/1714